ADVANCE PRAISE FOR GENERATION CITIZEN

"At a time when the future of our country and our world hangs in the balance, Scott Warren delivers a powerful, stirring, and deeply important call to action for our most vital and under nurtured citizen force: our youth. This book should be required reading for anyone under the age of thirty-five."

—JOSH TICKELL, author of *The Revolution Generation*

"Scott Warren is at the vanguard of a new movement called Action Civics, based on the all-American idea that the best way for young people to learn democracy is to practice it at the local level. In this timely and accessible new book, Warren deftly combines stories and strategies to show us that the rising generation is ready to exercise power—and save our republic."

—ERIC LIU, CEO of Citizen University and author of *You're More Powerful Than You Think: A Citizen's Guide to Making Change Happen*

"With incisive language, compelling stories, and a clarion call to action, Scott Warren's *Generation Citizen* offers a compelling argument for the essential role that government plays in our lives and the essential role young people can—and must—play in building the beloved community. A must-read for anyone worried about our shared democracy and hopeful about young people's power to change it."

—ERIC D. DAWSON, CEO of Peace First

"Through stories of his own and his students', Warren makes a compelling case that young people from all backgrounds can and should lead the change. Warren weaves many stories of young people leading the change in different places, using different means, and how pivotal education can be in giving young people the tools they need to activate their ideas and to 'right the wrong.' Warren has an enduring appreciation of the great American experiment and the republican form of democracy, and is absolutely set on making sure that every person gets the preparation they need to achieve their civic leadership potential. It is an inspiration and a call to action for young people and adults who want to see progress, to start believing in young people's ability to lead, not later when they 'grow up,' but today."

—KEI KAWASHIMA-GINSBERG, PhD,
director of the Center for Information and Research
on Civic Learning and Engagement (CIRCLE)
at Tufts University's Jonathan M. Tisch College
of Civic Life

"Warren, co-founder and CEO of the national political youth movement Generation Citizen, makes his book debut with a pragmatic, anecdote-filled guide for empowering young people . . . An enthusiastic, supportive manifesto to inspire political engagement."   —*Kirkus Reviews*

"Insightful, inspirational . . . A useful resource for aspiring political activists."   —*Library Journal*

"Scott Warren argues forcefully and eloquently that young people will save us all—and he comes with the receipts to prove it. By sharing his own lived experience and that of some of the hundreds of thousands of young people touched through his work at Generation Citizen, Warren lays out how we can take charge wherever we are, no matter our age. Following Warren's advice, any of us can and will change the world."

—AMANDA LITMAN, CEO of Run for Something and author of *Run for Something: A Real-Talk Guide to Fixing the System Yourself*

GENERATION CITIZEN

the
POWER
of
YOUTH
in
OUR POLITICS

SCOTT WARREN

COUNTERPOINT
Berkeley, California

Generation Citizen

Library of Congress Cataloging-in-Publication Data
Names: Warren, Scott, author.
Title: Generation Citizen : the power of youth in our politics /
    Scott Warren.
Description: First paperback edition. | Berkeley, California : Counterpoint,
    [2019]
Identifiers: LCCN 2018038401 | ISBN 9781640091276
Subjects: LCSH: Youth—Political activity—United States. |
    Teenagers—Political activity—United States. | Political
    participation—United States. | Generation Citizen (Organization)
Classification: LCC HQ799.2.P6 W375 2019 | DDC
    320.0835/0973—dc23
LC record available at https://lccn.loc.gov/2018038401

Cover design by Joan Wong
Book design by Jordan Koluch

COUNTERPOINT
2560 Ninth Street, Suite 318
Berkeley, CA 94710
www.counterpointpress.com

Printed in the United States of America
Distributed by Publishers Group West

10 9 8 7 6 5 4 3 2 1

To Mom and Dad—
for a childhood that taught me the power of politics

Change isn't something that happens every four years or eight years; change is not placing your faith in any particular politician and then just putting your feet up and saying, okay, go. Change is the effort of committed citizens who hitch their wagons to something bigger than themselves and fight for it every single day.

—BARACK OBAMA

CONTENTS

GENERATION
CITIZEN

A NEW POLITICS

Is Democracy a Dirty Word?

A s young people, our voices and actions can transform the conversation."

A'Niya Bankston's voice blasted throughout the entire schoolyard at Oakland Technical High School. Cheers from the masses below echoed the words.

A'Niya was speaking in front of more than five hundred students participating in a national walkout to advocate for gun reform in the wake of the deadly school shooting in Parkland, Florida. Students across the country were out of their schools, holding rallies and demanding action from their elected officials. A'Niya was helping lead the charge in Oakland.

A steady Bay Area drizzle broke through the perpetual fog, threatening to turn into a heavier downpour and put a literal damper on the event. But umbrellas stayed down—the students were enraptured by the words in a way that few classes could accomplish.

Just minutes before her big speech, A'Niya paced the halls of her school, unsure if she'd be able to address her classmates.

"I've never spoken in front of this many people! I'm not sure I can do it," she told me.

This, though, was not her first political rodeo. Only a ninth grader, A'Niya's political journey had started years earlier.

When she was in fifth grade, A'Niya could not believe that her elementary school in Union City, California, was not celebrating Black History Month. An African American girl in an overwhelmingly white school, A'Niya sprang into action, determined to honor her culture's heritage and ensure that the history of her lineage, wrought with oppression and activism alike, was taught as part of the American journey of democracy.

"I don't know how I found out what a petition was, but I started one anyways," A'Niya said. In conversation with her fellow fifth graders, A'Niya articulated the importance of celebrating African American culture and why it meant so much to her. A'Niya received hundreds of signatures on her petition in just three days, starting a mini-movement. As a fifth grader.

Using the petitions as evidence for broad support, A'Niya convinced her administrators to let her take over the intercom system for a morning. In her ten-minute address, A'Niya regaled her classmates with stories of African Americans leading change, from Harriet Tubman to Rosa Parks to Ella Baker. She emphasized how important it was that her peers studied and appreciated the role that African Americans had played in the country's founding and evolution. She closed with the hope that her address did not mark the end of the celebration, but rather a commitment by the school to teach these powerful stories consistently.

Her point had been made—the school decided that they would honor Black History Month going forward. Not a bad start to a political journey for a fifth grader.

The next year, A'Niya and her family moved to Oakland, where she began middle school. She quickly realized that this new school was not nearly as well resourced as her previous institution.

"Where were the pencils? The textbooks? Even paper? We had nothing," A'Niya reflected to me.

Despite her valid frustrations of a public school system lost in the bowels of a public-funding formula based on property taxes, A'Niya did see some positives.

"We did have community. I made friends quicker than I had in Union City. We were all really close."

Soon after, A'Niya learned that instead of putting more resources into the school, the city was planning on shutting it down. Dollars over community, or at least that's the lesson she began to internalize.

"We felt that no one cared about us. There was no hope in the classroom. It wasn't school. It was daycare."

A'Niya decided to take action. She worked to empower her peers, attempting to convince them to mobilize for their school's very survival. After all, she had already witnessed the powerful effect of advocating for an issue she cared about.

Her efforts, though, appeared to descend into the void. For their entire lives, her classmates had experienced a public system whose indifference to inequitable conditions reflected a reality to the students that their lives did not matter. Closing their school seemed to be only another stop on their interminable journey of witnessing an institutional disregard for their well-being.

"We didn't feel like the adults cared about us." The students' minds had been made up—the system did not care what they thought. So why should they participate?

But A'Niya defied this entrenched logic. She attended district meetings and pleaded with decision-makers, making her case that rather than shutting the school down, they should allocate more resources to it. She emphasized the tight-knit community they had formed and how equipping the school with paper and pencils and good teachers could help them overcome all their previous challenges.

"I was heard," A'Niya told me.

Sometimes, though, being heard doesn't necessarily lead to action. Later that spring, the school was shut down.

But rather than lose hope, A'Niya's strengthened her efforts.

"I had two feelings. I was disappointed and sad that our efforts were not successful," A'Niya started. While speaking to me, she paused, as if thinking out loud. "But I also feel like I did accomplish something. I used my voice. I became confident that I could make a difference."

And so, less than a year later, A'Niya was back again, addressing her new high school, filled with students she barely knew. Yet again, she was speaking up against an issue that had affected her Oakland community deeply but seemed unmovable: gun control.

"As young people, we deserve to be heard because our voices are the change for the future and today. Enough is enough." Her voice rose along with the cheers from the crowd.

"Your guns are killing us."

The cliché ending to this story would entail dramatic success. This is what we might see in a movie. Maybe her speech would have led the state of California to pass new effective anti-gun legislation. Maybe A'Niya's efforts would have been plastered on the front page of newspapers across this country.

But this isn't the movies; it's real life. And A'Niya recognizes that her political journey is just beginning. Gun reform won't transpire just because of a powerful speech, just like schools won't always be saved because of effective, galvanizing student testimony. Rather than hope for outdated, idealistic storylines, there are more realistic lessons from A'Niya's ongoing activism that we can hold on to and learn from.

The first is that real change takes time. A'Niya sees her efforts as a journey: no singular action will lead to the progress she wants to see. But the common through line, from advocating for the inclusion of Black History Month to lobbying for her school to stay open to speaking at the gun control rally, is that she will stay active. Always. We all need to lead political journeys. Not just when it's convenient or urgent. But all the time.

The second lesson, as she articulated at the speech at her school, is that young voices do transform the conversation. Whenever we see change in this country, and in this world, young people are at the lead. Always.

Right now, we, as young people, need to follow A'Niya's lead. In order to achieve change in this country, we all need to start our political journeys.

The road won't be easy. But the road is necessary.

BACK WHEN THERE WAS HOPE …

Ten years before A'Niya's speech, I was, like so many young people in this country, becoming incredibly optimistic about politics. I was participating in the historic 2008 presidential election, working to elect our first African American president.

I was entranced and inspired by the unprecedented election of Barack Obama. Perhaps a little too entranced. I put too much stock into one election. But it was electrifying to be a part of. And it was historic.

I followed the campaign daily, even hourly, and a week before the election I flew down to southern Virginia to help canvass with my former college roommate Rob, who had taken a job with the campaign after he graduated the previous spring. The week before the election, Rob, his girlfriend Posie, and I canvassed door to door all day and inputted data all night, doing everything in our power to make sure that Barack Obama would become president.

On Election Night, Rob, Posie, and I could barely move. More than a hundred young, idealistic campaign volunteers like us were crammed into the Roanoke bar that normally held about two dozen people. Only when nearby Virginia Tech played University of Virginia in their annual football game in Blacksburg was this sports bar as packed. But for tonight, a passion for politics had replaced the usual fervor for sports. We were all rooting for our democracy.

An hour earlier, we had knocked on our last door of the night. We offered to drive the couple that answered to the polls, but they insisted they were on their way, having just returned from work. As soon as they got into their minivan, we decided that we could safely call it a night.

We needed a drink. Or a few.

We arrived at the bar about an hour after the polls closed at 8:00 p.m. We knew the Virginia results would slowly trickle in over the night. As we walked in, we were handed cans of Bud Light by a pair of volunteers adorned in sweat-stained "Yes We Can" T-shirts. The bar had transformed into the headquarters for the entire southern Virginia Obama campaign team.

CNN news anchors reported the results from big-screen televisions. A nervous murmur pervaded the night. The three of us raised our beers and quickly toasted, not wanting to disturb anyone.

"We did our part," Rob said.

Our cans clanged in agreement.

Over the next hour, we nervously turned our attention to the news broadcast above the bar, barely engaging in conversation.

Finally, at around 10:45 p.m., Wolf Blitzer appeared on the screen with a pervasive, somber expression. His voice boomed from the speakers.

"This is a big one," he said. The bar went quiet.

"Senator Barack Obama will carry the State of Virginia . . . It hasn't gone Democrat in forty-four years, since LBJ in 1964."

"We did it! We fucking did it!" Rob cried out. He'd been working on the campaign since he graduated and couldn't contain his emotion. Obama's triumph justified all the sleepless nights and volunteer management and Domino's pizza lunch and dinners.

"I fucking told you, Rob!" I shouted at him mid-hug. He almost barreled me to the ground.

Fifteen minutes later, the polls closed in California. Wolf was back. Same look.

"CNN can now project that Barack Obama, forty-seven years old, will become the president-elect of the United States."

The bar erupted. Volunteers sprayed their shaken Bud Lights like it was champagne. Rob and I jumped in the air, hugging each other, before turning to strangers and doing the same.

Winning cures all. So does making history.

For over a year, we, and so many young people throughout the country, had dreamed of a moment we feared would never come. And here it was. A new American dawn brought on by an unprecedented victory.

Although I had canvassed in Virginia for only the last week of the election, taking a few days off from my senior year at Brown University, I was proud to have played some role in Obama's election. Obama had electrified and motivated me like no other public official ever had. His inspirational rhetoric and seeming ability to tackle the nuances inherent in complex issues provided hope for a new politics. His promises to bring a new bipartisan style to Washington, in addition to his unique global background, portended that hope and change would accompany him to the Oval Office.

The analysis on CNN continued, and so did our revelry.

"Virginia put us over the top, baby! It was all worth it!" Rob shouted to Posie and me. I refrained from noting that my home state of California had technically given Obama the electoral votes requisite for victory.

"All you, Rob. You were the difference," I sarcastically responded.

"I actually don't think Virginia would have gone blue had you two not come down this last week," he joked back.

Around us, there were shouts to focus once again on the televisions, which were now showing Chicago's Grant Park. Hundreds of thousands cheered, awaiting the remarks of our new president-elect.

"Yes, we can," they shouted.

We all joined in with the same refrain.

"Yes, we can!"

As Obama and his family walked onto the park's stage, the bar fell silent. We hung on to every word of his speech.

"I will always be honest with you about the challenges we face. I will listen to you, especially when we disagree. And, above all, I will ask you to join in the work of remaking this nation, the only way it's been done in America for 221 years—block by block, brick by brick, calloused hand by calloused hand."

I found myself nodding with every word. Just five months away from graduation, I knew that I needed to do my part. I would do what I could to, as Obama said, remake the nation from the ground up. After my family had moved abroad when I was eight years old when my father joined the State Department, I struggled to feel entirely American. And when I came back to the States for college, I felt my peers could not relate to my experiences growing up in different cultures, which had also given me a perspective on the disdain that much of the world felt for the United States during the Bush administration. In turn, I could not relate to their summer-camp experiences or interest in pop culture.

But, in that moment, I was so proud to be an American. I committed myself then to finding a way to engage in social change and justice work in the United States.

I could not wipe the smile off my face. Tears accompanied my smile before the speech ended.

But that feeling did not endure. How times change.

EIGHT YEARS LATER

On November 8, 2016, after a vitriolic, never-ending presidential cycle, Donald Trump was elected president. The elation that had overcome Rob, Posie, and me, and so many young people across this country, eight years earlier was now widely replaced by a dread and fear of what would come next.

I am a liberal Democrat. So I recognize that many others throughout the country greeted Trump's election with the same elation I did with Obama's victory. But regardless of your opinion on President Trump or President Obama, a starker reality has emerged in the wake of the 2016 election: people, especially young people, are sick of politics. We do not believe that our democracy works for us. The feeling of hope that I felt in Virginia seems to be a thing of the past.

In a sense, some of the same forces that had propelled Obama's election had helped Trump—namely, a lasting sense that politicians are not listening to the concerns of people across the country. Obama related to this sentiment from a place of hope. Trump related to it from a place of fear.

A country in which everyone has a seat at the proverbial table seems far from a reality. As citizens, we increasingly feel like our voices do not matter. We increasingly feel that we are powerless. We increasingly feel that the constitutional ideal that we were all created equal is just that—an idealistic premise.

These sentiments are especially true for young people, who

have become particularly distrustful of the public institutions that are meant to serve them.

Right now, regardless of party affiliation, perhaps the only area of agreement that we can hold is that our American democracy is not meeting its potential. The very premise on which our democracy is based—that individuals have the agency and opportunity to affect change—is at risk.

Indeed, the majority of Americans don't like politics. At the end of every election cycle, regardless of whether we're happy with the outcome or not, we're all exhausted. We're tired of the nonstop horse race of pundits reducing politics to a zero-sum equation that values drama over substance; that analyzes the cost of haircuts over the ramifications of policy decisions. We viscerally feel the lack of progress in solving the issues we care most about.

This political stagnation makes us wonder if democracy is the best form of government. The stasis makes us wonder if there's anything that we can do to improve our deteriorating political situation.

Can politics, or engaging with our government, lead to positive change?

Yeah, right.

How can we trust our elected officials to improve our communities if all they do is insult one another, engage in corruption and hypocrisy, and fundraise for the next election cycle before the previous one has even ended? Our politics have become defined by Twitter fights, insulting videos, and, yes, emails. Not the issues that we care about, or the ones that affect our everyday lives.

The very term *politics* has now become synonymous with

conflict, gridlock, entrenched and outdated institutions, and elites. We are incapable of talking with anyone who does not share our point of view. We don't trust government. We don't feel that our voices are heard, or that they matter.

All of this percolates as the conflicts surrounding issue after issue just seem to get worse. Our elected officials have been incapable of legislating on immigration, leaving DREAMers, who came to this country as young people, unable to secure their citizenship rights, and young children separated from their families at the border and placed in actual cages. The fight over gun rights continues, despite near-universal agreement on the need for expanded background checks, while school shootings have become a common occurrence.

While we hear substantial talk of bipartisanship and compromise, little has been done to solve the massive racial inequities that pervade our criminal justice system. The necessity to mitigate the effects of man-made climate change has become a potent talking point, but it's largely an issue that has evaded concrete, long-term action as politicians focus on short-term wins over real gains. Our country's debt continues to spiral out of control as politicians refuse to prioritize governmental spending or curtail tax loopholes.

Given our inability to solve these problems, our frustration with our democracy makes complete sense. Our representatives, public institutions, and systems are not helping us in the ways they are supposed to.

The subsequent choice to disengage makes sense as well, especially for young people. The logical reaction from young people is to discount the democracy we have experienced as a system that fundamentally is unfair and corrosive, especially to our interests. Democracy has become an abstract, ineffective, broad concept, rather than a community-centric, vibrant set of behaviors and practices.

Simply put, we do not understand how democracy is actually relevant to our lives.

This divorce from the political process does not mean we do not care. Young people do want to make the world a better place. We look around us and we see big, intractable challenges. We more than just see them; we experience them, deeply.

Millennials (of which I am one) are the first generation in a century that is predicted to fare worse than our parents economically. Astronomical housing costs make it increasingly harder to find a home. There are not enough jobs for us as we enter the job market, especially with rising student debt.

And that's to say nothing about climate change, which may threaten our very livelihood, and that of generations to come.

I could go on. And on. And on.

These issues affect the survival of young people across the country. So we do take action.

Sometimes, young people protest. Recently, young people have taken to protesting immigration bans, police brutality, Confederate statues that celebrate our racist past, and corrupt and greedy Wall Street institutions. Contrary to popular thought, young people do put down their phones and step outside their bubbles to take collective action.

Other times, young people look outside of government for change. We start companies, improve technology, and do what young people do best—become entrepreneurial. In search of solutions of our own, we've created Twitter and Facebook, Uber and Lyft, online grocery-delivery services, solar energy companies, and online education portals. All started by young people, designed to try to solve the problems around us. Young people innovate better than anyone else—when the system doesn't work, we create a way around it, developing better systems. We see the world for what it can be, rather than what it is today.

If government isn't working, then screw it. We'll just change things our way.

But here's the thing: protesting isn't enough. Neither is innovating outside of the system. We need to engage, deeply and constantly, with our democracy, with each other (even those with whom we disagree vehemently), and with our government. Not just on certain days, but as a habit and practice, just like going to the gym or learning to play an instrument.

Regardless of the current state of our democracy, we still need government. Protesting is important, but only sustained engagement leads to actual change. While innovative ideas might help make our lives more efficient, they don't solve the larger systemic problems.

If we want to change our country, we need to do more than show up on a Sunday at a park to protest, or create a few apps to expedite service delivery. We all need to live political lives in a quest to change and improve our government. We need to create our own political journeys.

GOVERNMENT MATTERS

Whether we like it or not, government still reigns supreme and shapes even the minutiae of our lives.

Think about a typical morning. We wake up to our alarms. We know the exact minute because the government-controlled

National Institute of Standards and Technology keeps the official time.

We eat breakfast. Our eggs could be at risk for salmonella, but federal regulations have ensured that we'll be safe after we've devoured our omelets.

We get on the school bus and go to school. If you're like 90 percent of kids in this country, you're at a public school supported by taxpayer dollars.

By the end of the day, we've walked home from school through a public park supported by the local Parks Department, watched television on publicly supported power grids, and talked on our cell phones, enabled by government wiring and technology.

When government works right, it makes our lives better.

But a lot of the time, government does not work as well as it should.

Sometimes the water isn't safe. Sometimes, like the kids in Flint, Michigan, discovered, public drinking water is contaminated at dangerous levels. Flint is unfortunately not a unique occurrence: too many communities across the country do not currently have access to safe public drinking water.

Sometimes, like in A'Niya's experience, public schools in certain areas don't receive the same resources as schools in more affluent areas. As a result, kids suffer. In some districts in Oklahoma, schools are open for only four days per week because of a lack of funding.

Sometimes public law enforcement officers are biased in their behavior, leading to unnecessary shootings and deaths. We see this in African American communities across the country daily.

Sometimes government does not do all that it can to ensure that we are safe. Sometimes people can buy guns way too easily because there's not enough government regulation.

Sometimes the government makes health care too expensive. Sometimes people even die from the flu because they cannot afford a $116 co-pay out of pocket.

Sometimes the government attempts to consolidate power or preserve control through restricting the vote or mapping congressional districts (a practice known as gerrymandering).

Sometimes those in charge prioritize tax cuts for those who are already wealthy, rather than ensure there is a more equitable distribution of resources.

So what can we do?

Despite the challenges, I still believe that democracy can work. I still believe it can work for us.

Why?

Because I know that young people can lead us to a better future.

Even in troubled and polarized times, the power of people coming together to make a difference, like A'Niya and her peers, is still evident. Every day, young people across this country are taking action to improve lives for themselves and for their communities. Just like they have all throughout history. Even recently, we have seen individual events—state elections, the Women's March, #BlackLivesMatter—and the birth of so many different movements, like the recent youth push for gun control in the wake of school shootings in Parkland and elsewhere, that give us hope.

We as young people need to use this hope to change the current narrative of our democracy. We need to create a better democracy. We can create this new normal by becoming power-ful ourselves. Gaining power will allow us to build a democracy that works for us rather than against us.

We can become powerful by overcoming our resistance to politics and participating, forcing our government to pay attention to the issues that we care about. We need to become politically active not just on Election Day, but on every single day of the year.

To make real change, we need to persist. We need to recognize that our democracy is messy. Change takes time. Whenever we see change in this country, it is the result of long, hard-fought battles and work. Especially as we deal with so many ingrained and oppressive regulations and laws, it is frustrating, and sometimes paralyzing, to reflect on the amount of work that is required to affect real systemic change. But this slog is the only way change actually happens.

This process, of changing the narrative of our democracy by becoming powerful and persisting over time, is our political journey. It is a journey that has no end, but it's one that can, and will, define our entire lives.

This book will try to convince you to become politically active. And then it will provide a framework for putting this passion into action, for becoming powerful through living a political life. The journey, while interminable in nature, can be defined by certain steps. We can learn these steps through studying real stories of youth-led political change, now and throughout history.

What's the common narrative throughout the journey of democracy in this country? It's that young people are always at the center of change. Always.

MY POLITICAL JOURNEY

As I lay out the importance of living a political journey, I will start by sharing my own. When I was twenty-one years old, as a senior at Brown University, I founded an organization called Generation Citizen (GC).

At GC, we focus on educating and empowering young people to become informed and engaged citizens, capable of driving progress in their communities by changing minds and affecting local governmental policy. Our mission is to ensure that all students receive an Action Civics education, giving them the knowledge and skills necessary to participate in our democracy as active citizens. We fulfill our vision by working in middle and high schools to teach young people about the political process by taking action on specific local issues they care about in their community. We also advocate for effective experiential civics education across the country, working to ensure that the subject becomes an expectation in our country's schools, just like math, science, or English.

After I graduated from college, I continued building GC. I now serve as the organization's CEO, and we've grown to serve young people across the country. For the last nine years, GC has steadily gained momentum and expanded our reach while deepening the quality of our program. We have opened offices in six different states, working with over fifty thousand young people since our founding. Our team has over fifty staff and hundreds of volunteers, all dedicated to pushing our mission forward effectively..

Our young people learn politics through doing politics, taking action on local issues they care about: police brutality, homelessness, the lack of teen jobs, the dearth of affordable housing options. Collectively, their efforts have impacted local policy in a real way.

This change, however, does not occur overnight. Young people, with reason, are skeptical about our democracy.

I once entered a classroom in Austin, Texas, and talked to a young Latino man about the program.

"This is dumb," he said. "No one actually cares about what we think; we're just young people. Besides, everyone in government is too racist to listen to me."

We engaged in a vigorous conversation about how change has to start somewhere, even when it's really damn frustrating. Even when there are a lot of racists and people who don't want to listen to young people.

Heated conversations like this one happen often, probably because young people are really intuitive and smart.

A typical narrative often takes place in a GC classroom: We enter the classroom. Students are skeptical change can actually happen. They are tired of being told parables and platitudes of how they can change the world. The reality of their lives does not match the rhetoric they hear asking them to participate in their communities.

We tell our students that their concerns are valid. Oftentimes, elders don't pay attention to young people. Structural barriers, like racist and sexist institutions, make change hard and slow in coming. The civil rights movement took decades. And racial-justice efforts are still ongoing, over fifty years after the passage of the Civil Rights Act. Sometimes this resonates. My voice, though, doesn't mean a hell of a lot. What resonates more is when young people begin to become political themselves.

Change can happen. Every day we see young people using

the political process to force government to improve. They are taking the lofty platitudes about the importance of young voices and turning them into concrete action.

At GC, our youth practice politics so that they can see the impact of their efforts. And then they start to believe in the power of their own voices and their own actions. In politics, seeing is believing.

Take a class of ninth graders I met in Providence, Rhode Island. Because so many students in their class (all under the age of sixteen) had been searched by cops on the way home from school, they became part of a coalition of organizations that pushed the Providence City Council to adopt a law requiring police to wear body cameras, one of the most comprehensive public safety bills in the entire country. They even worked in coordination with the police department to pass the legislation. They saw how their voices and personal experiences helped to move substantive legislation.

Another class in San Francisco was frustrated by the surge in housing costs throughout the Bay Area. Instead of just complaining, they urged their own city council member to oppose a housing moratorium that would have prevented more buildings from being constructed: they wanted more affordable housing built.

A class of ninth graders in Boston experienced increased gang violence in their community. Their peers felt targeted on the way home from school, and one unfortunately fell victim to gun violence. Reeling from tragedy, these students vehemently opposed extreme local budget cuts to a popular, effective program that used former members to engage in anti-gang advocacy throughout the city. Largely due to the student activism, the city restored funding to the program.

These stories do not illustrate catchall, silver-bullet solutions. Police brutality will inevitably still occur in Providence, and the efficacy of body cameras itself is in dispute. There seems to be no end to the escalation of housing rates in the Bay Area.

But the common element to these stories is that they all demonstrate progress. The stories demonstrate how young people can gain real power.

Regardless of our frustration in the face of inaction from our elected officials, the only way to solve the intractable issues of the day is through engaging, heart first and head strong, in our democracy. This democratic engagement will create our political journey—a process we'll be exploring throughout this book. It's a journey any young person can begin. Right now, it's a journey every young person must begin.

THE STORY OF POLITICAL CHANGE IS THE STORY OF YOUNG PEOPLE

I also understand that telling you to participate in politics and giving you the requisite steps to complete a political journey is not enough. Guiding you through this process cannot be like telling you to eat vegetables—do it because it's good for you. Words are empty unless supported by motivation. Ideas are meaningless unless they turn into real action.

So don't just take it from me.

To inspire action, we need to learn from actual stories throughout history of successful political movements led by young people themselves. These stories can both inform and inspire our future work. Our democracy does not provide a linear path toward progress—there are twists and turns, wins and losses. All people who engage in politics have their own stories of why they got involved, of their personal struggles toward progress, and of what they learned along the way.

The story of progress in this country is the story of the young people at the lunch counter in Greensboro, North Carolina, who refused to vacate their seats when they were declined service because of the color of their skin.

The story of progress in this country is the story of the young people at the Stonewall Inn in New York City, who fought back when police tried to arrest them solely because they were gay.

The story of progress in this country is the story of the young people who pushed for divestment from South Africa in the 1980s as a rejection to the government's racist agenda and jailing of Nelson Mandela.

The story of progress in this country is the story of the young people who have asserted that black lives do matter, in response to the surge in police brutality across the country, and who have begun to achieve concrete policy change.

Our country's history is the story of young people driving political progress. It has been so ever since our Founding Fathers conceived of the idea of the United States of America. More than a dozen of those who signed the Declaration of Independence were younger than thirty. The two youngest signers, Thomas Lynch Jr. and Edward Rutledge, were both twenty-six years old when they signed the Declaration.

Every single time this country has witnessed social or economic progress, from the women's liberation movement to the civil rights movement, from the gay rights movement to the push for international human rights norms, it has started with young people. Our country's founding is a story of young people acting to right a societal wrong—and, in doing so, creating their own political storybook.

Right now, we, as young people, need to look inward and take matters into our own hands. We need to create a citizen-centered politics in which individuals work together to solve problems. Or, better put by Jacqueline, a New York City GC tenth grader, "Politics is not the government making decisions for us; it's people pushing them to make decisions." We as young people need to start pushing.

When our founders conceived of the experiment of the American democracy, they did so knowing that the idea of self-governance was, well, almost crazy. Our country was the first in the modern world to be founded on the idea that citizens could come together as individuals to decide their collective future.

Sometimes, this citizen power does not go in the direction we want it to go. But we have the potential to (re)take control. And, as young people, we must become involved politically: it is the only hope for actual, lasting, systemic change. It is no longer our option, but rather our obligation.

I understand you might pick up this book as a political cynic. In this day and age, it's logical to be cynical. Cynicism will show up periodically in my voice too. But try putting that skepticism aside for a bit. Or let me try to convince you to harness that skeptical energy for concrete change.

This book will work to inspire you by showing how young people have always led our country forward. And it will provide you with concrete steps you can take so that you can also live a political life.

The result can be a revived American democracy, with young people at the forefront of change and progress.

2

DEMOCRACY IS US

Unpacking "We the People"

After having lived in five countries in ten years, due to my father's job as a foreign service officer in the State Department, I arrived at Brown University in September of 2005. At the time, I was struggling with my own identity crisis, trying to figure out whether I was an international student or an American one. Regardless, I was excited to be outside of the grasp of my parents for the first time in my life as I enjoyed all of the parties and socializing that define college orientation.

I was having so much fun I almost missed the news that thousands of miles to our south, Hurricane Katrina ravaged New Orleans and the Gulf Coast in one of the biggest American disasters of the twenty-first century to date.

Brown's president, Ruth Simmons, alerted students to the severity of the situation when she gave her convocation remarks at the end of orientation. President Simmons, who had attended school in New Orleans, was deeply affected by the disaster.

Fighting back tears, she told us, "Watching the tragedy unfold in the Gulf region, on some of your minds must be the thought: how guilty we feel to be safe, to be dry, to undertake our dreams."

All of my newly made orientation friends looked at each other contritely. The fact that I was largely oblivious to the situation before the speech provided evidence for her ruminations. I felt guilty ensconced in the privileged bubble of Brown University, just as I'd felt guilty growing up among so much inequality abroad. What was my role as a privileged young person to help as thousands suffered in New Orleans?

President Simmons offered one answer:

"One of the best things you can do in the moment of tragedy is to focus on your studies," she said, "to do what you know will ultimately do good for the world."

I am a big fan of Ruth Simmons and worked closely with her on numerous activism efforts related to ending the genocide in Darfur, Sudan. But this statement, then and now, bothers me. Too often we tell young people to leave it to the adults to solve the world's problems. Adults know best.

I understand the logic behind the sentiment. Some people may believe that young people do not have the knowledge or wherewithal to participate in complex issues. The argument follows that young people must experience the world before they can offer solutions on how to fix it.

Others may think that it's not worth putting a burden on our youth. Instead of being preoccupied with the most challenging issues of the day, it is better if they focus inward, developing themselves as people, and enjoying life before they have actual responsibilities.

The disaster in New Orleans helped me begin to see the fallacy of these arguments.

Eight months later, during spring break, I embarked on a service trip to New Orleans with other Brown students. Shortly after getting off the plane, we visited the Ninth Ward, an area of the city that had been most ravaged by the hurricane. Not co-incidentally, it was the part of the city comprised predominantly of low-income families of color. The city had not taken care of their own. Our country had not taken care of its own.

Almost a year after the hurricane, houses were still boarded up. On the outside of one house, "2 I" and "3 P" were spray-painted in white: two individuals used to live in the home, three pets. Long gone. Similar numbers remain painted on boarded-up homes throughout the city.

We drove past individuals who were still homeless. Government aid appeared nowhere. Throughout the week, we entered dozens of homes, talked to hundreds of individuals, and spent time rebuilding houses.

This is the United States? I kept asking myself. How did we allow this to happen?

The visit to New Orleans saddled me with a new identity, that of an American who had a responsibility to his country. I felt both the obligation to be an engaged citizen in my country of birth and the understanding that the United States needed me—and needed all of its citizens—to be engaged.

I could not believe that we had allowed a situation like the flooding in New Orleans to happen and, just as importantly, that we had allowed it to fester. I spoke with people still suffering from our government's neglect nine months after the hurricane ravaged the city. The ongoing devastation opened my eyes to an American poverty I previously did not know existed. It was beyond disheartening.

But seeing post-Katrina New Orleans did inspire me to want to make a difference. Additionally, it motivated me to take action politically. For while it felt good to help rebuild houses, this work was insufficient. I would go home. The situation would remain dire. Government needed to do more. Systems needed to change.

Although the situation in New Orleans was caused by natural events, it undoubtedly was worsened by the inaction of the federal government. As President Simmons also called for in her convocation, in an implicit rebuke to the government's response, "We must never become a nation impervious to the needs of the poor." A response to the plight in New Orleans required a commensurate political reaction. The federal government needed to make rebuilding the Gulf Coast a national priority and not just give the situation lip service (or fly-by helicopter visits).

As young people, we can help by engaging in community service and working alongside citizens to build houses. Volunteering in soup kitchens, rebuilding homes, cleaning up litter. All important. But, as young people, we should not stop there. We cannot stop there.

Idealistic young people see opportunities where others see barriers. There's a distinct yearning for justice and righteousness that sometimes fades with age. This attitude can also manifest itself as a certain irreverence and impatience, helping to sustain the fire that the long, slow process of change requires.

President Simmons told us that the best response to New Orleans should have been to concentrate on our studies.

I disagree.

We should have been pushing for the government to enact a response that demonstrated a willingness to help all of its citizens, rich or poor, black or white.

Instead of consistently pushing young people to the sidelines, we need them at the front of efforts to change society for the better. We need young people to be engaged politically. And we need them to be engaged now.

GENERATION Q?

New York Times columnist Thomas Friedman attempted to define my generation in an October 2007 column entitled "Generation Q." Friedman, oft lambasted because of his habit of making sweeping generalizations after conversations with cab drivers, frustrated my peers and me with his labeling of young people as "Quiet" (ergo the *Q*). His main thesis in the column was that he was both "baffled and impressed" with the latest generation of young people (now commonly known as millennials).

"I am impressed because they are so much more optimistic and idealistic than they should be. I am baffled because they are so much less radical and politically engaged than they need to be," Friedman stated.

He argued that young people do want to make the world a better place, volunteering abroad and at home, trying to find meaning in their own lives. But they are not organizing politically. Thus, Friedman concluded, they are Generation Q, the Quiet Generation. In a sense, he was describing some of the response to New Orleans. Young people were rebuilding houses. They were not pushing for radical shifts to how our country treats the poor in the aftermath of disasters.

As a millennial myself, the op-ed came across as condescending. Friedman seemed to imply that all we needed to do was act like him, and his generation, to solve the problems of the day. The act of attempting to define millennials, and tell us what to do, is quite the tried-and-true trope. The op-ed seemed like quintessential Friedman.

But, as with most criticism, there is some truth. Young people are more likely to go on community service trips to New Orleans than protest the government's response to the situation in the first place. Indeed, by a two-to-one margin, young people consider volunteering as a more effective way of finding change than participating in politics. Volunteering is a good thing, but we will not see systemic change in this country without political engagement. We, as young people, need to show up politically.

This is a tricky argument to make, especially from my vantage point as a white male who has been provided numerous privileges and power as I navigate the world. The reality is that making a difference has always been easier from my end—I know that. This is not meant to be an assertion that I have all the answers on how to create a better political climate. But I'm hopeful to shed light on some of the issues.

It is indisputable that young people are not as politically engaged as other generations, at least in the traditional ways of measuring engagement. In the 2014 elections, 20 percent of eighteen- to thirty-year-olds voted—the lowest rate since the voting age was lowered to eighteen in 1971. Eighteen- to twenty-four-year-olds voted even less—at a 12 percent rate.

While it is sometimes argued that Barack Obama helped to galvanize a youth political movement, this is an incomplete picture. The reality is that a greater percentage of young people voted in the 1992 presidential election than in Obama's historic 2008 victory. Youth turnout dipped again dramatically in 2016 without Obama on the ballot. We cannot rely on charismatic individuals to inspire youth participation: even inspiring presidential candidates do not reverse the long-term trend of lower voter turnout.

So why don't young people participate?

Oftentimes, young people do not believe that politics affects their everyday lives. Many are busy trying to get jobs, support their families, and enjoy their youth. They don't see how voting, or engaging with politicians, will make a difference. Peers often justify their lack of participation with versions of, "Yeah, I want to help make things better. But is my vote actually going to matter?" Or, "I just don't have time to pay attention to everything going on. So I can't participate if I'm not informed." Or, "Whenever I turn on the news, all they're talking about is tweets and drama, not the real issues I care about. What am I supposed to do?"

The subtext to all of this commentary is that in the laundry list of things to worry about, care about, and do something about, our democracy is not at the top.

Young people are also tired of being exhorted to participate by adults, while simultaneously being told that they are ruining the country. According to older generations, young people today are too selfish, or too self-absorbed, or too entitled, or too social-media obsessed, or too apathetic—the list goes on and on.

Young people have become a convenient whipping target for older adults, who talk about how hard life used to be back in the day, and about how politically active they used to be. But contrary to the opinions cast by the walking-to-school-in-the-snow-uphill-both-ways-touting adults, the research objectively demonstrates that young people are not apathetic, that they are not too consumed with themselves to want to make a difference, and that they volunteer at a higher rate than almost any previous cohort of young people. Indeed, a 2014 study by the Brookings Institution found that 64 percent of millennials assert that it is a priority for them to make the world a better place. Millennials just don't see politics as the best way to make change. But it doesn't help when we feel that adults are telling us what to do through lecturing, without inspiration.

Elected officials too often follow this same trope of conde-scension. They are apt to treat young people as pawns, forgetting they exist until two months before an election, and then pandering to them by addressing singular issues like astronomical college debt. We rarely, if ever, see a comprehensive youth agenda focusing on issues like access to college, quality of education, affordable housing, or climate change. Politicians are not inspiring young people to participate.

Beyond just exhorting young people to contribute politically, there are serious and real structural barriers that have impeded participation: it is indisputable that gross inequalities often prevent young people from engaging in the process. In recent years, there has been an explicit attempt to restrict voting rights, and this extends to, and sometimes focuses on, young people. Many states have made it challenging and confusing for college students to vote, sometimes requiring them to vote in person in their home district. Despite living in a democracy, our government actively makes it more challenging for people to vote.

Additionally, economic, social, and racial inequalities remain prevalent throughout society. It can seem like regardless of which political party is in charge, real and systemic change remains elusive while those in power consolidate their rule. We, as young people, feel like we have nothing or nobody to vote for.

In other words, previous generations have dealt us a pretty bad hand. To claim that our democracy can solve all of our problems seems unrealistic and, perhaps, naive.

So it's a complicated state of play. Objectively, we, as young people, are not participating in the political system as much as we used to. But at the same time, we're tired of being told how terrible we are by adults and ignored by politicians. And we're also faced with real structural barriers to our participation that make it difficult to participate. This all adds up to a feeling that the system is too irrevocably corrupt and broken to repair.

So it makes total sense that we doubt democracy can actually work.

A DEMOCRACY AT RISK

The current crisis in our democracy comes at a time when the system is at a historical precipice. Perhaps more so than any other time in recent history, democracy itself, both in the United States and around the world, is at risk. The behaviors and values associated with good citizenship are in short supply, and citizens are wondering whether better systems of governance may actually exist.

In order for democracy to hold, people must believe in it. After all, the entire concept is predicated on the notion of self-governance: government of the people, by the people, for the people.

Thus, perhaps most problematic is that we are witnessing a weakening belief in the concept of democracy itself. Fundamentally, citizens in the United States, in the midst of challenging economic and political conditions, are questioning whether democracy can actually improve our lives. People doubt whether their actions can, or should, make a difference in the act of governance.

This distrust of democracy is not just American—it is a global phenomenon. International trends measured in various surveys over the last ten years demonstrate a dramatic surge in support for a "strongman," an authoritarian leader with few checks and balances in place to limit executive power. People seem to increasingly believe that a strong leader can circumvent the institutions in place to achieve change more quickly. Relatedly, this questioning of democracy is occurring in the context of authoritarian states, like China or Indonesia, demonstrating that economic gains and security can be realized without a completely open democracy in place.

In the United States, unsurprisingly, young people are the demographic most distrustful of democracy. In 1995, surveys demonstrated that 16 percent of American young people born in the 1970s thought that democracy was a bad idea. In 2011, 25 percent of American millennials born in the 1980s said they did not believe democracy can work. That's an alarming increase, to say the least.

The distrust toward government is also at historically high levels. During the Great Depression, 50 percent of individuals polled pronounced their faith in their government to improve the economy; only 29 percent did not believe elected officials could improve circumstances. At the time of the Reagan-era recession, 41 percent of Americans were confident that the economy would soon recover, while 22 percent were not convinced. Americans thought government could help them.

In 2010, two years after the Great Recession, the percentage of optimistic Americans fell dramatically, with only 35 percent believing that the government could help the economy show signs of promise.

This data indicates that moments of crisis and economic turmoil do not inherently yield distrust of or disillusionment with the government. Instead, the American public over time has lost faith in the power of our democratic government to solve widespread problems and improve challenging conditions for its citizens.

Overall public trust in government was much higher during the 1950s and '60s, peaking at 74 percent in 1964. Today, only 19 percent of Americans say they can trust the government in Washington to do what is right and beneficial for all citizens. Citizens indicating distrust in government might not be wrong, especially right now. But in the long term, these types of opinions don't allow the system to hold.

WE'VE STOPPED PARTICIPATING

The increasing skepticism of democracy has resulted in diminished citizen participation. In an analysis from the U.S. Census, voter turnout for presidential elections has decreased consistently from 1964 to 2012 for every age group, except for citizens over sixty-five years old. Looking back to 1972, when the voting age was lowered to eighteen, almost 50 percent (49.6 percent) of eighteen- to twenty-four-year-olds participated. In the 2012 presidential election, only 38 percent of that same demographic voted. In current times, in all elections, more than half of the young voting population is not showing up.

On the aggregate, 55.7 percent of eligible voters participated in the 2016 election. Approximately 65 million people voted for Hillary Clinton. About 63 million voted for Donald Trump. And over 95 million people did not vote. Compared to developed democracies, the United States now ranks twenty-eighth out of thirty-five democracies in voter turnout.

At the local level, numbers are even more disconcerting. The Who Votes for Mayor? project out of Portland State University has collected data from fifty cities across the country on voter participation in municipal elections. Findings show that for local elections, turnout in ten of the United States' thirty largest cities was less than 15 percent.

Exacerbating this drop-off, young people are not showing up in local elections. The youngest (youngest!) median voting age of any of the cities surveyed was forty-six years old, in Portland. The average median age of a voter across all the cities in the study was fifty-seven years old. Our cities are not paying attention to young people, and young people are not showing up to participate.

WE DON'T LIKE EACH OTHER

Compounding our democratic challenges is the reality that we are increasingly unable to relate to people who do not think like us. A democracy cannot hold if its citizens do not interact with people who espouse divergent beliefs. In recent years, as political strife increases, Democrats and Republicans have become more ideological, steadfastly aligning themselves with their parties and developing negative, and even hostile, views of the "other."

Today, 58 percent of Republicans have a very unfavorable impression of Democrats, all the way up from 32 percent in 2008. Democrats have followed a similar trajectory; 55 percent currently view Republicans in a very unfavorable light, up from 37 percent in 2008.

In a similar vein, a recent study indicated that 77 percent of citizens consider their political rivals to be less evolved humans than members of their own party.

One clever historical poll has asked people over time if they would approve if they had a child who married a member of the other party. In 1960, 5 percent of Republicans would be displeased if their child married a Democrat, and 4 percent of Democrats would be unhappy if their child married a Republican. By 2015, these numbers had climbed astronomically, to 49 percent and 33 percent respectively. One could assume these numbers will only continue to increase. We have effectively othered individuals of other political parties—we actively do not want to be associated with them.

When the conversation becomes more about which of two sides is right or wrong, it becomes impossible to uphold the democratic practice of productive deliberation and values of open-mindedness and inclusivity. We cannot expect citizens to productively engage in democratic dialogue, debate, and decision-making if they are unable to interact with each other, or even respect those who disagree with their perspectives.

These statistics all portend incredibly worrisome trends.

Sometimes, we in the United States have a tendency to see democracy as a fixed state. It is not. Democracy is an idea. And as such, democracy needs to be constantly molded, cultivated, tended to. It has not been.

And right now, subsequently, democracy is at a potential breaking point. We are seeing an unprecedented lack of belief in democratic systems and forms of governance, historically low participation, high levels of polarity, and an inability to interact with a diverse citizenry—all worsened by structural barriers to actual participation. We are in the midst of an unprecedented breakdown in democracy. And as a result, democracy itself is at the precipice.

WHAT NOW?

What can we do about the fact that democracy itself may be at risk? As young people, we need to change the very narrative of what democracy actually means.

We are often taught about democracy and politics in boring civics lessons focused on the founding documents, like the Declaration of Independence and the Constitution. Democracy, we are told, is a constellation of historical documents that dictate how we should live our lives.

With this flaccid definition of democracy, it makes sense that young people aren't excited; this so-called democracy doesn't include them. Young people are cast as the audience members rather than players in the game itself. We are told what to do, and how to participate, rather than having the option to help change the way the game is played and to influence outcomes.

We're also told that democracy is just about voting. Wait

until you turn eighteen, and then vote. That's all politics is. It's hard to get worked up about something you can participate in only one day every two to four years.

To save democracy, we need to change its narrative. Instead of the system defining how we live our lives, we can define democracy as its original intention: a system in which people work together, collaboratively, to make collective decisions for how society can and should act. A system in which people, not politicians, are at the very core.

In this new narrative, we can make democracy exciting and something that happens every single day. I've been privileged throughout my life to see citizens working to do just that. For me, democracy is not static, and it is not an ugly concept. It is an everyday activity, and there is truly nothing more exciting.

Democracy is the hundreds of Kenyans I saw, as a fifteen-year-old election observer, waiting in line at 6:00 a.m. to cast the first votes in their lifetime in the rural town of Rongai.

Democracy is the Ecuadorians I saw in the streets, on the way home one afternoon during my senior year of high school, frustrated by a government rampant with corruption and rife with false promises, refusing to back down until the president left the country. They did not retreat, and the people won.

Democracy is the Zimbabweans I met as a college student, plotting in secret, attempting to force out an oppressive dictator. Democracy was an ideal for which they put their lives on the line.

Even in this country, with all of our challenges, we still see democracy at work every day.

Democracy is conservative Tea Party activists organizing in

the wake of Barack Obama's election, ascending to statehouses, the governor's mansion, and Congress.

Democracy is the unprecedented number of women who have taken to the streets and pledged to run for office to fight back against Donald Trump.

Democracy is the members of the #BlackLivesMatter movement, who refuse to accept the status quo of police brutality and have organized to push for legal reforms in a move toward racial equality.

Democracy is NFL players kneeling during the National Anthem to protest police brutality and provoking a national conversation about the true meaning of patriotism.

Democracy is the #MeToo movement, which has started to reshape the role of women in politics and society. Women are standing up to the men who have abused their power for generations.

Democracy is victory, when our favorite leaders are elected and policies are passed and when our lives are changed. And democracy is defeat when, despite sweat and hard work, we lose.

Democracy is challenging. Beautiful. Frustrating. Painful.

Most of all, democracy is a reflection of us. Democracy is people coming together to participate in collective governance, embodying the notion of "We, the people." It is the actions we collectively take to move closer to the inspiring refrain that helped to found our country but that we have never yet reached: that all of us are created equal, with certain unalienable rights.

The notion that democracy is about "We, the people" is not a given. Many have believed that citizens are too uninformed and mercurial to govern themselves. In fact, many of our Founding

Fathers were nervous about the ramifications of a citizenry run amok and strove to create a permanent divide between the ruling class and the people themselves. Luckily, those voices did not prevail. Instead, the Founders focused on a system in which citizens themselves reign supreme.

To that end, it may be wise to take former prime minister of the United Kingdom Winston Churchill's oft-repeated adage to heart: "Democracy is the worst form of government, except for all the others." Even if we don't like the democracy we have right now, we have the opportunity to change it. We can create a new narrative that puts young people, and our beliefs and values, front and center.

Perhaps, most of all, it is crucial to remember that democracy is us.

Reflecting back on President Simmons's speech about New Orleans, the natural response to the problems in our democracy may be that we should turn inward. It may be that we should learn all about our democracy and society's problems, and then emerge from our labyrinth ready to solve them.

We don't have that luxury. With democracy at the precipice, it is up to us, as young people, to take action and create a new narrative. Starting now.

3

GENERATION CITIZEN

A Reluctant Entrepreneur's Journey

Hi, Ed," I nervously choked out the words as I picked up my cell phone and stepped out of the restaurant. I was enjoying a post-graduation dinner with my parents in San Diego, marking the first time we had eaten together in my hometown in two years.

Ed was calling yet again to see if I'd accept the $50,000 he'd offered me to run Generation Citizen full-time, enabling me to build it up as a real nonprofit organization. No one had ever offered me close to that kind of money before. But I felt torn, especially since I'd already accepted a teaching job in New Orleans. I had spent two weeks worrying and deliberating over Ed's offer. I knew I had to give him an answer.

"Hi, Scott. What are you thinking?" Ed was not one to mince words.

I paused for a few moments. It seemed like an eternity to me.

Walking back into the restaurant, I smelled freshly cooked fish, caught from the nearby ocean earlier that day. I sat down, my eyes focused downward, as if I were analyzing the floor patterns. I finally raised my head to meet my parents' anxious looks.

"Here goes nothing," I said.

BECOMING POLITICAL

When I was eight years old, my father tired of his job as a criminal defense attorney and, embodying the definition of a midlife crisis, became a foreign service officer with the U.S. State Department, changing the course of my childhood. We left the comfortable environs of San Diego, and our family began moving around the world, living in a new country every two to three years. We began in the Dominican Republic, moved to Argentina, then Kenya, before I graduated from high school in Ecuador.

In each new home, I attempted to adapt quickly, learning about each country through meeting its people and immersing myself in its customs and politics. Along the way, of course, I learned a lot about myself as well. In the Dominican Republic, for example, I quickly realized that I was not a star baseball player as soon as I joined the local Dominican Little League. I was the only gringo, or American, in the entire league. Relatedly, while my batting average dipped to astronomically low levels, my Spanish, and knowledge of Dominican trash talk, increased exponentially. The opportunity to learn so much about the world at such a young age was exhilarating.

As a high school student in Nairobi, I'd discovered the complex, fragile nature of the political process in an emerging democracy through observing the country's first democratic elections. I'd also studied atrocities across the continent—for example, the 1994 genocide in neighboring Rwanda. I was shocked that the international community allowed eight hundred thousand innocent civilians to die in less than ninety days.

I learned about another ongoing genocide after my junior year of high school in 2004. In the western region of Sudan, called Darfur, government-supported militia groups, known as the Janjaweed, were systematically targeting and killing Muslim-majority populations that they felt threatened their power. Whereas the onset of the conflict had escaped the focus of the international community, it was becoming challenging to avoid the fact that this was Rwanda in redux, and in slow motion. This time, the international community could not look away.

When I first learned of the genocide in Darfur, I thought of President Clinton's promise of "never again." It was a pledge he made in the years after Rwanda, which he declared to be the biggest regret of his presidency, as the United States did nothing while the genocide took place. Never again, he claimed, would the international community allow genocide to occur. Similarly, during the first year of his presidency, President Bush wrote "Not on my watch" in the margins of a report describing the United States' lack of response to Rwanda.

But, as Darfur unfolded, we were *there* again. The international community was again doing nothing. I felt an obligation to take action.

I returned to the States, and during the first three years of college, I decided I would not stand idly by. I put everything I had into building and sustaining a student movement to end the atrocities in Darfur. Lots of emails. Lots of phone calls. Lots of retreats with other student activists. Lots of writing op-eds.

I did good work, I think. I also think I probably lost out on college as a result. I left college on the weekends to go to rallies, cut my winter break short to lead a retreat of youth activists, and spent a lot of time on the phone with my fellow student activists from across the country.

Before long, I became the national student director for an organization called STAND, Students Taking Action Now: Darfur. We led efforts for the hundreds of college and high school chapters across the country trying to take effective political action. Along with other youth activists, I appeared on CNN, spoke at conferences, and attempted to mobilize other young people.

I helped to organize a rally in front of the White House in April of 2008. We decided that enough was enough, and we wanted to make a big statement. As a rally with over one thousand young people ended, nineteen of us marched to the front of the White House. We chanted and urged President Bush to do more, as part of his legacy, to end the genocide. The National Park Police told us to leave. We continued chanting until we were arrested for civil disobedience and taken to the Anacostia prison. We received national press attention—this was the cause of the day.

In addition to these efforts to rally public support, I also helped lead national efforts to convince university, city, and state pension funds to divest their assets from companies doing business in Sudan. While American companies could not conduct business in the country, predominantly in the oil industry, international companies continued to do so, providing funds to the genocidal regime as it pillaged, looted, and killed the Darfurian people. We worked to ensure that pensions were not invested in these international companies.

This divestment work included convincing Brown to become the fifth university in the country to divest. Providence became the first city in the entire country, and Rhode Island one of the first states, to follow suit, and divest their assets from international companies doing business in Sudan. Due primarily to the efforts of young people across the country, the divestment movement rapidly gained traction, becoming the largest and fastest-moving divestiture campaign since the move to divest from South African companies during apartheid in the 1980s.

I believe we made a tangible difference in bringing attention to the atrocities in Darfur. I also think that the divestiture efforts caught the attention of the Sudanese government and might have helped to actually curb, in at least a small way, their genocidal behavior. In this case, as in so many others, money talked.

I also know that I was burning out. And I was allowing some of the media attention to get to my head.

By the time my term as student director of STAND officially ended on April 30, 2008, I was a little disenchanted by the lack of progress we were seeing in Darfur. And I was tired. The sleepless nights had caught up with me.

Had we actually done any good?

The genocide, in all its complexity, continued. Despite the fact that I had spent so much of my life abroad, I wasn't sure if I wanted to continue to put energy into international activism. It was difficult to evaluate whether our efforts were leading to change, and it was impossible to become an expert on an issue so far away. I began to doubt whether I, as a white American who had never been to Sudan, could actually advocate for solutions for a people who lived on the other side of the world.

My experience in New Orleans also continued to weigh on me: there were so many problems in the United States; I found myself asking, what should my role be in improving conditions in my own country?

This is a tension that continues to arise, and is always worth reflecting upon, in change-making work. What was my role as an ally in the cause?

I wanted to make a difference in Sudan, and I feel genocide is the ultimate threshold of moral action (or inaction, in this case). But I am somewhat circumspect of my own actions now. I wonder how my personal ambitions—in this case, to "Save Darfur"—may have been arrogant or misplaced. This is to say nothing of the historical role of white westerners in Africa and the deep, lasting ramifications of colonialism throughout the entire continent. There are no easy answers, but it is always critical to assess personal motivations when engaging in any sort of political work.

I do know we could have done more to enlist Sudanese themselves in the effort to end the conflict in Sudan. With expertise and knowledge of Sudan, they should have been leading the charge. We should have been learning from them.

Regardless of my existential reflections, my activism did change me on a personal level. The act of passing a bill in the Rhode Island legislature provided an intimate and effective crash course on the realities of local politics. I witnessed firsthand how a bill actually becomes a law. This wasn't *Schoolhouse Rock!* style, or what you learn in a textbook. Instead, it was the behind-the-scenes lobbying that involves everything short of promising your firstborn to political representatives to accomplish legislative change. Along the way, I discovered how challenging it can be to get adults to take young people engaging in politics seriously.

Our coalition of divestment advocates, comprised of community organizations and young Brown students (including myself as a nineteen-year-old), was able to get Democrat and Republican state legislators to introduce Sudan divestment legislation. There seemed to be traction—we figured that the moral imperative of the bill was obvious, as over four hundred thousand had died in the atrocities, and for the first time in U.S. history the president and Congress had declared that the ongoing atrocities met the definition of genocide.

Accordingly, to push the bill forward, almost every Tuesday and Thursday, I would walk down College Hill to the statehouse with peers and community members to lobby legislators to support the bill on the floor of the House and Senate chambers. We composed a binder with every legislator's picture in it, and over the course of a few weeks, we approached every single one for their support. We felt we were close; the majority of legislators seemed to be in favor of the bill. One week before an important hearing, I felt like we were on the cusp of something momentous.

Then a woman at least twenty years my senior walked up to me on the House floor and introduced herself as the policy director for the treasurer of the state. I was (again) stoked—I had been trying to get a meeting with their office for a long time, since they actually controlled the pension fund.

"I'm so glad to meet you," I said. "I would love to talk to you and the treasurer about the merits of the bill and see if we could get you to support it. This movement is gaining traction across the country, and Rhode Island can play a leading role."

She looked at me, then laughed. The laugh transformed into that condescending look that young people are all too used to receiving when engaging in political activism.

"Is this a cute student project? What class are you doing this for?"

She thought the whole thing was a joke. Flustered, I stammered that we were actually trying to pass it.

I quickly walked away.

A week later, alongside experts and other community members, we faced off against that same woman at an official legislative hearing for the bill. We explained the moral imperative behind the bill and used statistics from other state decisions, as well as specific language in the bill, to drive home the fact that the state's pension fund would not be harmed.

This time, as she testified, she was the one stammering.

"The activists have provided very clear evidence from other states that this type of bill does not negatively affect the state's pension fund. Why are you arguing against this?" the head of the finance committee pushed her to answer.

"We know this would not be good for the state," she replied, without elaborating.

The legislators looked on skeptically. They visibly shook their heads.

I snickered in the back of the room. Some student project, I thought to myself.

But, in the end, the treasurer's office had more political cache than a nineteen-year-old college freshman and our troupe of activists. They defeated the bill soon thereafter, but I knew that our testimony had made them nervous.

The fact that they had originally laughed off our efforts motivated us to work even harder. In the next year, we organized folks from across the state, held rallies, published op-eds, and met with every single legislator in the state. Fortuitously for us, the old treasurer reached his term limit and left office. When the next legislative session began, a new treasurer held the reins. This time, largely because he had heard so much about our efforts, he made Sudan divestment a key priority, even campaigning on the issue.

Before long, I was back in the statehouse. But this time, I was at a ceremony with the governor of Rhode Island, who was signing into law an unanimously passed piece of legislation that required the state to divest its holdings from companies doing business in Sudan—one of the first states in the country to do so.

After helping to successfully pass a bill in Rhode Island, my faith in the potential of democracy was heightened, if not totally confirmed. Unlike so many of my peers, I came to see politics and participation in our democracy not as a bottomless abyss of inaction, but rather as a primary mechanism to sustainable change. As disenchanting as it could sometimes be, this hands-on work empowered me. As an active citizen capable of taking action on issues that I cared about, I learned how to achieve real change politically. As a twenty-year-old, I had played a major role in passing state legislation with global repercussions.

Still, I realized that the majority of young people did not feel the same way. Not because the young people I interacted with didn't care about making the world a better place. My peers constantly talked about their dreams and aspirations to create a more equitable society. But often their passion for change stopped at the level of talk.

This inaction manifested itself not because of apathy, but rather, because many, or most, of my peers saw politics as fruitless. They perceived elected officials as incompetent, inaccessible, racist, corrupt, and largely out for themselves. And so they thought the best way to affect change was to work outside of the system.

My experience was a little different. While we may not have ended the genocide in Darfur, our efforts to organize and mobilize thousands of college students had fundamentally changed the political calculus of genocide prevention in the United States. And we had done so through engaging in the political process.

Maybe our political system wasn't working. But the way to fix it, I decided, was to become more political. The question was how to convince other young people to do the same.

TURNING DOMESTIC

I began to have conversations with fellow activists about the lessons we had learned through STAND and the challenges we encountered in convincing other young people to participate in the political process. My friend Elizabeth, who went to school in Chicago and had led our efforts to engage high school students in Darfur activism, drew my attention to the fact that one of the main reasons the majority of young people did not feel the same way we did about politics was because they did not have effective civics education when they were growing up. I had never thought about the lack of civics education until Elizabeth brought it up, but it made sense logically.

We also reflected on the elitism and privilege inherent in the movement. Too many youth activists came from, well, similar backgrounds: they attended elite colleges, and they had time and money to spare. True democracy could not flourish if only more affluent young people participated in the process and only their efforts were uplifted.

We began to conduct research on the topic and found that affluent students were acclimatized to formal political education whereas poorer students received little, if any, civics education at all. Our conversations continued as we thought about our Darfur activism and the political process in which we'd participated. We wondered if we could translate our own experiences into a class. Could this experiential form of civics be something that every young person could receive?

On May 1, 2008, the day after I ended my term as student director with STAND, I put together a proposal for an initiative I called the Generation Citizenship Project. With Elizabeth's help, I outlined a program that would encourage young people to become excited about politics. First, we'd ask students which issues they cared about most. Then, after helping them conduct some research, we'd train them to take action on that issue.

We did not want this civics education to be extracurricular. Our Darfur activism, which had been a voluntary activity, had appealed predominantly to privileged students who had the capacity to engage in this type of work in their free time. Instead, we conceived of a sort of political-socialization class. Our goal was to have students take this class just like they would take math, science, or English. We would call it Action Civics, and it would be something every single young person could receive.

As we were coming up with the concept of Generation Citizen, a summer trip to see my parents in Zimbabwe, during which I visited with political-opposition members in the midst of a violent, runoff election, caused me to continue to reflect on the limitations of my international activism. When I returned to the United States, my mind was fully set on developing and growing Generation Citizen. I would work to do what I could to improve democracy at home. I wrote a skeletal five-page curriculum and composed a training manual. I was grateful to realize that other Brown students thought the idea could work. We quickly formed a volunteer team of seven.

Despite this momentum, the reception was not universally positive, at all.

I had conversations with numerous advisors before officially launching Generation Citizen. They offered similar, discouraging feedback:

"It's a good idea, but you're too young to make it happen."

"Maybe let someone with more experience start this out."

"Wait your turn."

Despite their doubts, our group piloted the Generation Citizenship Project (the later name change was a necessary one, for the organization and this book) in four classrooms in Providence that September. I began by teaching tenth graders at Central High School. The school was a mile away from Brown, but I quickly realized that none of the students had set foot on Brown's campus. And vice versa.

Students were doing everything they could to not pay

attention on my first day. Reluctantly, I tried to harness their energy by telling them what we were trying to accomplish.

"Throughout this semester, you all are going to choose an issue you care about and take action," I said. "We're going to make a change together!"

My attempt at inspirational rhetoric fell flat. A few students looked up from their desks. Not many. There were scattered laughs.

"Well, you all care about politics, right? What do you all think about the current presidential election?" I had been following the 2008 election nonstop, so I assumed that they had been as well.

I received more than a few blank stares, so I kept explaining.

"So Barack Obama and the Democrats had their convention last week, and John McCain and the Republicans are having their convention this coming week." I was ready to launch into the new phenomenon of Sarah Palin and hear their opinion on the presidential race.

A hand shot up, and someone asked, "Who's John McCain?" A room full of students looked quizzically at me.

I realized I had a lot of work to do. I had tried to inspire the students by describing the national political horse race that I followed so closely. But they didn't care about that. Their issues were located where politics should reside: in local communities.

I realized how insular and privileged my bubble had become, assuming everybody's existence revolved around politics. I also realized that perhaps they had more important things to care about than the presidential election—issues that actually affected them in a more immediate and visceral way.

The next class, we moved from the national drama to the relevant local issues. After an intense debate on topics ranging from the lack of summer jobs to the quality of the cafeteria food, our students voted to take action on public transit—an issue that I had no idea was even a problem in Rhode Island.

Because of recent budget cuts, the Rhode Island Public Transit Authority, or RIPTA, had been forced to disproportionately cut routes in low-income neighborhoods. Additionally, a policy was in place that provided free bus passes to students who lived at least three miles away from their school. Which meant that, somehow, if you lived two and a half miles away from school, you were expected to walk. In the snow, in freezing temperatures during the winter.

After conducting research, our students contacted their local officials, and they ultimately convinced one of the board members from RIPTA to come into class about halfway through the semester. I was nervous about how they would react to an actual decision-maker in their presence, especially given the fact that, throughout the semester, each class was a complete wild card. Sometimes only three students would be engaged while the other twenty slept on their desks. In these particular classes, democracy and politics remained an abstract, boring concept. A budding educator without much experience myself, I probably was not helping matters.

But this class was not that. For this class, every student was wide-awake. It was almost as if they had been paying attention all semester.

The students asked the director informed questions, clearly surprising him with their knowledge of the intricacies of the funding of RIPTA:

"Why is the free pass radius three miles?" asked one student. "What if it's freezing in winter?"

"Why is the Number 20 bus running half as often as it was last year? It makes it really hard to get to school on time!"

"Why does RIPTA get 40 percent of their revenue from the gas tax? Doesn't that mean that you make more money if more people drive cars?"

The barrage continued.

The board member was first surprised, and then impressed, with their knowledge. He realized that they knew their stuff and eventually invited them to come to a meeting.

"He actually cared about what we think!" recalled Quai, a student who was ecstatic after the meeting. "I think we got him to change his mind on a few things."

My students were not accustomed to adults caring what they thought about the problems happening in their communities. And despite their passion, change to the public transit authority did not happen right away. But over time, routes were restored and funding increased. The radius for free passes was eventually, years later, reduced to two miles. The students played a role in reforming the system. This was politics at work. The class proved that the idea of educating young people to participate in local politics had promise.

Still, I didn't expect to stay with Generation Citizen. I was faced with the challenges of senior year. After roughly sixteen years of churning away at school, I had to sort out my next steps—steps that would not, for the first time, be outlined for me.

So began the constant interrogation from professors, family members, peers:

"What are you doing next year?"

When I started looking at jobs, the notion of continuing with GC did not really cross my mind. Since I enjoyed my experiences in the classroom, I decided to apply to teach. And that's how, two weeks after graduation, I came to be in possession of a job and a one-way plane ticket to New Orleans.

ED

When I started GC, I had a partner in crime, Anna, who was a fellow Darfur activist. Compelled by GC's vision, she became GC's indispensable cofounder. She also introduced me to her friend's father, Ed Cohen.

Before meeting Ed one Saturday for breakfast in October, Anna explained that he was a titan in the social entrepreneurship arena. He knew everyone, and apparently, he knew how to smell success.

Ed was not your typical banker or consultant, who you might expect would pull up with a fully pressed suit and coiffed hair. When he shook my hand, I could feel his fingernails, completely caked with paint. Ed had become an artist.

He grilled me, but not on what I thought he'd press me on. He asked about my background, my family, my passions. He seemed interested in my international background, and my anti-genocide activism efforts. GC barely came up. He did have a few ideas on ways we could learn from similar organizations. And then, as abruptly as it had begun, breakfast was over.

"It's a good idea," he said, without any tone in his voice that would actually convince me that he thought it was a good idea. "You should stick with this after you graduate."

Over the next few months, we emailed back and forth. In every exchange, Ed returned to his persistent desire for me to make GC an actual organization. Usually in very few words or complete sentences.

When I told him in March that I was planning to teach, the emails stopped.

Yet, almost as soon as I accepted the offer to teach in New Orleans, I began to have second thoughts. Did I actually want to teach? Would I actually be a good teacher?

Then came graduation weekend.

My parents flew in from Zimbabwe, and we had a weekend chock-full of plans: a campus-wide dance, lectures, dinners with friends, and then graduation itself. Festivities began on Friday night with a reception at Brown's Swearer Center, the hub of community service, which had helped to incubate GC's work. As part of the reception, a group of seven seniors were asked to make quick pitches describing their work. I was among those asked to speak.

I stood up in front of a crowd of more than fifty, and I described GC. I recounted how I'd help teach Action Civics to area middle and high schoolers. We were asked to end by declaring our postgraduation plans.

"I will be teaching middle school social studies in New Orleans," I announced to the crowd.

As the speeches ended, Ed appeared. I was angling to get to the reception to begin drinking for the night, but he would not let me leave.

"Hey, Scott," he said sternly. "You really need to stick with GC after you graduate." He really had no idea how to make small talk.

I smiled uncomfortably. "Ed, I appreciate all the support. But I'm really excited to be teaching in New Orleans." I was trying to convince myself.

"You really need to stay," he insisted.

He was appealing to my oppositional streak. After all, I had always loved succeeding against the odds and in spite of what people said I could do. Advisors had insisted I was too young to start GC, so I piloted it a few weeks later. Politicians had said we could never pass divestment, so we did.

"Look," he said, "I'll give you fifty thousand dollars over the next two years for you to grow Generation Citizen."

I couldn't speak.

"Think about it. I'll be around all weekend."

I put it out of mind. My future was in New Orleans, teaching. I didn't even reach out to Ed. What a completely ridiculous offer.

On Monday morning, the day after I graduated, fate intervened. I walked to a friend's house to help him move out.

Somehow, Ed was across the street. Seriously.

He called me over.

"I really appreciate your offer," I said, "but I made a commitment. I'm going to teach."

"Scott, stop being ridiculous. Any sane entrepreneur would jump at the offer I made." This was the most passionate I had ever seen him. His usual stoicism, or detachment, was gone.

"What's holding you back?" he asked.

"I'll think about it."

Ed shook his head and walked off.

But over the next week, Ed kept pushing me. With a few phone calls, he set up a day of meetings for me a train ride away, in Boston. He wanted to test me. Could a person this reluctant to take his money actually build an organization?

That day, I met with numerous people: the founder of Health Leads and a MacArthur Fellow (Rebecca Onie), the founder of City Year (Alan Khazei), the head of a huge foundation, and a dean at Tufts University. It was both exhilarating and nerve-racking. I needed to make a decision. The uncertainty was killing me. Although obviously it was all my own fault.

Halfway through the day, Ed called.

"How's it going?"

"I'm enjoying meeting these folks. I think I can see myself doing this," I told him, though I wasn't sure I meant it.

"Rebecca was not impressed. You didn't ask her enough questions. She doesn't know if you have what it takes. I'm tired that you are taking this long to make a decision. You better do well the rest of the day."

I realized later that the MacArthur Fellowship is known in common lexicon as the Genius Grant. So I had officially failed to impress a genius.

The gauntlet had been thrown. I might shy away from starting a nonprofit on my own. But I did not shy away from a challenge. Especially from a genius.

Rebecca's doubt ended my own. I doubled down in my meetings the rest of the day. I was focused. I was passionate.

At the end of the day, I was on a plane to San Diego to see my parents. I was exhausted: in the last week, I had graduated from college, bid farewell to all my close friends, and contemplated leaving a secure job for complete uncertainty.

I knew that this was an opportunity that I could not pass up.

It would be challenging as hell. I would fail, more times than I could count.

But I believed in the ability of young people to make a difference in our democracy.

And so that evening in San Diego, after Ed's phone call, I sat back down at the table with my parents, full of enthusiasm and hope.

"I'm in," I told them.

4

A FRAMEWORK FOR CHANGE

The Advocacy Hourglass

Although it was early May of 2016, the cold thunderstorm outside made it seem like the brutal New York City winter had not yet ended. Upon my exit of the overcrowded subway, in what was becoming a weekly occurrence, I cursed my East Coast residency, wondering when I'd have the sense to move back to the better weather of California.

The inevitable morning subway delays meant that I was running late, so I began jogging from the Jackson Heights stop to I.S. 230, a middle school in the heart of Queens. After three blocks, I stopped in a local coffee shop for some caffeine. Consuming sufficient coffee was more important to me than being on time.

As the barista made my drink, he laughed. I had not brought an umbrella.

"I hope you are not walking too far!" he said.

I grimaced. "Didn't check the weather before I left this morning." Truthfully, I never brought umbrellas anywhere. Felt they were a nuisance—and would lose them frequently anyway.

I downed the double shot of espresso and ran back out into the winter abyss.

Eight blocks and five minutes later, I barged through the heavy school doors. Councilman Daniel Dromm, the chair of the Education Committee in the city council, was waiting along with two Department of Education officials in the lobby. The security guard handed me a paper towel with a pitying look in his eyes. Great first impression to make in front of incredibly important city officials.

I introduced myself nervously. They laughed, probably wondering how this guy could actually be the CEO of the organization they were present to observe. Not an uncommon occurrence in GC's early years. Or perhaps even now.

After niceties and the inevitable small talk about the weather, we took the creaky elevator up to the fifth floor. Once there, we passed rowdy students chasing after each other in the hallways, and we made our way into a classroom.

Eighth graders were running around, not unlike the students in my first class in Providence years before. This time, though, they were excitedly practicing presentations with one another. They grew quiet as we entered. The ringing bell signaled the start of the class period.

The thirty students were all dressed in their Sunday best—boys in suits and ties, girls in dresses. The four of us found seats at the back of the class. The room was already packed with people. I almost fell off my desk as I sat down—one leg was much shorter than the rest. The students around snickered. A kinder one passed me one of his notebooks, and I placed it under a leg to steady the desk.

Written student presentations covered the walls. There were five-paragraph essays on gun control and drawings of the neighborhood that indicated local expertise and art acumen. I noticed an essay on the contemporary meaning of the Declaration of Independence. Another paper examined the recent protests in Ferguson, Missouri, and across the country, as the Black Lives Matter movement had started to spread. I also saw a delegate tracker that counted the race between Bernie Sanders and Hillary Clinton. A separate one from Republicans already had a big red circle around Republican nominee Donald J. Trump. Sign of the times.

The teacher, Ms. Alvarez, attempted to quiet the rowdy students. She raised her right hand in the air.

"It's time!" she said. "Please take your seats for our guests!"

The shouts did not totally abate, but they did turn into murmurs.

The students quickly took their seats at the front of the room. These eighth graders, having participated in Generation Citizen for a semester, were presenting their action plans to a panel of Queens community leaders.

The first group of five students nervously shuffled their way to the front of the room. They described their plans to advocate for regulations to ensure more nutritious cafeteria food in New York City public schools. Disgusted by the plastic-tasting pizza they generally receive, they had contacted their food-service contractors to ask for healthier options.

"We have rights!" they said. "And we deserve better food. What we have now is unacceptable!" As they sat down, the class applauded. Clearly, this was a popular issue. And not just to their school. Basically, every Generation Citizen class starts with students wanting to tackle the issue of cafeteria food.

The next student moved to the front of the room. Maria described how she had come out as a lesbian during seventh grade. After coming out, she was taunted, a victim of bullying and abuse. She said she'd thought about taking her own life.

But she had persisted, and had now become an advocate. She thanked her classmates for supporting her.

"I once was scared," she admitted. "I thought there was something seriously wrong with me. I could not even talk to my parents about it. I now feel proud of who I am. And I want to help other young people feel comfortable in their own skin, regardless of how old they are."

In front of the first LGBTQ staff liaison for New York City schools, Maria turned her personal struggle into a call for action. She and her class had decided to lobby for more resources for the LGBTQ department in the Department of Education. She wanted to foster a more understanding environment among young people and ensure that young girls like her felt more comfortable being themselves.

"One liaison for the entire city is not enough," she said. "Young people should not go through what I went through. I want to help make a difference."

The class clapped. The liaison leapt up and shook her hand.

"I need to get you in front of my boss. You can help me get more support in my office!"

Maria beamed. It was clear that, in that moment, she felt powerful.

And then, a young girl with shy but powerful eyes slowly walked to the front of the room.

"I am from Bangladesh," she said. "My family moved here when I was four years old because they were in search of a better life for me and my sisters. But life here has been very difficult."

The whole room focused on Laila as her voice began to rise.

"I used to be shy," she continued. "I used to be afraid to speak for what I cared about. I am no longer afraid."

Laila recounted how her class, through the GC curriculum, decided to focus on racial discrimination. Many students had experienced ramifications of the City of New York Police Department stop-and-frisk initiative, which allowed officers to search individuals if they were suspected of engaging in illegal behavior. Laila's classmates, some as young as eleven years old, were stopped by police because of the color of their skin and the neighborhood they lived in. They were searched, and, in some cases, their rights to privacy were violated.

Laila, as an American Muslim, keenly felt this discrimination. She saw people look at her differently, nervously, in the subway because of the hijab that covered her hair. She saw family members targeted by the police. All this, and she was only in middle school.

Laila and the class looked at statistics that demonstrated the real racial disparities in both police stops and sentencing laws, and then they decided to focus on a specific law before the city council that would change the quota system for police officers. Instead of police officers only receiving credit for arrests and searches they made, they wanted to ensure that the officials received credit for more positive behavior they engaged in, like responding to citizen concerns. They reached out to their local officials and encouraged them to cosponsor and push for passage of the bill.

Laila closed with a powerful statement in support of the cause, and in support of youth activism generally:

I was afraid too; maybe I still am. But I know I have people who are there for me and that someone needed to come up and say something, and I took that place of someone. My voice right now is not only mine. But the voice of a thousand other people. My voice right now represents those people who can't speak up for themselves.

This country is our responsibility. This country depends on us as much as it depends on you. We won't let anyone take away our identity from us. We won't let anyone come in our way to success. We won't let anyone take away our smiles from our faces.

Rather we will make a positive difference in this world. Whether it is alone or together, we'll do it. Never be afraid to stand alone if you must because one person can make a difference!

Laila pumped her fist in the air as she closed. She was more inspiring and powerful than most politicians I've seen.

On cue, the politician in the room, Councilman Dromm, stood up and started clapping.

"This is the next generation of leadership!" he said. "I hope you wait a while before you decide to run against me!"

Laila beamed. I'd have voted for her that day. So would have the entire class. She was proof of youth power.

Laila's ability to speak truth to power, especially as a fourteen-year-old in a city and country that has continually and increasingly discriminated against American Muslims, is democracy. In a tumultuous political time, Laila reminded all the adults in that room that young people matter. And that their voices can be more important and more powerful than that of any adult.

THE ADVOCACY HOURGLASS

We need more Lailas. We need all young people to lead us toward a brighter political future. We need to take action on issues that we care about. And we need to show the rest of the country how to build a better democracy.

Generation Citizen created a framework we call the Advocacy Hourglass to help guide us through the process of taking effective political action. When we first started teaching our Action Civics class, we found that students were eager to speak about the issues they cared about. Students, for example, would articulate a concern about gun violence, because friends in their community had been shot and killed. They wanted to take immediate action.

But they wouldn't know what to do. Maybe they would propose writing to President Obama or raising awareness on the issue in some general way—not the most effective courses for action. While President Obama might care about a student shot in the Bronx, he wouldn't be able to do anything concrete about it. And while raising awareness is important, it doesn't necessarily lead to immediate action to address the root causes of the problem.

Citizens throughout the United States often use similar logic. We all can articulate the broad issues that we care about, from climate change to immigration. But we often fail to analyze these issues and focus on the root cause. And we often look to our most senior national officials, like the president, to solve local issues. In a country of over 350 million people, this approach doesn't work. In fact, a focus on the national can be disempowering when we see nothing done to help local communities.

The reality is that the most effective way to take action is still local, to paraphrase former Speaker of the House of Representatives Tip O'Neill. There are over five hundred thousand elected officials throughout the country, most of them in local positions, like city council, school board, even coroner, and they are all accountable to everyday citizens. We need to appeal to officials in our communities.

The Advocacy Hourglass, below, is an attempt to bring the local back to politics. We use it with all our students, and its overriding philosophy can be used by citizens in all walks of life:

The shape of the Hourglass is purposeful: we begin by thinking about broad issues in the community, such as climate change, police-community relations, and, yes, even cafeteria food. We then narrow the topics to one local issue and identify a root cause of the problem. Finally, to address the root cause, we identify a specific main goal and develop strategies to achieve it. The tactics, again, are broad. There are many potential ways to achieve your articulated specific goal.

The Hourglass is meant to encourage substantive political action. While signing petitions or going to rallies are all forms of action, they are not enough. More robust, sustained, local tactics will allow us, as young people, to create the new politics we need for this country's democracy to ultimately succeed.

The Hourglass supported Laila and her classmates in their shift from the broad issue of racial discrimination to specifically lobbying for a bill that would address the requirement for police to meet certain arrest quotas each month. This progression works for classes across the country progressing through Generation Citizen's curriculum. It can work for citizens across the country as well.

A recent class in New York City utilized the Hourglass in an innovative way to address the omnipresent issue of their school's awful cafeteria food. A popular issue, though, can sometimes prove difficult to tackle from a systemic perspective. What can you do, besides clamor for healthier food?

Eighth graders at Williamsburg Collegiate decided to research potential ways to take action. They discovered that school cafeterias in the city are graded on their cleanliness, with a system similar to the letter grades that restaurants receive for their sanitation: A, B, C, D, or F. These scores, however, are not public, and there is no ramification, positive or negative, for the grades that school cafeterias receive.

So these eighth graders got smart, and they got political. They contacted their local state representatives and lobbied for the introduction of a bill that would require the Department of Education to publicly publish grades for every school's cafeteria. As the bill worked its way through the legislature, the students organized phone banks and lobbying meetings while also educating their peers about the bill's merits. Eventually, the bill passed. Cafeterias across the state are now required to publicize their cleanliness grades.

Using the Advocacy Hourglass, the students started with the giant, vague issue of school lunches. They narrowed it down to a specific root cause: the lack of transparency in the state's cleanliness grading reports. They then determined specific goals and tactics.

Advocating for a state bill to publicize cafeteria cleanliness grades is not the sexiest issue in the world. It also will not automatically and immediately lead to better food. But it is a start. And the way that the students approached taking action on a local issue is a necessary means of tackling political change, for young people and in our society at large.

Another middle school class in San Francisco chose to attempt to reform police brutality, an issue that has rightfully galvanized young people across the country. Again, this is an expansive problem without a clear and specific solution. So they began to break it down using the Hourglass. Specifically, they learned about a young Latino male, Alex Nieto, who was shot dead by police in a public park in San Francisco in 2014.

They identified deeply with the incident, which was reflective of broader trends in the city, in which gentrification and housing costs were bringing in more white people, who were more suspicious of the Latino individuals who had long called San Francisco home.

The students wanted to draw attention to the issue of police violence in the demographically changing city, while simultaneously honoring the man. They began a movement to lobby for a memorial for his life. They felt that this specific goal would bring awareness to the horror of police brutality and inspire subsequent action. A clear and powerful memorial to the cause would mean that it would be impossible for regular citizens to ignore the issue.

Christina Fogel, a senior at the University of San Francisco, worked with the middle schoolers as they made their way through the Hourglass. She emailed me in December of 2016:

> A few days after Civics Day, a San Francisco district supervisor reached out to one of my students and told her she was touched by all of the messages from our class and because of it would be voting in support for Alex's memorial. Her response was incredibly powerful in making my students realize their voices truly matter and that there is tremendous power in advocating for what you believe in.
>
> Last Tuesday, the SF Board of Supervisors voted on the memorial. It passed 9-1, which we view as a huge victory. I arranged a phone call with the teacher to congratulate the class the next morning. I am so proud of them—they helped make history. This will be the first

government-sponsored memorial honoring a victim of police brutality in California.

There are a few important stages that all of these effective, youth-led changes have in common. These steps all lead through the Advocacy Hourglass. Using stories of real youth change, we'll explore these steps throughout this book. They'll comprise the framework for our political journey.

FOCUS ON AN ISSUE

Young people who have made change have historically fought for something that affected their everyday lives. The politics becomes personal—a key tenet of effective political action. In GC, young people focus on immigration because a relative has been deported, gun control because a peer tragically fell victim to violence, or public transit because they cannot afford to travel to school. The politics of the personal is the most effective way to inspire us all to become active and engaged citizens.

It is important to note that we don't all have a story like this to inspire us to action. We all, however, can be empathetic. In addition to focusing on the politics of the personal, we can listen to our neighbors, community members, and those around us, and we can learn the issues that deeply impact their well-being.

When picking an issue, it's critical to keep in mind that change starts locally. As citizens, we have a much greater ability to affect change at the local level on issues that matter more to us.

Your local school board is responsible for ensuring your schools are equitable and offer a high-quality education. Your local police chief is responsible for law-enforcement behavior, good and bad. Local city council members set the public transit budget. In many ways, your local officials affect your daily life much more than the president does. Our political journey will almost always begin at the local level.

DEVELOPING EXPERTISE

Through comprehensive research involving interviews, historical records, and the news, young people decide the best way to take political action. Any time reform occurs, it is because young people have interviewed stakeholders and constituents, reviewed existing laws, and followed the news.

When we see real change, we see that young people have determined the root causes of their issues, identified decision-makers, determined specific ways to act, and pushed the appropriate decision-makers to listen and learn. They did not solely raise awareness or talk about their issues—they became experts on their issues. They met with local officials, conducted petitions, and organized rallies.

TELLING AUTHENTIC STORIES

Critical to engaging in effective change-making is persuading others to join your journey. Expressing compelling stories, through use of a personal narrative, allows others to empathize with your issue while also inviting others on the journey and galvanizing them to action.

When young people lead change, they inspire others to join through their own personal stories. For example, the story of the civil rights movement includes the young people who organized in Selma and captured the attention of an entire country. These young people did not simply exhort people to follow them because of an obligation; they told compelling personal stories that convinced people of the merits of their issue. They followed a persuasive narrative framework to change hearts and minds. The art of storytelling, which has accompanied every political movement in this country's unfolding history, is essential to any political journey.

The challenge is to tell a story that does not simplify but rather addresses the complexities inherent with any road to change. An intellectually honest recounting, devoid of glitz and glamour, characterized by authenticity and vulnerability, is the most powerful form of storytelling—one that can effectively move others to action.

BUILDING A TEAM

Change does not happen just because of one person. Oftentimes, the leader is not the most important person in a movement—it is the followers who turn a crazy, radical idea into something that actually has momentum and legs. Young people always enlist others in their cause as they push for a better tomorrow.

One person pushing for change is an activist. Enlisting others to join as part of a team is integral toward building an actual movement. Whenever young people are able to affect change, it is because they have been able to organize a mass of young people, all passionate about the same issue, all possessing the requisite expertise, and all pushing for change.

Starting on a personal political journey is necessary. But the reality is that, especially in a democracy, the only way to reach political success is through collective action. Part of this includes, and necessitates, talking with people who disagree with you and who challenge your core convictions. Moving past our extreme polarization is a necessary component to a political journey and is one which young people may be uniquely positioned to achieve.

BECOME POWERFUL

Much of political life is associated with power—who holds it and what they do with it. Rather than seeing power as a dirty word, young people who have made a difference have used their collective energy to harness it for good. Power, as a concept, is not inherently good or evil. Instead, it is a necessary component to marshaling change. Young people have recognized it as a force and leveraged it to achieve positive outcomes.

Creating power involves all of the previous steps: when you select an issue, become an expert, and mobilize others, you will be creating power. The next step is unleashing that power. Sometimes that involves convincing decision-makers to push for the legislation you want. Sometimes young people use and consolidate power by actually running for office.

Once we get past the idea of power as an evil and recognize that it's a political entity to harness, we can begin to achieve real, systemic change.

DON'T TALK ABOUT CHANGE; LEAD IT

Finally, and most importantly, young people lead the change. Despite the fact that adults often don't take young people seriously, when young people make change, they do not wait for adults to tell them they are old enough to act. They take matters into their own hands. They create a better government by participating in the process. They meet with local officials and lobby them to sponsor legislation. They conduct petitions to assess which issues affect their communities. They organize rallies and demonstrate the power of youth voice.

These steps begin the path toward a better politics led by young people. These steps can make up your own political journey.

It is easy to be cynical about politics right now. Perhaps it's even necessary to be a little cynical about politics right now. But if middle school students can engage in the methodical work to lobby for local political change, so can all of us. The work of political change is challenging. Results do not come immediately. But the fate of our very democracy depends on the ability of us, as young people, to participate in the process—and more than that, to lead the process.

We possess the idealism to turn these challenges into campaigns. As young people, we can bring back the citizen-centered democracy that adults have failed to realize. Passionate, committed, responsible young people have the opportunity, the zeal, the vision—and the obligation—to rebuild our democracy.

We can begin the process of rebuilding our democracy by leading our own political journeys. These journeys start today.

5

THE (REAL) POLITICAL JOURNEY

The Fallacy of the State of the Union

n a world rife with uncertainty and conflict, we are constantly in a hurry to know more. We desire instant gratification through efficiency: we want to know exactly where we are going, via a concrete path that tells us exactly how to get there.

The transformation of various industries through technology demonstrates our societal need for certainty. Uber and Lyft allow us to get from Place A to Place B easily. Dating apps use complex algorithms to match us with people who indicate similar interests. Food-delivery apps result in gourmet dinners brought to our very doorsteps. Streaming services offer videos on demand and use our prior viewing habits to make educated guesses on what we want to see next. We are making everything in life easier, more certain, and more efficient.

Often, we are asked to change the world in a similar spirit.

We're told that if you want to positively impact society, and change things, there are specific things you need to do:

Sign this petition.

Attend this rally.

Send this tweet.

Like this post.

It feels good. We know how to make change, and it's become increasingly comforting in an uncertain world.

As Gandhi says, be the change you want to see in the world!

In this world of linear thinking, change becomes just like the composition of water or the answer to a multiplication question: a logical and concrete journey. And like using Netflix to help decide what to watch next or Tinder to decide who to date, there are increasingly easy ways to participate in the political process. You can like that Facebook post, sign three petitions, and even call your senator—all during your lunch break. And then you can feel satisfied about your efforts.

I don't mean to demean this work. But politics is not meant to be easy. The road to change is neither linear nor efficient. There is no equation that I, or anyone, can present that will give you the exact steps to follow in order to achieve political change. Even when you're on the right journey, it's going to take a lot of time to get to where you want to go. Google Maps won't get you there quicker. Uber or Lyft isn't going to pick you up and take you there. There's no algorithm that tells you how to achieve immigration reform.

Sometimes, we think we're achieving progress. But the progress we witness can be deceptive. We think everything is moving in the right direction, but then an unexpected setback changes everything.

When Donald Trump was elected to be the forty-fifth president of the United States, many thought his rise to power positioned the country on the wrong track. President Trump, they argued, would steer us away from progress on the economic and social issues that President Obama had championed. Others, though, thought the complete opposite.

The morning after the election, President Obama gave voice to these contradictory sentiments. Speaking outside the White House Rose Garden, in front of hundreds of stunned, crying White House staffers, he calmly expressed his thinking: "We zig and zag, and sometimes we move in ways that some people think is forward and others think is moving back, and that's okay."

Trump, in so many ways, is the antithesis of the inclusive, forward-thinking politics Obama represented. Trump's very slogan, "Make America great again," is indicative of this stark break. Millions across the country awoke on election morning convinced that the apocalypse was coming. Obama took a different tact, however, and did not give voice to these fears (at least out loud).

Given his preelection speeches in which he warned about the existential dangers of Trump in the White House, Obama must have been worried about the state of the country. But in his postelection statements, Obama tended away from hysteria. Instead, he recognized that social and economic progress does not follow a linear path. He focused on the long political journey, rather than the immediate political moment, betting on the fact that, over time, his vision, and not Trump's, would succeed.

"The point, though, is that we all go forward, with a presumption of good faith in our fellow citizens—because that presumption of good faith is essential to a vibrant and functioning democracy . . . And that's why I'm confident that this incredible journey that we're on as Americans will go on," Obama ended.

Perhaps he's right. But that doesn't mean any of this is easy to stomach. Especially in the moment.

It is challenging to accept the zigzag theory of change. It's difficult to tell people who have experienced hardship, discrimination, and inequality that their struggles are part of the inevitable march and slog toward justice.

"I know it's hard right now, but just hold on—we're getting there. We're moving in the right direction!" is a generic message that can reek of privilege at worst, or a lack of sensitivity at best.

Yes, gay marriage is now the law of the land in this country. But it took decades of discrimination and hardship for that to become a legal norm. And, indisputably, LGBTQ people still do not receive equitable treatment in many parts of American life.

Yes, women can now vote (which wasn't even allowed just one hundred years ago) and are increasingly in positions of leadership. But their salaries are still much lower than men's, and they encounter structural and cultural barriers to equality every day.

I say this to acknowledge the inevitable tensions that accompany any effort to drive change. It can be said that African Americans in this country are certainly better off now than they were when they were enslaved through the mid-nineteenth century. And the civil rights movement, led largely by young people, helped to create much more equitable conditions, including laws that protected the right to vote and prevented discrimination at private establishments like restaurants and hotels.

However, at the same time, this country still has rampant racial inequities that pervade every level of society. Approximately 12 percent of the American population is African American, but they make up 38 percent of prison inmates, largely because of the unjust way we treat mandatory minimum sentencing for minor crimes.

Similarly, our educational system remains deeply inequitable. Low-income and minority students receive fewer resources for their educational pursuits. As a result, there's a persistent achievement gap that has only worsened over the past two decades. The unemployment rate for African Americans is more than double what it is for the rest of the country, and wage levels are much lower.

Better off is not good enough. But we're supposed to tell people, especially young folks, to keep on keeping on? Is better off better than nothing?

How do you tell someone to show up in a system that does not value his or her input? How do you tell young people to show up when the message they have been sent, fairly explicitly, through public institutions, is that they do not matter?

However paradoxical it may seem, the answer may be that the more progress zigs and zags, and the worse things become, the more important it is to show up politically.

On one hand, the message to young people is *all you have to do is participate, and you'll see results.* The problem with this messaging is that it's not true.

On the other hand, the message is *the system is too broken to actually achieve change.* This is completely disempowering. What can you do to affect change if the system is broken?

The answer must lie somewhere in the middle. We need to be honest about the limitations and flaws of our political system, and their costs every day on marginalized individuals in this country, while working like hell to improve it. We can understand that change won't come right away while insisting that change must eventually come. Yes, our public systems are not fair and equitable. But, yes, we can change the systems.

We have to change the systems.

This book will be using GC's Advocacy Hourglass to focus on the notion of a political journey. There are no *easy* steps to affect change. But by the end of this book, I hope that you'll understand how real political journeys unfold and how you can start toward the path of change. As with any journey, there will be forks, setbacks, and unfair rules to fight back against.

Rather than pretending that democratic change stems from an easy, joyful process, we need to embrace real challenges. These journeys include suffering, disappointment, and disillusionment alongside inspiration and real change. This is how we live political lives.

THE DANGER OF A SINGLE STORY

Anthony Mendez represents the power and importance of the long but necessary slog to real political change.

I met Anthony in December of 2013 when he was a senior at a high school in the Bronx participating in Generation Citizen. Anthony's class concentrated on criminal justice issues and lobbied the City of New York Police Department to end their

policy of stop and frisk, which they felt unfairly targeted minority youth. The same issue that Laila's class took on: stop and
frisk was, understandably, a hot-button issue in New York City
for young people.

I first encountered Anthony at the end of Civics Day, our
end-of-year event during which students present on the issues
they've taken action on over the course of the semester. The day
always provides much-needed inspiration to the students and
participating judges. And to me. After weeks of fundraising and
traveling, I'm able to be present in a room of over 250 bustling
young people. And they always fill the room with an infectious
political energy.

After the closing speeches, Anthony approached me at the
front of the auditorium that housed the events for the day.

"Hey, how can I help you?" I said, loosening a tie that was
probably too formal for the celebratory but student-centric
occasion.

"Hi, Scott, my name is Anthony," he said. "I've loved Generation Citizen this year and leading change in my school and
community. I really want to find a way to stay involved."

Of the 250 students who attended the event, Anthony was
the only one that approached me. I immediately recognized the
potential Anthony possessed. He had natural charisma, the
confidence that he could get stuff done, and a smile that made
you want to help him right away.

I gave him my business card, and three days later, I received
an email:

Tuesday morning, I had the opportunity to take part in Civics Day. I want to first take a minute to thank you for the

opportunity. I am inspired to make a positive change in my community.

I had the opportunity to converse with you in regard to the controversial issue of inequality in Specialized High Schools. Low-income students do not have the same opportunities that students from wealthy parents have when it comes to enrolling into Specialized High Schools.

I'd like to know if you could recommend ways for me to become involved in activist work, which will allow me to make positive impacts for students of color.

Awesome, I thought to myself. What a motivated student. I immediately connected him to our staff and to resources to continue his journey. We always want students to remain politically engaged after the semesters conclude. In GC, we do not see success in terms of how effective student projects are, but rather in how politically engaged young people become over the long term. This was a kid who could demonstrate the power of being politically engaged for the long haul.

Anthony wrote back: "I really appreciate the opportunity to begin my journey in making a change."

He was already thinking about the notion of a political journey before I had even been able to articulate the concept in my own head.

Over the next few months, Anthony became one of our star students and a youth-activist success story. He received one of our Community Change Fellowships: a paid summer internship in a political office and expanded organizing training with our staff. As part of this fellowship, he worked with a New York City councilman and began to engage in his own activism.

He also traveled with us to Albany, personally lobbying for a bill that would allow sixteen- and seventeen-year-olds to serve on New York City community boards. He impressed every legislator he met, helping to convince them that young people could be effective political actors. The bill ultimately passed, thanks in no small part to Anthony's efforts.

He was becoming a political star—our political star.

Anthony's personal journey, or what I knew of it at the time, was raw and powerful. He had grown up with his mother and three siblings, moving around frequently. His father was never around. Days before he started eighth grade, one of his best friends had been shot and killed in his neighborhood. Soon after, Anthony and his family were evicted from their home. They moved into a homeless shelter, far from his school.

None of these external challenges prevented Anthony from moving forward with his journey. While he was at the shelter, he would get up at 4:30 a.m. to make it to school on time, and he'd tell his friends that he was staying with an aunt. He would run track after school, then return to the shelter for a night of homework, often working until midnight. Then: rinse, run, repeat.

His political, academic, and athletic efforts paid off: Anthony was awarded a scholarship to the University of Hartford to run track. He credited becoming involved in politics and activism as one of the reasons he was able to prosper—he had found his voice and wanted to give back to his own community. Through political engagement, he began to recognize how education was relevant to his own life. The critical-thinking skills and ability to communicate persuasively, which he had cultivated in history and English classes, allowed him to become a powerful political actor. Civics, as we say at GC, is more than just one class.

We stayed in touch with Anthony sporadically, wanting to ensure that he would continue as a youth leader and activist. And, if we're honest, probably so that we could continue to use his story as we got in touch with supporters and donors.

Then, in January of 2015, just before his spring semester of freshman year, we received a phone call: Anthony would be the personal guest of First Lady Michelle Obama at the State of the Union Address. We were beside ourselves. Our Anthony. We were so proud.

We immediately sprang into action, telling all of our stakeholders about Anthony and his success. We sent an email to our entire Listserv with the subject reading, "From Generation Citizen to the White House."

To me, Anthony showed that our program worked. He had become motivated and inspired to participate in politics, and now he was at the State of the Union. What further proof could I need that educating young people to be active politically was important and powerful? What further proof could I need to show that Generation Citizen was a wild success?

That night, our staff watched the speech together. Anthony sat directly next to the First Lady. The camera panned to both of them repeatedly. The smile never left his face. I don't remember the contents of President Obama's speech—I was too focused on Anthony, wearing that same smile from ear to ear that he did when I first met him.

He called my colleagues later that night, thanking them for the experience of GC, which he said had put him on the path that led to the White House.

"This was awesome," he said. "And I'll be back here some-day. Not just as a kid."

We didn't doubt him.

In the months that followed, we promoted the hell out of Anthony. We told every single donor about him. We featured him on our website. He became the keynote speaker at our next Civics Day, inspiring the attendees with his story.

"After the speech, I met the president himself," Anthony said. "I will never forget what he said. He gave me a hug, we took a great picture, and then he looked at me and said, 'You're an inspiration to all of us.'"

We got a lot of mileage out of our chief success story.

Then, in August of 2015, six months after the State of the Union and only three months after Civics Day, Anthony visited me at our offices.

"Anthony, great to see you, man!" I told him. "How are you doing? We're so proud of everything that you're doing."

The strong handshake was still there. The ear-to-ear smile was not.

"I'm so sorry, Scott," he said. "I dropped out of college." He looked down at the ground, evading my eyes. "I feel like a failure," he continued.

We sat down, and, for the first time, Anthony told me his story—his real story. Not the glossy one we had put on the front page of our annual report.

When the White House called to invite him to the State of the Union, he had a grade point average of just over 1.0 and was about to drop out. When President Obama told him that he was "an inspiration to all of us," Anthony knew that he was at risk of not returning to Hartford. He did not know how to handle the attention. He did not know how to reconcile the fact that he was at risk of dropping out of school with the fact that the president of the United States was calling him an inspiration.

How could he be? He was eighteen.

Hartford gave him a second shot, predominantly because of his newfound celebrity status. The president of the college invited him into his office and offered to do anything in his power to help Anthony succeed.

But, like so many first-generation college students, Anthony had a difficult time dealing with the stresses of navigating the completely foreign system that higher education represented. He also felt overwhelmed by the pressure or expectations that came with being Michelle Obama's personal guest at the State of the Union. Suddenly, he was a celebrity all around campus, with everyone wanting to talk to him about his time at the White House.

Despite the offering of support, and perhaps because of all the attention, his grades did not improve. Anthony was forced to drop out at the end of the spring semester.

When he spoke at our Civics Day, regaling the young people with his story, he already knew he would not be returning to college. But he did not know how to tell us.

I felt terrible. I felt that we had exploited his story. I felt guilty.

Anthony and I continued to stay in touch in the months to come. He was struggling, trying to figure out how to live back at home and provide for himself. But he did eventually land on his feet, becoming a barista at a local coffee shop, and thinking, critically, about his journey. His self-awareness is remarkable and is a valuable aid in thinking through the importance of surmounting obstacles on any long road to change.

Anthony threw himself into writing, a discipline that he says allows him to clarify his thinking. He ended up writing a piece for *Vox*, which ran with the headline, "The White House Made Me a Poster Child for Beating the Odds. Then I Dropped Out of College."

Anthony wrote:

> Even though I had attended the State of the Union, even though the first lady and the president of the United States knew who I was, I was still right back where I had been before the phone call from the White House. I wasn't in school. I didn't have a job. My mother was still struggling week after week, living paycheck to paycheck. For a moment, I'd believed that the trip would change not only my life, but my family's life as well.

The reality was obviously different. But the person who has come out on the other end is a young man incredibly confident and humble, articulate about the challenges of young people participating in politics. He no longer sees himself as a failure. He no longer sees himself only through the vantage point of being a guest at the White House. He ends the article eloquently:

> I am more than any one event in my life. I am more than a former homeless kid. I am more than a success story that sat next to the first lady at the State of the Union. I am more than a former college dropout. I am the sum total of all the

events and decisions of my life. And I know that everything that has happened to me will only make me stronger.

To this day, Anthony inspires me. His views on political engagement have evolved. He still is passionate and wants to make a difference. But having seen how the sausage is made, he is more realistic about the challenges inherent in making change. He knows it will take a long time to improve his community.

He says that when he first got involved in politics, through his Generation Citizen class, he was hooked. For him, seeing the statistics on the deep inequality that persisted throughout American society was essential. As a low-income young person, he did not even know that an alternative reality could exist. He did not believe that poor schools could actually receive expanded funding. Until he dove into the research, he assumed that all students went to schools like he did.

Achieving actual, real change is hard. It is not just about individual leaders and heroes and inspiring stories. It is about the inevitable failures we experience on the path to change, and how people pick themselves up and continue to push forward.

I am not going to pretend that there are specific levers that you can push to make change happen. I will not tell you that engaging in political work will always be fun, or worthwhile, or rewarding. Sometimes it will be boring, disheartening, and even infuriating.

After watching Anthony, I became much more conscious of our organizational tendency to reduce a complex story into a compact narrative. I can still say that one of Generation Citizen's students sat next to First Lady Obama at the State of the Union, and that he credits GC with his transformation and lifelong commitment to living a political journey. All of that is true.

But it's also incomplete. It's misleading.

A press release can't do justice to Anthony's story. It's too complex. Let's acknowledge that and lean into the discomfort that accompanies our journey into democracy. As Anthony told me, "Failure is part of life. To make a change you have to fail, I don't know how many times."

As we move forward, and think about our own political journeys, I want us to remember Anthony's story. Yes, there's the inspirational part—he's someone who found his political voice at an early age and, because of that, met the president. But Anthony also encountered challenges and unrealistic expectations along his way. Those challenges have made him the man he is today. He's thriving while beginning to discover a more nuanced version of his political voice.

That is the political journey. Not a straight shot to change or a moment captured in a glamorous press release. But a real journey, with all the ups and downs on the long road to ultimate progress. That is the real journey we all need to lead.

6

A POLITICAL AWAKENING IN KENYA

The Power and Fragility of Democracy

Long before the sun rose in the coastal port town of Mombasa, hundreds of Kenyans gathered outside the school that would serve as the polling site for the day. By the time my team of PeaceNet poll observers arrived at the Nyali-region polling place, fifteen minutes before the official opening, thousands of Kenyans stood patiently but restlessly in a line that stretched kilometers down the highway.

It was 5:45 a.m. on Tuesday, August 8, 2017—Election Day in Kenya (a holiday—unlike Election Day in the United States). I was traveling with two Kenyan observers, Caroline and Molly, and my best friend from high school in Kenya, Tobin, now a professional photographer. Our role as observers was to travel to election polling sites throughout the region to ensure that the process was fair and free and that it respected the integrity of the Kenyan voters. Tobin's job was to capture photos that newspapers throughout the world could use. His work seemed a little more glamorous than ours, but I convinced myself that both were important, despite the fact that his photographs would later be featured in the *Washington Post*.

Holding up our bright green official observer badges, we walked to the front of the line. Tobin hung out in the back, capturing the massive lines and infectious energy for all to see.

As observers, our first job was to ensure that the Kenyan authorities had properly prepared for the commencement of the electoral activities. The people standing at the front of the line told us they had arrived outside the school at midnight. We naively thought we could enter the polling facilities before everyone else would. This wasn't going to happen.

As we approached a locked metal gate, we became ensnared within the masses. There were thousands of people around us. We were locked shoulder to shoulder with the expectant Kenyan voters, unable to move. I continued to hold my green badge up but realized it was fruitless, so I hung back with the crowds. Or rather, I was stuck among the crowds. I felt like I was in Times Square at New Year's.

A countdown did start as 6:00 a.m. neared, and it actually felt more crowded than Times Square ever did.

"Five minutes left!"

"We want to vote!"

"Do not cut the line!"

"Ten seconds!"

As soon as my watch showed 6:00 a.m., the guards quickly opened the gate, jumping to the side in the process. Everyone rushed forward at once. Caroline, Molly, and I were unprepared. We fell to the dirt. I tensed my feet so that my shoes wouldn't be torn off. I felt future voters trampling over me, more excited to vote than to pay attention to a wayward American observer. I tensed into a ball. Gun shots rang out—the guards fired into the air in an attempt to inspire order.

Seconds later, several concerned citizens pulled me to the side. I warily stood up. My shoes were still on. My clothes were caked in the red dirt that made up the schoolyard.

I looked for Caroline and Molly, who had similarly been trampled upon. We were all shell-shocked. Molly clutched her shoulder, in pain. Physically, Caroline was intact, but her expression was one of bewilderment. We looked at each other in suspended disbelief. And then we burst into laughter—physical relief that we had survived the onslaught of voters. This was Election Day.

As we prepared to finally enter the polling stations, I noticed a pile of shoes by the gate: voters had lost their footwear in the stampede but kept going to ensure they could vote, leaving their sneakers behind.

Though the lines gradually grew more orderly, the energy and excitement outside the polling station remained palpable. People ran up and down the lines. They feverishly conversed with their compatriots, sharing their opinions. Some silently read the newspaper, analyzing their choices one last time before they walked into the voting booth. They would look up to yell at me, imploring me to speed up the process, which, as an observer, I could not do.

Carrying out our respective duties, Caroline, Molly, Tobin, and I moved to polling station after polling station. Throughout the day, thousands of Kenyans greeted us, waiting patiently but eagerly, sometimes for hours upon hours. This was democracy in action.

There were old men who could barely walk. They entered the small schoolrooms with their canes and pressed their thumbs down into an electronic machine to prove their voter registration. There were young mothers whose babies remained strapped to their backs as they exited the cardboard polling stations and carefully placed each of their six votes in the appropriate sealed plastic baskets. There were eighteen-year-olds jostling to have their pinkies marked in indelible ink, a sign they had voted. On television, for the first time in Kenya's history, prisoners cast their votes from jail.

As night fell, poll workers meticulously counted votes, showing each and every ballot to a panel of eight party advisors, all of whom had to agree on the result of the ballot before moving forward. For many, the process lasted until at least 3:00 or 4:00 a.m.—the poll workers worked twenty-four-hour shifts. In the days that followed, the poll workers and party advisors moved on to county tabulation centers, waiting as the boxes arrived, and officers tallied the votes together. They slept on-site. Democracy was too important to go home.

I was thirty years old when I served as an observer during the 2017 Kenyan elections, returning to the country where I had spent my high school years. I went back to learn more about how Kenya conducted elections. I went back to try to help as an official observer. But more than anything, I went back to become reinspired by the possibility and potential of democracy itself after a period of nonstop tumult in the United States in the first year of President Trump.

And I went back in order to return to the place where my own political voyage started, engaging in the exact same activity that had motivated me to start the journey I continue today.

As we begin to examine the concept of a political journey, and learn from others, I think it's relevant to talk about my own path to political engagement. And despite the fact that I'm American, the journey actually begins in Kenya. My own story shows that we have much to learn from democracies around the world in our path to creating a better American political reality.

THE POLITICAL AWAKENING

Every journey starts with a spark, an idea, an itch to scratch. Many of us have stories of civic awakenings—moments or events in which we first felt called upon to participate in our political process for the greater good. For some of us, a political awakening is facilitated by our families; parents often take us to the polls or city council meetings for the first time. For other young people, awakenings come in response to anger, in the wake of injustice, when trying to right a wrong.

Many times, these awakenings occur when we are young; we're idealistic and able to envision a better world, rather than accepting of society for the way it is.

President Obama traces his own political awakening to a talk he gave at the age of nineteen, urging his school, Occidental College, to divest from apartheid-era South Africa. In a 2013 speech in Cape Town, South Africa, Obama recalled being embarrassed by the content and delivery of the speech, but he also recognized that "I know now that something inside me was stirring at that time, something important. And that was the belief that I could be part of something bigger than myself; that my own salvation was bound up with those of others."

Every person who is passionate about politics has a similar story of his or her own awakening and the first time he or she engaged politically. Perhaps out of concern for their child's school, they ran for the school board. Many Republicans who ran as Tea Party candidates and were elected to Congress in 2010 became involved through a passion to reduce the United States' debt and a belief that the political system treated them unfairly. In the wake of Trump's 2016 election, an unprecedented number of young people and women decided to run for office, seeing his election as an affront to their values while internalizing a need to do something to fight back.

While we often disagree on how to achieve progress, the reality is that almost everyone can trace his or her first involvement in politics to a desire to create positive change. It is worth focusing on this notion of positive motivation; despite all of our challenges and turmoil, the vast majority of people do get involved for the right reasons.

I had my own political awakening as a fourteen-year-old living in Kenya, observing the first democratic elections in the country's history. The experience showed me the transformative potential of individuals coming together to make a collective difference. The opportunity to witness the election in action inspires me to this day, allowing me to recognize how democracy can work and causing me to reflect on my responsibility to participate in the political process. I believe in democracy today because of what I saw in Kenya in 2003.

I continue to believe in democracy because of what I saw again in 2017. The good. And the bad.

THIS IS CIVICS

I originally did not want to go to Kenya. After successive two-year stints in the Dominican Republic and Argentina, my parents told me that we were going to move to Washington, D.C., where my dad would work at the State Department and I would start the eighth grade.

However, midway through seventh grade, my parents sat me down and presented a change in plans.

"I am not moving to Kenya!" I protested. "You're depriving me of my American childhood!"

No joke. I said that.

Not surprisingly, my parents prevailed. Also not surprisingly, they were right to insist on the move.

At the time we arrived, Kenya had been independent from Great Britain for thirty-seven years and had been led by only two presidents. Jomo Kenyatta, known as the father of modern Kenya, ruled from independence until his death in 1978. He was succeeded by Daniel arap Moi, the then sitting president, who led what amounted to a single-party democracy. Moi had "won" a total of five elections from his perch as leader of the Kenyan African National Unity (KANU) party. Objectively, none of the elections were free and fair, or had any semblance of real opposition.

Kenya's evolution into a more fully formed democracy accelerated when the courts forbade Moi from running again in 2002, providing hope for an actual democratic election. Led by the United Nations, the African Union, and the United States, the international community invested significant resources into building a free and fair election process, a task that included providing funding for modern voting technology, training an independent judiciary, and sending independent election observers. Despite these efforts, significant doubt and cynicism persisted both within the international community and among Kenyans themselves. Many doubted that a free and fair election could occur. In the months leading up to the December 2002 presidential election, opinion articles in Kenyan papers questioned whether the reforms would be sufficient, and the international community weighed how much stock to put into the electoral process, skeptical of the outcome.

The two leading contenders were Mwai Kibaki, the leader of the opposition party called the National Rainbow Coalition, and Uhuru Kenyatta, running as the establishment party's nominee. Kenyatta was running both as founding father Jomo's son and as part of an effort to keep the presidency with Moi's KANU party.

Leading up to the election, informal polls, conducted by international groups like the European Union and National Democratic Institute, indicated Kibaki held a wide lead. The Kenyan people desperately craved change after years of economic stagnation, high unemployment, and an unequal corrupt system in which they felt that the voices of the masses were marginalized at the expense of the powerful.

But the country had never held an actual democratic presidential election, and opposition candidates rarely win elections in emerging democracies. Generally, those in power ensure that they remain in power. Unsurprisingly, people throughout the country generally assumed that Kenyatta would somehow prevail.

Until this Kenyan presidential race, the only other time I had felt personally invested in a political election was during the infamous 2000 American presidential race, which took place just one month after we arrived in Nairobi. The son of loyal Democrats, I spent the day after the election with my friends, shuttling back and forth between the computers in the library and our classes. Due to the time difference, we followed the States' evening chaos in real time on Yahoo.com, a website that had just been launched. We refreshed the site with incredibly slow and sporadic dial-up internet, excitedly waiting for updated results. Before our morning classes, Yahoo had declared Florida for Gore. By lunch, Florida had gone to Bush.

By the end of the day, early morning in the States, it was a toss-up. We passed the next few weeks desperate for our version of justice to prevail, only to end up devastated when the Supreme Court ruled against the Florida recount.

The experience, as a young person, left me bitter and distrustful of politics. It felt like the process had ended in a way that did not ensure that every vote was counted fairly, and I became doubtful about the ability of individual citizens to affect change.

Less than two years later, in 2002, as the Kenyan election consumed the country's attention, I was a tenth grader, more invested in my fledgling athletic pursuits, studies, and girls than in politics. Who cared about democracy? It had already disappointed me once. I wouldn't let it happen again.

While I had left politics behind, I had started to like life a little more. Kenya had grown on me, and I had begun to even acknowledge, begrudgingly, that my parents were right in moving us there. I had a close group of diverse friends at my international school: my grade was comprised of fifty-six students from thirty-four different countries. I loved traveling throughout the country, rock-climbing on Mount Kenya with Tobin, and learning about the country from local Kenyans. I was becoming an avid tennis player, learning to cope with the five-thousand-foot-high altitude of Nairobi by lathering my shots with topspin that would allow the ball to reluctantly stay on the court. The diversity of my classmates, combined with the juxtaposition of natural beauty and immense poverty throughout the country, taught me more than any classroom experience could.

But when my dad told me that he had signed up to be an official observer of an election in the rural Rongai province over Christmas break and wanted me to come along to witness Kenyan history in the making, my youthful instincts resurfaced, and I protested. After all, I didn't care about politics.

"It's so far away!" I complained. "And all my friends are playing basketball at school on Saturday and then going to the movies at Sarit Centre." The argument seemed substantive and persuasive to me at the time.

"You're going to look back on this and be grateful that you had this experience," my dad insisted.

Right, I thought.

On Thursday, December 26, the day before the election, my dad and I drove off in our four-wheel-drive Land Cruiser to the northern region of the country. We traveled with three Foreign Service Nationals (Kenyans who worked at the American Embassy) who would also be participating as observers. It struck me as important that Election Day would be a holiday—even at the time, it seemed that the United States was one of the few countries in the world that couldn't figure out that it's important to give citizens the day off to ensure that they can vote.

Our role as observers was to make sure that the election stations were set up fairly, that people were able to vote freely and fairly, and that the polls were tabulated accurately. Most countries, including the United States, allow for observers to prove the validity of their democratic elections, and even to educate other countries on how their elections work.

En route, we stopped by a roadside restaurant where we ate the traditional Kenyan fare of *nyama choma* and *ugali*, roasted lamb and a starch-filled, potato-like dish. My dad and I were the only white people in the restaurant, as tourists generally avoided local Kenyan haunts for more formal meal destinations. There was barely a free seat: law at the time required Kenyans to vote in their home provinces, so Kenyans were out in droves as they traveled back to their home rural areas from their jobs in the city.

Over lunch, our Kenyan colleagues confessed their mixed sentiments about the election. They had voted early in their home provinces so that they could now serve as official observers. They were excited about the prospects for democracy but doubted their hopes would be realized.

"I think that this time, elections will work," said one Kenyan woman who was traveling with us. "But I have thought that before, so I am more cautious this time. I am not sure what will happen if they do not work this time."

"The country's so tense. I am so excited, but also nervous. I literally do not know what it means to have a free election—we have never had one," said another one of our fellow Kenyan observers.

Listening to them, I began to absorb the magnitude of this election for Kenyan voters.

As we devoured our lunch, the Kenyans told my dad and me how impressed they were with the aftermath of the 2000 election in the United States. For them, it was unfathomable that an election that was decided literally by hundreds of (disputed) votes could result in a peaceful transition of power.

"I do not understand how someone would concede the election if he won more votes than the other person! How does the American system even work?" one of the Kenyans asked quizzically.

"Well, in the United States, we have something called the Electoral College," my dad started to explain. "Each state gets a certain number of votes that help determine who the president will be. It's about who wins more of those state votes, not the overall vote total."

Attempting to explain the Electoral College to a foreigner is a helpful exercise in understanding its total absurdity in these modern times.

"But I still don't understand why he would walk away when it was so close! Were there protesters on the street? Why would citizens accept that?"

"The courts spoke," my dad explained. "In our democracy, there is nothing more powerful than the courts." My dad was still a lawyer at heart, even though he'd left the profession years before when he joined the Foreign Service.

Our fellow observers were hopeful that the next day might

bring a similarly peaceful result in Kenya, but they were still doubtful that the day would result in free and fair elections.

"We are optimistic. But we are taking our role as observers seriously," they told us.

We nodded along. I began to realize this was a little more high stakes than my usual weekend basketball game with friends.

OBSERVING HISTORY

By the end of the day, we arrived up north in Rongai and checked into our bare-bones hotel. There was nothing in the room except a queen-size bed and a wooden couch, which would be my accommodation for the night. A solitary portrait on the wall of a lion in the midst of a kill reminded us that, yes, we were still visitors in Kenya.

Most of my travel in Kenya up to that point focused on tourist destinations—safaris in game parks and beachside resorts. Rongai was not your standard Kenyan vacationer experience. A small rural town that had been created as a midpoint for a railway line between Uganda and Kenya, Rongai had not caught up to globalization and modernization. As my dad and I took an evening stroll through the small town, citizens gawked at us from the roadside kiosks scattered throughout and excitedly shouted hello, while also trying to convince us to buy call time for our cell phones. They rarely saw *mzungus* ("white people" in Swahili) and figured that we must be in town because of the election.

We ate in our quiet hotel restaurant, which had the only food we could find in town. Our television flashed talking heads discussing the next day's events. My dad drank a cold Tusker beer. I convinced him to allow me to drink my own—as long as I could order alcohol, I was fine by Kenyan drinking laws.

My dad helped us to reflect on our privilege, and responsibility, in being foreigners observing an election that was not our own. He advocated that we were there to learn and observe. We did not, for a second, want to pretend that we knew best, or that our democracy was better. It was a lesson I would try to take to heart, both the next day, and for the rest of my life.

The next day, Election Day, my dad cajoled me out of bed at five in the morning. We drove through town as the sun rose in the distance. All I could see from my window was more and more dirt and plains—no people.

I curled up in the corner of the passenger seat. But before I could fall asleep, my dad shouted out, "Wake up! We're here!"

When I opened my eyes, the vastness of the rural plains had completely transformed into the hustle and bustle I was accustomed to in Nairobi. We parked outside the small schoolhouse serving as the poll center for the area. As we stepped out of the car, it was impossible to miss the sight of hundreds of people in a single-file line. We began to walk down the line, which would have spanned blocks if it weren't in the middle of the plains. It was still a quarter to six in the morning—the polls would not open for another fifteen minutes—but citizens were already chattering excitedly as the poll workers conducted their final preparations.

In a country still plagued by misogyny and male-dominated politics, it was striking to see more women in line than men. We saw older women being pushed in wheelchairs, men in suits, Muslim women in burkas. They shouted at my dad and me as we walked down the line.

"Hello, *mzungus*! Welcome to our election day!"

"Will everything work today? Please make sure our votes count!"

"Rainbow Coalition to victory! Kibaki is the future of Kenya!"

"KANU will win! Kenyatta will return!"

"Can you make the lines shorter, *mzungus*? I have been here for hours!"

At last, the poll workers unlocked the shaky wooden door at the front of the school, and the voters shouted and jostled in line.

"One at a time! Everyone will vote. Patience, please!" the solemn poll captain declared, dressed for the occasion in a fully pressed black suit and a bright green vest that signaled his status.

Using the status provided to us by our official badges, we entered the schoolroom to see the election in action. The room held only about twenty people: six clerks to carry out the actual duties, a presiding officer to manage the proceedings, representatives from the various political parties, and observers. With the sun still rising, a single kerosene lamp provided the only light in the middle of the room as the officials sealed the ballot boxes and put the final touches on their election preparations.

Democracy was playing out in a one-room schoolhouse lit up by a kerosene lamp.

As voters entered the room, the officials sprang into action— their serious demeanor conveyed the gravity of their roles. The first clerk took the voter's name and country identification card, cross-checking them against the records in their voter binder. The next clerk stamped and handed out three official ballots—a presidential ballot, a parliamentary ballot, and a civic ballot for local positions. After receiving the ballots, a voter retreated to one of two voting stations: a box on a school desk, enclosed by a torn beige curtain.

The actual voting process was simple. The voter would mark an "X" on each ballot, voting for one person as the candidate of his or her choice. I soon realized, however, that some voters were illiterate. These people could either have a close friend or relative vote for them or have the presiding officer read out the names of the candidates and mark the declared choice for them. Whenever an illiterate person voted, the party representatives gathered around and took care to ensure the voting process remained fair and that they were not being unduly coerced to voting for a specific candidate.

After their choices were recorded, the voters inserted their ballots into a sealed wooden box before making their way to the end of the schoolhouse, where the final clerk would dip their pinkie fingers in indelible ink to ensure that Chicago-style "vote early, vote often" tactics would not occur in Kenya. The party officials stood to the side, eyeing the process, prepared to pounce if they observed any irregularities.

My dad and I watched for a few minutes. We then stepped outside to the other side of the schoolhouse to see the recent voters excitedly showing each other their black-stained pinkies.

"It worked! I voted!" One elderly woman shoved her pinkie in my face.

"All right, time for the next one," my dad said as he tugged me away from the action.

We visited several polling places throughout the day, ensuring that the practices were in place to maintain order and fairness. Each station proved similar: a one-room schoolhouse, replete with broken windows, dirt floors, and sometimes the absence of a door. Somewhat ironically, one of Kibaki's most popular campaign promises was to guarantee free primary school education, which was not yet available.

Despite the conditions, the process itself felt incredibly professional. The Kenyans took this duty seriously. They wanted to make this first election work, to be a model for the rest of Africa and for the world.

At six that evening, after we had visited more than ten polling places, the sun began to set. Before long, stars appeared over the prairies, lighting up the sky. People gathered in the streets around radios, anxious to hear the results as the election was officially over. It seemed that the day had proceeded smoothly; the test would rest in the counting and reporting.

Our observation team journeyed over to a small school gym, the largest venue in town. After election officials carefully examined our badges, we were escorted to the spectator seating. About forty observers spanned the bleachers: half were local Kenyan observers, and the rest were from around the world and had served as election monitors for other countries or the United Nations. The gym equipment had been cleared, except for the ten-foot-tall basketball hoops, lacking nets, which towered over the proceedings. Local journalists spoke quietly into tape recorders. Rongai was too remote for the international coverage that had descended upon other parts of Kenya.

Over the next hour, the plastic ballot boxes were carried into the gym from across the region and placed at what would have been midcourt. Security remained tight. Whenever new people entered the room, guards patted them down.

Once all boxes were in the room, the officials announced that the counting would commence. The election officers unsealed one of the boxes and proceeded to count each ballot. One. By. One.

"Kibaki."

"Kibaki."

"Kenyatta."

"Kibaki."

I'm not sure if I'd given any prior consideration to how they would count the votes, but I was fairly astounded that, throughout the country, each vote would be counted by hand.

I turned to my dad and said, "Maybe they should have used this process in Florida."

No one around us laughed. He did.

Everyone paid careful attention to the counting, ensuring that no noise was made to disrupt the tabulations. I calculated that it took about an hour to count six hundred votes, a rate of ten votes per minute.

We stayed for two boxes. After ensuring that someone on our observation team would hold the fort to ensure the counting process remained fair and impartial, we decided to leave.

As we drove back to the hotel, I reflected on the day, the experiences, the sights and sounds. I could hear the clamor of the Kenyan people chatting before they cast their votes. I could still see the elderly, illiterate woman who proudly showed me her pinkie after voting for the first time in her life. The six-year-old boy who accompanied his father into the polling place.

The family of six who stood in line for hours and made voting a community affair.

This democracy thing, I thought, as our car pulled into the hotel parking lot, is pretty damn cool. Better than a basketball game, even. Maybe.

The political cynic that had emerged in the aftermath of the 2000 election fell to the wayside.

I looked at my dad before we opened the car doors.

"Thanks for bringing me," I said.

HOOKED FOR LIFE

On the drive back the next morning, my dad and I tuned in to the local radio as the results began to pour in. I was riveted. Seeing individuals lining up to vote and watching the counting process had taught me more than watching pundits discussing politics on television or reading textbooks about postcolonial Africa ever could. As we entered the streets of Nairobi, which were eerily calm and empty for a Saturday, the radio announcers sounded increasingly animated.

The early tabulations indicated that Kibaki was the clear victor. The opposition had won, and it wasn't close. More than 60 percent of the vote had pointed in the direction of change.

"Kibaki could actually win!" I told my dad.

"We'll see," he said. "But it's looking good."

The question remained as to whether the indisputable results would lead to a peaceful transfer of power. My dad remained optimistic, but my Kenyan friends were apprehensive. There were too many incidents where previously undemocratic countries refused to turn over control.

But two days after the election, my friends and I walked through a local mall and saw citizens rejoicing, hugging each other, and flashing us the V sign, signifying victory for the opposition. Local vans, or *matatus*, proudly waved the Kenyan flag outside the windows as they drove by. Televisions showed the preparations for Kibaki's inauguration.

Two days later, on Monday, December 30, only three days after the election, my mom and I drove through downtown Nairobi on the way back from a dentist appointment. Traffic was at a standstill. Horns sounded off incessantly.

We were in the middle of a celebration. People ran through the streets, over cars, to the adjoining Uhuru Park. The inauguration would take place that afternoon, and everyone wanted a front-row seat. Newspapers later declared that some two hundred thousand Kenyans showed up to see their country enter a new phase in its history. We turned on the radio.

"Corruption will now cease to be a way of life in Kenya," Kibaki declared in his inaugural remarks.

History had been made.

NOT SO EASY

Although I didn't realize it at the time, the experience hooked me on politics for life. It convinced me of the power of individuals coming together to make a collective difference. It sold me on the power of democracy.

To this day, the memory of the individuals lining up to cast votes at dawn, the counting of the ballots one by one, and the jubilation of citizens throughout the streets convinces me of the power of politics. Kenyans taught me the importance of ensuring that every young person recognizes his or her own power to change the world through political participation. Democracy can work. The spirit of the people I met in Kenya mirrors the principles we try to hold close in our work at Generation Citizen. Politics can be positive. And communities and individuals should be empowered to solve their own problems.

At the same time, however, Kenya's story of democracy is not linear. The very next election, in 2007, was not nearly as democratic. There were widespread reports of rigging and voter intimidation. Rather than participating in a huge celebration in the streets of Nairobi, people stayed in their homes. Mwai Kibaki took his presidential oath only hours after the polls closed, indicating he believed trouble was afoot.

In the weeks that followed, the opposition, feeling like they'd been robbed of victory, took to the streets in protest. Police closely guarded the same Uhuru Park that had been home to such a momentous celebration five years earlier; they didn't want to allow any unrest or protests to occur. Citizens who only five years earlier had celebrated the success of democracy now felt that democratic values had been relinquished and forcibly taken from them. They felt like their voices did not matter. Violence erupted in towns across the country. A church was burned to the ground. In the end, over one thousand people died in Kenya in postelection violence.

Similarly, after observing the power of Election Day in 2017, the outcomes were not as auspicious as they had been during my first observations. As Kenyans waited days for the results, unease built. The citizens were not convinced that the process of vote counting was legitimate. Tension throughout the country mounted, stores stayed closed, and the streets remained empty.

Days later, the Supreme Court of Kenya declared the election results to be invalid—the election authorities had not followed the right procedures in tabulating and reporting the votes. Governmental officials failed the people of Kenya. Many blamed international observers for too quickly declaring that the results were fair and free. I reflected on my own role in the process—was I too optimistic at the end of the polls? Did the palpable excitement of the voters cloud my judgment? I still think about whether my excitement clouded my conclusions.

A follow-up election held two months later resulted in sustained anxiety throughout the country, violence, and the opposition candidate pulling out. Democracy in Kenya remains in peril.

But, perhaps, democracy always remains in peril.

Fifteen years earlier, I left Kenya completely convinced of the power of democracy. This time, I left wondering if the process could actually work.

Herein lies the tension of democracy. It is an incredibly powerful idea based on the premise that individuals can participate in their own self-governance and make their own decisions. But it is an idea whose actualization is much harder than its idealistic principles might make it seem. It is an idea whose actualization is never complete and never will be complete.

Both Kenyan elections I have observed provided so much promise, and its people showed how powerful the idea of self-governance can be. The aftermath has not been as inspiring as the citizens I met throughout the day.

The dichotomy between the ideals of democracy and the reality of disappointing and lethargic results has become the evergreen democratic conundrum. This dynamic is playing out in the United States right now. Even in troubled and polarized times, the power of people coming together to make a difference is still evident. We see glimpses of promise: first-time candidates running for office and winning; the birth of new movements, like a push for gun control or protections for immigrants, led by young people.

The United States' democracy is sometimes declared as exceptional, and we, as a country, often attempt to teach others how to govern themselves. In troubled democratic times, however, it is worth looking beyond our comfort zone, and beyond our borders, for new ideas. It is worth learning from the Kenyans, who were waiting at midnight to claim their place in line to vote. Their unwavering energy, in the face of numerous obstacles, inspires belief in the power of democracy—the power of individuals to self-govern and make change.

No democracy's path leads straight toward progress. Kenya's tumultuous recent history is a reminder that politics is not a one-day activity: one election won't make or break a democracy. Kenyans inspire me to remain committed to living a political life—they remind me that the fight for democracy is an everyday affair that will be marked by highs and lows, but that it will hopefully, eventually, lead toward progress. This belief in both the promise and fragility of democracy inspired me to found Generation Citizen, a pursuit I continue to this day. I wanted to do my part to bring the same hunger and vigor that I saw in those Kenyan elections to the United States, while recognizing the complexity of democratic change.

7

"OUR WORST FEAR BECAME OUR REALITY"

Choosing an Issue

In 1998, thirteen-year-old Cristina Jiménez, her parents, and her six-year-old brother decided to leave their home in Ecuador. For years, Cristina's parents had struggled to find stable jobs in the economically depressed and politically unstable Latin American country. They'd remained jobless for months at a time with barely enough money for food, let alone housing, health care, or school supplies. They'd moved from city to city, searching for a better life. Nothing had worked.

Ultimately, they decided to risk everything for the possibility of something better. They fled to the United States, journeying up through the Mexican border and eventually settling in Queens, where other family members already lived. Anything would be better than the perpetual uncertainty of Ecuador, they thought. Even coming to the United States without proper documentation.

"My parents tried everything to give us a better life," Cristina reflects now. "It was really difficult. Their sacrifice inspires me to this day."

Upon settling in their new home, Cristina immediately realized how challenging it would be to adjust to life in her unfamiliar surroundings. Because she spoke English better than the rest of her family, she led the effort to navigate their new home, albeit a home where they lived in fear as undocumented immigrants. The questions and challenges seemed endless.

How do you register for classes at a school without an address? Cristina's family was moving from week to week, as they did not have enough money to rent a home. They lived with extended family some weeks and in shelters other weeks. Cristina kept this information to herself at her new school, pretending that everything at home was steady and calm as she tried to fit in and make friends.

How should she fight for wages for her father when the factory refused to pay him? Her father's first employer took advantage of the fact that he did not have a social security number by frequently threatening to withhold wages while simultaneously increasing his hours. He had no leverage, and could not speak English, so the negotiations fell to teenage Cristina.

How could she succeed in a country that did not seem welcoming? Cristina did not feel like she belonged here. She did not feel American. Her family felt the same. Despite all of the challenges they faced in Ecuador, she missed her home.

While attempting to deal with the other struggles that emerged daily, Cristina and her family lived in constant fear of deportation. Cristina's father left his first factory job due to the persistent wage theft and discriminatory treatment. To make matters worse, Cristina and her family felt frequently profiled by the police, who they assumed targeted them because of their skin color.

Despite this adversity, the potential for a better future in the United States remained more appealing than the life of continual abject poverty they left in Ecuador. Possibility still existed. Cristina's parents did eventually find more stable jobs. Cristina continued to do everything she could to succeed in school, determined to graduate high school, attend college, make a living for herself, and, eventually, support her family. She wanted to make her parents proud.

YOU CAN'T GO TO COLLEGE

Now seventeen years old and in eleventh grade, Cristina waited in her overcrowded Queens school hallway to meet with an advisor to start the application process for college. She was excited for this next step in her academic career. Her sterling work ethic had resulted in consistently good grades, participation in a variety of extracurricular activities, and a steady dosage of volunteer work that any college would embrace. Graduating from an American college would make all the sacrifices her parents had undertaken worth it, she thought.

Because there was only one college counselor for the more than 450 students in the school, she waited over an hour for a meeting. She nervously looked over her transcript, again and again. She peeked around the line, calculating how long she had to wait.

She finally entered the room. She exhaled a deep sigh of relief and placed her transcript on the desk. Barely pausing to greet the counselor, she began describing her hopes and dreams.

She had done extensive research on the colleges she thought could help her achieve them.

"I want to be a lawyer and give back to the immigrant community that has given me so much. I'd love to go to a college that has a good pre-law program. I have many in mind."

Her college counselor looked up from Cristina's transcript. She interrupted her midsentence.

"What's your social security number?"

Cristina froze.

"Green card? Any proof of citizenship?"

Cristina's smile left her face.

"I don't have any of that," she nervously stammered.

"You don't have papers. You can't go to college."

Cristina sat in silence. The counselor showed no emotion. This was obviously not the first time she had crushed a young immigrant's dreams.

"Can you please step outside? I have dozens of other students to get to."

"There's nothing I can do?"

"Good luck."

Cristina walked through the hallways of her school, stunned. Her family had left everything behind so that she could go to college. So that she could succeed.

Cristina was humiliated. She had played by the rules, worked hard, endured adversity. And now, she could do nothing. She felt a deep sense of injustice. The system had failed her.

She understood that her parents, as undocumented immigrants, would face challenges in assimilating to a country in which they did not hold formal papers. But she was thirteen when she came to the United States. Should she be punished for actions her parents took when she was just a child?

"I was very disappointed," she told me. "Educators are there to help you. This one did not."

She never talked to her counselor again.

As Cristina reflected in the days to come, she decided she would turn her anger and frustration into action. She resolved to use that visit to the college advisor's office as motivation.

Her counselor's assessment that Cristina could not attend college led to the first step in her political journey. She'd found the issue that would define her life's work for years to come: ensuring that young, undocumented, immigrant people would receive equal rights and, ultimately, be able to pursue their dreams as real Americans.

And so, Cristina got to work. In her school, and in her Queens community, she found other young people who were in the same situation, largely in the shadows, too nervous to publicly proclaim their undocumented status for fear of governmental ramifications, including deportation. She started conducting research and found that her status as an undocumented immigrant did not technically preclude her from attending college. The problem, however, was that the state of New York did not extend in-state tuition rates to undocumented immigrants. College, therefore, would become unaffordable to Cristina.

But possibility existed: the New York state legislature was considering a bill, called the DREAM Act, which would extend in-state tuition for public colleges to undocumented immigrants. Alongside other young people in similar situations, Cristina began leaving school early some days and taking the bus up to

Albany. She testified in front of members of the legislature and told her story of playing by the rules and working hard.

"I was organizing without knowing that I was organizing," Cristina reflected. Her innate passion for the issue paved the road forward to her own political journey.

Led by youth activism, the bill, SB 7784, passed in the state of New York in 2002. Cristina's dreams were now within reach. Before she knew it, Cristina was accepted into Queens College. She could now pay in-state tuition, making it affordable.

As with any political journey, the road did not end with one success. In college, Cristina became a youth immigration advocate. Although she was now in college, her immigration status had not changed. The fact that she was undocumented meant that she continued to live in fear that her family and friends could be deported at any time.

Cristina continued to connect with immigration advocates across the country. Recognizing their newfound power, these young immigrants decided to host their first-ever national conference in Chicago to build solidarity and plan the next steps for their burgeoning movement.

Cristina was excited to be part of a national campaign of young people in the same situation as her, but she was nervous about traveling too far outside of New York City—Albany pushed the northernmost boundaries of her comfort zone. She ended up staying home, but her friend and classmate Walter traveled to represent the New York contingent of activists. Walter did not want to fly and risk having to produce identification before going through security. So he got on a train to travel to Chicago.

When conceiving this new plan, however, Cristina and

Walter did not realize that this train veered through upstate New York, through places like Rochester and Buffalo, where immigration officials were stricter as the train approached the Canadian border.

At the Rochester stop, U.S. Immigration and Customs Enforcement (ICE) officials sternly entered the train. They began to search passengers, and, unsurprisingly, focused on those who were not white. They were looking for individuals who might not have their immigration papers.

They quickly found Walter. He obviously did not have citizenship information. Before he knew it, they hauled him off the train and took him to a deportation center near the Canadian border.

"Our worst fear became our reality," Cristina said.

Upon receiving a phone call from Walter, who told her of his predicament, Cristina immediately sprang into action. She contacted her fellow activists, and they formulated a plan. They would use every ally they knew in an attempt to free Walter. He did not have a criminal record, so legally, there was not a concrete reason that the government should deport him.

They mobilized, calling senators, faith leaders, and celebrities. They started a letter-writing campaign geared toward their elected officials. They received media attention throughout the region. They took concrete political action. They were able to gain and deploy power.

After four harrowing days and nonstop political pressure, Walter was released. He returned to New York City. In this specific part of the political journey, Cristina was victorious. "That event motivated me to a long-term commitment to the cause," she told me.

She had seen the human costs of the fight and had also tasted success from activism. Cristina's journey had begun with self-interest: being able to afford to go to college. Walter's experience in the deportation center made her realize that she was fighting for something so much bigger than college admission and affordability. She was fighting for the future of young immigrants throughout the country. She was fighting for what it meant to be an American.

THE POLITICS OF THE PERSONAL

Our political conversation today is so often dominated by the crude and vapid analysis of a nonstop horse race. Democracy can start to feel like a reality TV show.

What did Trump tweet?

How did the Democrats respond?

Who's up in the polls?

Who will win the House?

Who will run in the next presidential election?

Politics has become like a sporting event. We focus on style over substance, the drama of the day rather than how issues affect real lives.

When we focus on drama, the corresponding action becomes relatively shallow. Mainly, we are exhorted to vote. That's what political action can become: the act of voting every two to four years for candidates whose quest for power is analyzed and reanalyzed by cable television pundits and newspaper editorial writers.

Or, sometimes, we go to protests and rallies. Events like the Women's March or March for Our Lives are powerful. But they fail to produce real change if not accompanied by the requisite follow-up work, not all of which is as fun or as motivating.

The way many of us treat our political engagement is the equivalent of being a basketball fan but not being able to practice or play. You only hear about the games from so-called experts. Then, every two to four years, you find yourself in a game for just a minute, just to get a taste of the action.

Before you know it, the game is over and you're on the bench again, watching how it turned out. It's not participatory, and it's not exciting. Politics is being done to you.

Politics can't be a once-every-few-years engagement. Rather, it's a game that needs to be both practiced and played every single day.

Indeed, one of the more prevailing themes to Cristina's journey is that, as an undocumented immigrant, she cannot even vote. But that has not stopped her from becoming one of the most inspirational and powerful youth political advocates in the country, recently awarded a MacArthur Fellowship and named one of *Time* magazine's "Most Influential People of 2018." She has found other ways to influence the game.

To get in the game, we need to get beyond the superficial drama. To get in the game, you start by picking a specific cause that you care about. The road to change almost always starts with a single issue.

At Generation Citizen, we start students on their political journeys by asking them what they want to change. This is the top of the Advocacy Hourglass: issue selection.

"If you were in charge of your school, your city, or your state, what would you change? What would you want to improve?" We ask those questions at the beginning of every semester.

The answers always vary: Cafeteria food. Climate change. Public transit. Immigration comes up frequently in a place like Austin, Texas, close to the Mexican border. Sometimes, students will choose a niche political issue, like the proliferation of the wild turkey population on Staten Island (seriously). Or water quality in schools outside of Oklahoma City.

The most powerful advocates are always those who focus on issues that personally affect them—like Cristina did by focusing on immigration. Students have focused on gun control because their friends have been murdered. School funding because the drama program was cut from their school. Teacher pay because their favorite educators have been forced to leave the state as a result of low salaries. Seeing eighth graders advocate for higher wages for their teachers because their teachers keep leaving is incredibly moving. It also is an issue that comes up way too often, everywhere from California to Oklahoma.

As we start our political journeys through the process of issue selection, it is imperative that we don't solely adopt a deficit perspective. Low-income communities aren't the only communities with problems. Those with fewer resources at their disposal often present more pressing problems, usually due to the lack of public funds and sustained institutional neglect, and need help more urgently. But they aren't the only communities in peril.

Low-income communities should not be blanket labeled as conflict zones. Instead of focusing on a language of deficiency and calling low-income students disadvantaged, under-resourced, and under-everything, there is an opportunity to focus on the positive. These young people, like Cristina, possess a wealth of resiliency, tenacity, and grit. These positive traits are indispensable when solving the political issues of the day.

We need the unique energy, talent, and vision of young people—all young people—to solve the many intractable issues prevalent throughout society. Not every person is at risk of being deported, like Cristina and her family. Many people in this country are well-off, with stable incomes in safe communities. Part of the process of becoming passionate about an issue is developing and refining a sense of empathy, recognizing that the issues that affect those around us also affect us personally. We cannot rely on only certain people becoming politically engaged.

THE INTERSECTIONALITY OF OUR ISSUES

It is also crucial to recognize that problems are fundamentally intertwined. If you decide that climate change is the issue that you want to focus on, you will find that the changing climate disproportionately affects poverty-stricken populations. Indeed, low-income people often live closer to power plants, waste sites, and other areas affected by natural disasters due to segregation and low levels of public investment in their communities. By focusing on climate change, the intersection with other political realities, like poverty and housing, becomes apparent and unavoidable.

A similar acknowledgement of intersectionality becomes apparent when examining a broad issue like education. For example, a movement of "no excuses" charter schools emerged at the onset of the twenty-first century: the theory being that, regardless of where one comes from, schools can level the playing field. Schools attempted to do this through a heavily controlled environment, focusing on a combination of intensive academic coursework and rigid disciplinary policies.

While sometimes this type of education can lead to better academic test scores, the notion of a "no excuses" school has been largely disproven in recent years. It is impossible to level the educational playing field without taking into account issues like poverty, racism, housing situations, or access to healthy food. All of these public problems are related to young people receiving high-quality educations, in addition to the types of schools they attend. Schools cannot solve everything.

It is sometimes hard for us to articulate this intersectionality compellingly. Everybody thinks his or her issue is the most important. When I engaged in Darfur activism, I thought that stopping the genocide mattered more than anything else. Sometimes I would ignore, or even become resentful of, other issues. But truth be told, there were a lot of other important issues out there—from the economy collapsing to the war in Iraq to climate change. Additionally, these additional issues actually affected our response to Darfur. Part of the challenge in the region was caused because of a lack of water due to climate change. And the Iraq War meant the United States was less likely to become involved in another international conflict.

Similarly, when I began work at Generation Citizen, I thought educating young people to be civically engaged mattered the most. But it was virtually impossible to get others to care in the same way. No one would pay any attention to our work.

This reality has turned on its head since the last presidential election. In recent years, as our democracy has become more at risk, interest in civics education has increased. But other issues have emerged—from the Movement for Black Lives to #MeToo and a focus on assault against women to ever-increasing income inequality. Our issue of educating young people to be passionate and engaged citizens isn't the most important issue in the country. There is no "most important issue" in the country.

The reality is that we need individuals focused on all of these issues. We need passionate people finding the issue they care most about and taking real action. The problem is not too many issues. The problem is that not enough of us are engaging in these political journeys in the first place.

THE FIGHT CONTINUES

Cristina's fight for immigration rights continues to this day. She has become one of the preeminent national leaders of the movement as the executive director of a nonprofit called United We Dream. She's still motivated by the fact that both she and her parents remain at risk, every day. Her passion pervades everything she does because of the urgency that accompanies her activism. She remains undocumented and has now become a very public undocumented youth activist. If her efforts are successful, life will be better for her, her family, and the millions of undocumented young people in this country. If they are not, deportation becomes a real risk—for herself, for her family, for so many of her friends.

The DREAMer movement now has close to five hundred thousand formal, active members—all immigrants who care deeply about the issue from a personal vantage point. In this movement, young people have taken the mantle of leadership and are pushing the country to address the issue of immigration in ways we have never considered before.

When Cristina began organizing on the issue, immigrants—particularly undocumented immigrants—were seen almost singularly as criminals breaking the law. People to get rid of. Even the often-utilized, official governmental term *illegal aliens* literally indicates that they are less than humans.

Young undocumented people, the DREAMers, through their intensely personal activism, have completely changed this narrative and become one of the most powerful groups in the country. For many, these immigrants are now seen as some of the linchpins that bring different factions together, and, through their diversity, they are uniquely American. Their activism has been critical to this reframing. The DREAMers have consistently shown up at congressional offices, met with officials, and refused to back down until their issues are addressed. They have worked to become real influential political actors, rather than bit players in their own futures.

Polling now shows that, by overwhelming majorities, the public thinks that undocumented young DREAMers like Cristina should be protected and should ultimately become naturalized American citizens. Relentless activism, led by young people like Cristina, has transformed the political calculus. It has changed lives.

As Cristina notes, the fact that young people have led is significant. "The most marginalized groups are taking center stage," she told me. "We are not witnessing this. We are the protagonists. Young people are front and center in this movement because we have experienced it."

After Cristina's work on the New York law to ensure that

undocumented immigrants had access to in-state tuition, the DREAMers began an effort to provide expanded rights to undocumented immigrants at a national level. The culmination of their activism became the Deferred Action for Childhood Arrival program, or DACA, announced and implemented by President Obama in 2012. The DACA program allows individuals who entered the country as undocumented minors to receive a renewable period of deferred action from deportation and to be eligible for a work permit. The program directly impacts people like Cristina, who came to the country with her parents as a young person, through no choice of her own. DACA ensures that young people like Cristina will be able to stay without threat of deportation, work legally, and attend colleges across the country at in-state tuition prices.

This monumental policy decision occurred because Cristina and her peers did not stop. They did not make their issue about an election but rather made political engagement a nonstop endeavor.

"Our communities are being deported every single day," Cristina said. "We are at work twenty-four/seven. There hasn't been a moment where we can stop."

Cristina and other young people from across the country made the issue that affected them personally their life's work. They elevated the issue to the extent that the president of the United States implemented an executive order with the sole purpose of protecting young undocumented immigrants. That is power.

This is not to say that Cristina's stance on immigration is indisputably the correct one. Part of living in a democracy is exchanging viewpoints, finding compromise, and engaging in spirited, but respectful, debate. Immigration is an incredibly challenging issue that affects so many people. There is no silver-bullet solution.

The debate about how the United States should address immigration, and youth immigrants, is a deliberation worth having. Cristina's knowledge, personal experiences, and deep passion for the issue help to expand the debate. She does not shy away from a deeper, more substantive conversation—she welcomes talking to opponents and persuading them to take her point of view.

This debate must occur within the confines of the political process—through government. The fact that Cristina took her passion from the frustrated halls of her overcrowded school into the political realm matters. The only way that substantive immigration change will happen—the only way for Cristina and other DREAMers to receive legal protection—is through the political process. No amount of community service or volunteering can change immigration policy. Whether we like it or not, government reigns supreme in determining the fate of immigrants across the country.

This political journey does not necessarily have a happy ending yet. While Cristina's journey has included many successes, challenges continue to mount. President Trump's very campaign was based on an anti-immigrant sentiment—with the president continuing to blame undocumented individuals for almost every ill that befalls our country today, despite evidence to the contrary. Unsurprisingly, shortly after taking office, President Trump revoked DACA, putting Cristina and undocumented young people across the country at risk for deportation again. The anti-immigrant rhetoric has resumed in full force.

The situation worsened in the summer of 2018, when the Trump administration began implementing a zero-tolerance policy for all border crossers. Suddenly, all undocumented persons who had crossed the border would be tried as criminals. Practically, this led to a situation in which children as young as eight months were separated from their parents, who were brought to trial. Across the country, ICE has ramped up its efforts, conducting raids in communities and forcibly deporting long-term community members, people like Cristina and her family. Immigration has become essentially a wedge issue, with the Trump administration utilizing its controversial policy to provoke the public and consolidate its base.

Cristina wonders if her efforts have been successful, or if her community will continue to be set back. She knows people who have been deported and fears deportations will only increase in the months and years to come.

And so the zig and zag of the political journey continues. The push for immigration reform won't end anytime soon. Neither will Cristina's fight.

PICKING YOUR ISSUE

Using Cristina's story as inspiration, here are some tips to keep in mind as you find your own issue and start on your own political journey:

CHOOSE WHAT YOU WANT TO CHANGE

Like we do in Generation Citizen classrooms, ask yourself what you would change if you were in charge of any of the institutions that affect our lives—your school, your city, your state.

What aggravates you? What injustices do you wish you could right?

Do you wish you could reduce traffic in your city? Virginia state representative Danica Roem ran for the legislature on that issue alone and won in 2017.

Do you wish that the public transit system worked better? In New York, activists and citizens have realized that in order to improve the subway system, they need to take matters into their own hands.

Do you wish that we paid more attention to climate change? Young people will be uniquely affected by the long-term effects of climate change.

Do you wish you had more say in your school's curriculum-revision process? All too often, young people are sidelined on issues that directly relate to their own education.

The possibilities are endless. The key is not to accept the world for how it is but instead to envision a better tomorrow. Cristina refused to accept the fact that she would not be able to afford college because of her status, and she pushed forward.

ASK HOW THE ISSUE AFFECTS YOU

Think about how the issue affects you personally. In Cristina's case, this was very obvious; she became an activist because she and her parents could be deported any day.

There might be other issues that affect you intimately: A lack of school funding could influence your ability to take specific classes or extracurricular activities. A lack of affordable housing options could impact you and your family. College tuition costs could negatively influence your ability to afford higher education. You'll be a more powerful advocate if you are intimately aware and affected by the issue. You'll also become an expert on the issue and provide relevant content knowledge that can help move the issue forward.

LISTEN TO HOW IT AFFECTS OTHERS

Sometimes, you might select an issue that relates to others more than yourself. When I became an activist to end the genocide in Darfur, Sudan, the issue did not affect me personally, but I felt a sense of humanitarian kinship and an obligation to take action. Empathy for those around us is a crucial part of effective and long-lasting political activism.

Think about issues that do impact others that you care about. These could be issues that affect your neighbors or people thousands of miles away.

Then talk to the people who are affected. Make sure that you really understand how your issue affects them. And then make sure that they are at the lead. Cristina needs allies at the table who are not undocumented immigrants to help push the issue. But she, and other DREAMers, need to lead.

CHANNEL YOUR PASSION

As you navigate the inevitable bumps of the political journey, you have to be passionate about the issue you choose. Don't pick an issue because you think you should, or because it has become popular. Pick an issue that you'll be so fired up about that you'll be able to sustain your activism when the going gets tough.

8

"OUR CONDITIONS WERE NOT RANDOM"

Developing Expertise

Darius Craig was born and raised in East Baltimore, a neighborhood replete with community and character but largely economically under-resourced. Even at an early age, he recognized the divide between affluent and poor. He knew his upbringing was materially differently from other young people's who lived only blocks away.

Walking to school alongside Monument Street, the road that divided the two communities, Darius observed abandoned homes, walked over trash lying in the street that was never cleaned up by public authorities, and passed by dilapidated warehouse buildings. His parents expressed anxiety about letting him walk alone at night and forced him to travel with adults.

Meanwhile, whenever he traveled to Federal Hill, just a few blocks away, he saw pristine streets, ornate housing developments, and just-opened fancy coffee shops. Safety was an afterthought. His friends' parents from that part of town had no qualms about their kids walking home alone at night.

At first, Darius thought that this was just the way things were—that he was predestined to a life of scarcity on Monument Street. Like most of his neighbors, he was African American. Most of the kids in Federal Hill were white. Most of his neighbors had little money. The kids in Federal Hill had a lot. He focused on one day to the next rather than dreaming of a brighter tomorrow. He thought that kids like him grew up facing the challenges he saw every day.

But as Darius grew older, he became more acutely aware of the links between geography, community, and inequity. His lot in life was not arbitrary. He was not predestined to live a life worse than the kids on the other side of the city just because of his race or because of where he grew up.

"I actually befriended a few students from these neighborhoods," Darius told me. "It was then that I realized just how sheltered they were from disadvantaged neighborhoods in Baltimore. Many of them usually didn't travel deep into the city."

Both a passionate and reflective young soul, Darius began high school and, by his own account, "started to get an understanding of deep inequality. But more importantly, I began to understand that our conditions were not random."

Darius recognized that the disparities in Baltimore were predominantly the ramifications of an oppressive history of government policies that had lifted up one segment of the population while taking from another. The best way to reverse the disparities would be to reverse the actual policies. He could participate in a trash cleanup on his street to improve the short-term surface-level conditions, but real governmental engagement would be the only way he could ensure that the debris wouldn't return.

"That was my big realization. Policy impacts inequality. Or, more accurately, policy causes inequality," Darius told me.

Darius's belief that his zip code did not have to indicate his destiny was strengthened as he began to dive into extensive research. Some of this exploration took the form of gathering data: even as a high school student, he read newspapers, examined policy briefs, and read books about the history of Baltimore. Some of the research took place through interactions with fellow community members: he visited prisons, conversed with his peers, and visited other schools. Darius unearthed data that confirmed and provided context to his anecdotal observations from walking around town.

He studied the sometimes racial and cynical motivations that underpinned mass incarceration in the state of Maryland. He learned how Baltimore's burgeoning prison-industrial complex, defined by an increasing number of private prisons, preyed on young African American men like him, arresting them for petty crimes and using mandatory minimums to keep them imprisoned for years. He realized that, according to a 2013 American Civil Liberties Union report, Baltimore had Maryland's highest rate of arrests for marijuana possession, and Maryland had one of the highest rates in the country for such petty drug offenses. Indeed, African Americans on his side of the community were imprisoned much more frequently than his white peers on Federal Hill, despite the fact that they statistically did not commit more crimes.

All of these facts only confirmed that the economic, social, and political inequality that pervaded Baltimore was caused and perpetuated by unjust policies that lawmakers had set in place, perhaps in an effort to maintain the status quo and consolidate power that had historically rested with white power brokers.

For example, because of long-standing funding formulas dependent on property taxes, the city spent less on schools in Darius's part of the city. As a result, the schools were becoming more segregated than they had been in decades. More affluent parents would move their children away when they could, exacerbating the problem by further segregating the schools and decreasing the property-tax income the city used to help fund Darius's school.

Additionally, he found that 59 percent of black men between the ages of twenty-five and fifty-four were employed, compared with 79 percent of white men between the same ages. Only 10 percent of black men in Baltimore have a college degree, compared to more than 50 percent of white men. The median income for black households in Baltimore is less than $33,000. For white families, it's over $65,000. The deeper into the research Darius dove, the more the disparities became apparent. It was clear that policymakers did not prioritize the concerns of young people who looked like Darius. These facts were not just statistics. Darius personally experienced the effects of these unjust policies.

"I know what it's like to walk to school and see heroin needles on the street," he said. "There aren't that many people from my end of the city who make it out and go anywhere other than our local high school. I want to make the situation different for those that follow me."

As he progressed through high school, Darius decided that he had an obligation to speak out about the policies that had led to this inequality. He began to see the fight for more equitable conditions as *his* fight. The inequality that pervaded Baltimore became his issue—the one that motivated and propelled his political journey.

Assisted by a teacher who saw his potential, became his mentor, and encouraged him to apply for the National Honor Society, Darius developed into a leader at his school, eventually becoming vice president of the Society. He himself began to mentor younger students and to attend community meetings. Having a mentor, someone who challenged him and pushed him forward, made a difference.

Darius began to engage with the issue that defined his political journey. And he found, unsurprisingly, a system comprised of governmental officials that did not look like him—they were overwhelmingly white and older. For Darius, the fact that white people faced better conditions in Baltimore than their black counterparts could not be divorced from the fact that the majority of public officials were white.

Darius began to meet with city council members to urge them to pay attention to his side of the community. He entered meetings armed with facts and statistics. But, like Cristina's meeting with her college counselor, his passion was not necessarily shared. He learned that those who claimed to represent him exhibited no desire to bridge the gap between the two Baltimores. Unsurprisingly, the council members saw Darius as a young advocate they did not have to take seriously.

Engaging with the city's leadership allowed Darius to understand the policy implications of a system that for ages had systematically deprioritized his needs as well as those of his community. And he began to understand the reasons for the neglect.

"We elected people who don't care," he said. "When you don't care who you elect, or don't pay close attention to what's going on, you elect folks who are narcissistic and self-involved. I needed to teach young people what is at stake."

Darius's moment of political transformation occurred when it looked like his city might be torn apart.

On April 12, 2015, Freddie Gray, a twenty-five-year-old African American male, was arrested by the Baltimore Police Department outside the Gilmor Homes housing project, blocks away from Darius's home. When the police approached Gray, they noticed a knife clipped to his pants, which they later alleged was an illegal switchblade. Video footage captured by bystanders showed Freddie screaming in pain as the police arrested him and forced him into their van. One police officer bent his legs backward. Another dug his knee into Gray's neck. By the time the police forced Gray into the van, witnesses noted that Gray was unable to walk on his own.

While he was being transported to jail in the back of the van, Gray fell into a coma. The destination subsequently changed—he was transported not to jail but to a trauma center. A week later, on April 19, 2015, he died. Medical reports confirmed that Gray suffered traumatic injuries during his post-arrest trip.

Reports suggest that the police officers staged a "rough ride," an illegal practice in which a handcuffed passenger is placed without a seatbelt in an intentionally erratically driven vehicle. In this case, the police turned and sped up the van in an attempt to harm Gray on the ride to the station. The city coroner officially concluded that the ride caused his death.

Baltimore took to the streets. Gray's death had come at the same time as numerous high-profile incidents of African American men dying at the hands of police officers. Less than a year before, Eric Garner had died in Staten Island after a police officer put him in a chokehold when arresting him. Gray's death occurred just six months after Michael Brown had been shot by a policeman in Ferguson, Missouri. His death occurred just five months after twelve-year-old Tamir Rice had been killed at a Cleveland recreation center when police opened fire when he showed his toy gun. The list went on. And on. And it will continue to be added to.

Police brutality had become a pressing political issue, largely thanks to young people who, through protest online and offline, refuse to let the issue be ignored. They are tired of a system that has habitually and disproportionately targeted black people and treated them as criminals just because of the color of their skin. While these crimes have occurred for generations, the ability to draw attention to them through cell phone videos and social media created a new public consciousness of the severity of police bias.

The ubiquity and pervasiveness of social media in the wake of these killings helped to spawn the #BlackLivesMatter movement, which began when George Zimmerman was acquitted for the shooting of Trayvon Martin in Sanford, Florida, in 2013. This movement had begun to transform into a national calling for young African Americans like Darius, who felt that American society had, for too long, not valued black lives.

This tumultuous political context was about more than Freddie Gray—people were tired of the unequal Baltimore that Darius had come to know so well. The vast majority of those who took to the street, like Darius, were peaceful. Some, however, turned violent.

One night, soon after Gray's death, numerous local businesses were looted and burned, and fifteen police officers were injured. The situation became so chaotic that Maryland governor Larry Hogan issued a state of emergency and called in the National Guard, and Baltimore mayor Stephanie Rawlings-Blake established a curfew.

Darius knew he needed to do something. Baltimore was an unequal and unfair city. But it was a city he loved.

In the aftermath of Freddie Gray's death, Darius felt that older adults were not leading, or even helping. Darius decided to organize a march to show support and solidarity for Freddie Gray. He did want to bring attention to the scourge of police brutality and advocate for potential community-oriented solutions. But, more than that, he wanted to show the country that Baltimore would use this incident as a way to look itself in the mirror and holistically and finally begin to address the challenges that had divided the community for decades. The divisions that he had observed on his everyday walk to school.

The then seventeen-year-old Darius reached out to his principal, local community groups, and city council members. Impressed with Darius's initiative, they all agreed to participate in the march. He arranged a walkout from his school, leading all of his classmates out of the building while classes were ongoing. Thousands of young people joined Darius in marching through the streets of Baltimore. His words rang loud and clear in a powerful speech he gave before the masses:

We stand here in the heart of a city fractured but not broken . . . Today we stand together with politicians, members of our community, and our teachers denouncing all of the violence and crime that's fallen on our city.

However, we'd be lying to ourselves if we say that we don't understand. Many of those who faced off with the police needed to release the anger that's been built up in their generation, and the generations before them.

We are seeing the outcry of people who don't feel protected by a system designed to protect them.

There is anger because they don't feel that people like Freddie Gray or Michael Brown or Tamir Rice are getting justice. They are angry that our elected officials seem to protect the police and not hold them accountable . . .

We, the youth of Baltimore, hold the responsibility of taking the lead of Baltimore's future. The only way to fix a broken system is by working the system yourself.

The rally was featured prominently in newscasts across the country, helping to broadcast a more positive image of Baltimore nationwide. The message Darius delivered resonated especially with young people across Baltimore. They could bemoan and complain about a system that belittled their existence. This was all true. The public institutions had systemically oppressed people of color for generations. But their response could be to organize and work to fix the system itself.

The rally was only the start. Darius knew that the Freddie Gray incident was not an exception but rather indicative of broader injustice. This reality of wider discrimination didn't just occur on the streets of Baltimore but within the school walls themselves.

"What happened with Freddie Gray is a similar issue with our school policing, but on a larger scale," he said. "In the outside world, some people are being killed. But in our schools, they're just being beaten, assaulted, and arrested."

Indeed, research demonstrates that while Baltimore schools account for 10 percent of Maryland's students, the district accounts for 90 percent of Maryland's school-based criminal referrals. It would be naive, and incorrect, to think that Baltimore students are responsible for that high percentage of crimes. Studies confirm that African American students across the city, and the broader country, are disproportionately targeted for school-based criminal offenses. The statistics demonstrate how broken and unequal the system has become.

Darius continued his advocacy and testified at a school board meeting. He spoke out against a bill to arm school police officers.

At the hearing, he testified forcefully, "There are many students who feel as if the school police are out of line, they take their power out of hand, that it's more like outside policing rather than school policing. What we want is for the police to show the students that they care, that they're here to help, to keep us safe."

Darius had taken on the spark plug issue of Freddie Gray's wrongful death, and, through his research and expertise, brought it very close to home and into the literal schoolroom.

To this day, Darius remains involved in efforts to reform the system by participating in it. While attending the University of Maryland, he has become chair of the Maryland Youth

Advisory Council. He has advocated for topics like legislation to address the mental health crisis among young people and harsher punishments for people who commit hate crimes.

Every step of the way, Darius has demonstrated the importance of developing expertise on the issues he cares about.

"Growing up in poverty, I know what it's like to live in neighborhoods with boarded-up properties, trash lining the streets, lack of healthy food options, and an abundance of drug traffic. However, I was blessed to be able to ignore those temptations and have remained committed to fighting the injustices that so many of my peers have fallen victim to. This experience has helped me understand how prevalent these issues actually are."

Darius personally experienced the inequity that has pervaded Baltimore. He walked into schools where police officers hovered over metal detectors and understood how this affected the psychology and well-being of young people. His research has proven that the policies that the city of Baltimore has executed and perpetuated over decades have contributed to an environment in which too many people like Freddie Gray die at the hands of police.

"The most effective way to combat an issue is to be an expert at it. You need to know all of the important details: the history, the stakeholders, the prevalence, the causes, and the effects. You must be prepared for all rebuttals and counterattacks," Darius told me.

He continues to learn more about the issues every day, both from his own experiences and from continuing to conduct research. But he understands, intimately, the importance of backing up his activism with real stats. He wants to change the unjust systems that surround his everyday life. But he knows he must do so by understanding the systems intimately.

"You cannot take down a building without tools," he told me, paraphrasing Audre Lorde.

THE MUDDY MIDDLE OF ADVOCACY

The shape of Generation Citizen's Advocacy Hourglass is purposeful. The top of the Hourglass, which focuses on the selection of community issues, is broad because of the array of public problems we currently face, from climate change to racial inequality to school funding. The bottom of the Hourglass—tactics—is also comprehensive. You can consider innumerable actions, ranging from petitions to rallies to letter-writing campaigns.

The middle is much narrower: determining a root cause and articulating a specific goal that will address the problem. Because these aspects of the framework for change are more specific, they are also harder to determine and act upon.

For example, selecting the issue of hunger and volunteering at a soup kitchen is a fairly popular, and important, way to take action. That's good—we need volunteers at soup kitchens.

But examining the reason that hunger exists, identifying a root cause, and taking concrete action requires much more work. It may involve analyzing the way the government provides food stamp benefits, or finding incentives to combat food deserts, or even ensuring that individuals have access to a basic income to afford good and healthy food. This type of action is more complex, but it's necessary if we're going to make sustainable, long-term change.

When we first become politically engaged, we tend to reside at the broad ends of the advocacy hourglass. We take action on big issues through general means. We care about climate change, so we join a Climate March. We are passionate about education, so we participate in a call-in day to work to protest against Betsy DeVos becoming the secretary of education. We care about the Nigerian women abducted by Boko Haram, so we sign a petition to #BringBackOurGirls. We read a political article that frustrates us, so we rant about it on Facebook.

These aren't wrong ways of taking action. And, to be honest, just starting on the Advocacy Hourglass and committing to a political journey is more than most do. By participating in any way, you're already on the right track.

Substantive political action, though, the type required for long-term systemic reform, requires more than that. The type of activism that we need to enact true systems change involves moving beyond the broad poles of the Advocacy Hourglass and into the nitty-gritty middle. It requires developing expertise on the issues you care about and determining the root cause of why certain issues exist in the first place.

Darius has become such an effective advocate because he dove into the muddy middle. He did rally and organize the community for racial justice and peace in a time of immense unrest and tumult. But he didn't stop there. He also became well versed on racial and economic inequality by uncovering the statistical and policy realities that underscore the differences between the economic and social conditions where he lived and where others resided. He determined, for example, that the intense police presence in schools statistically helped to perpetuate the treatment of African American students as preordained criminals.

And he found a root cause of these unjust policies: young people, and people of color, are drastically underrepresented in the policy process. Their lived experiences are not seen as what is needed for combating entrenched issues of economic and political inequality. Darius has dedicated his life to changing this harmful and inequitable dynamic.

The Movement for Black Lives, emerging out of this most recent spate of police killings, has revealed the importance of understanding the root cause of challenges that continue to plague society. The top of the Advocacy Hourglass for this specific issue centers on racial justice. The bottom, in terms of tactics, has included many protests to bring the injustice of police brutality into the public consciousness.

However, advocates, most of whom are African American, have intricately explored the root causes of racial inequality and police brutality in the United States. Their expertise begins with their own experiences with the criminal justice system. Building on their personal encounters with racial injustice, they've developed a deep knowledge of its root causes.

Diving into criminal justice reform, the statistics become overwhelming. In 2015, while racial minorities comprised 37 percent of the U.S. population, they accounted for 63 percent of victims killed by police.

Additionally, African Americans like Freddie Gray are much more likely to be arrested for drug consumption or distribution, even though they are statistically not more likely to use or sell them. While 13 percent of the overall American population is African American, they comprise 40 percent of the incarcerated population, despite study after study that demonstrates they do not commit more crimes than their white counterparts.

Incontrovertibly, our criminal justice system treats races differently. Why are African Americans subject to such intense brutality by the police? Why are minorities arrested at such high rates?

There is no one reason. There is no one root cause. Some of this inequality is due to individual root causes: people possess an unconscious bias that influences how they react, especially in times of perceived crisis. The fact that police departments are disproportionately white lends itself to an unconscious racial bias that plays a role in law enforcement and police behavior.

And some of these unequal outcomes are due to the implementation of policy that explicitly contributes to a climate that unjustly targets certain groups more than others.

Recognizing the need to move past broad rallies and into concrete changes that could mitigate and ultimately solve entrenched inequity, a group of Black Lives Matter advocates created a campaign focused on the middle of the Advocacy Hourglass. The ultimate goal of the campaign? A country in which we see zero police-related deaths. The effort is called Campaign Zero.

To achieve their ultimate goal, Campaign Zero examined the root causes of police violence. In turn, they proposed specific policy changes that communities and states can implement that will lead to immediate solutions. These policy proposals were compiled thanks to research drawn from the communities themselves, research institutions and think thanks, and from President Obama's Task Force on 21st Century Policing, which was set up in the wake of all of these killings. The ten distinct policy solutions all stem from an analysis of some of the different causes of police violence. They all go beyond the broad poles of the Advocacy Hourglass and into the narrow middle. Some examples include the following:

- Recognizing the fact that more than a quarter of police-involved killings occur during the arrests of people committing minor offenses, like sleeping in a park or loitering, the advocates articulated a specific goal of ending the policing of minor offenses, or the "Broken Windows" theory of policing. They advocate for a more holistic, community-centric policing strategy.

- Acknowledging that fewer than one in every twelve civilian complaints of police misconduct results in any disciplinary action, Campaign Zero advocates for the creation of official local civilian oversight structures, establishing formal liaisons between police departments and civilians.

- Noting the reality that video evidence has drastically altered the public perception of police–civilian relations, the campaign lobbies for legislation that would require police officers to wear body cameras to record all interactions with subjects they encounter. The proof on the efficacy of body cameras is still up for debate, but the activists want more data points from which to draw evidence.

- Campaign Zero found that white men comprise more than two-thirds of U.S. police officers, even though they represent less than one-third of the entire population. Their solution to this root cause is to implement policies to increase the number of police officers who represent the communities they serve, and to create mechanisms to ensure that community feedback informs police department practices and policies.

There are many more root causes than the ones articulated above. And not all of these solutions may contribute to the ultimate goal of ending needless deaths at the hands of police. Regardless, the Movement for Black Lives exemplifies the importance of moving into a substantial, complex political journey. In addition to mobilizing citizens across the country to care about their issue, they have developed expertise in the work that needs to be done to tackle the problem of racial inequity at its roots. In the midst of any political journey, developing expertise is both necessary and challenging.

COMPLEXITY MATTERS

Becoming an expert as a means to determine specific public solutions is hard work. Conducting research, talking to other experts, investigating root causes: it's worth asking whether all this work is totally necessary. Can one be an advocate without being an expert? Can one participate in the poles of the Advocacy Hourglass without becoming mired in the details and root-cause analyses? In other words, is it sufficient, or even okay, to attend a rally to support #BlackLivesMatter if you're not totally well versed in the policy recommendations that the movement has articulated?

Like any element of the political journey, the answer isn't simple. When Darius rallied throughout Baltimore with thousands of young people, he needed a broad coalition of allies who supported his agenda and pushed for a more equitable criminal justice system. Not everyone at his rally could have understood his nuanced positions on the issues he cared about most, like the importance of limiting the use of force in the Baltimore Police Department or curbing racially motivated school disciplinary policies. In order to most effectively and efficiently mobilize a mass of people and demonstrate the breadth of the movement, he had to simplify his message. In this case, his message centered on showcasing a positive Baltimore while recognizing the necessity of addressing the plague of police brutality. It was a message easy to rally behind.

Even when advocating for specific policy changes, like in the case of Campaign Zero, the reforms are critical and oftentimes insufficient. Policies alone will not change innate racist behaviors and tendencies. In this case, implicit bias in police departments, which has been ingrained over centuries of American life, will not evaporate with the passage and implementation of specific public policies. More robust and culturally sensitive police training will help. But real reform requires a cultural transformation and full recognition of the ramifications of a country that was built on the premises of white supremacy.

We can, though, start with changing the policy outcomes. And in order to live a fully political life and push for the policies that adequately address the problems that concern us, we need to develop expertise in the issues we care most about. As we dive deeper into the problems, we realize that solutions are incredibly complex and begin to appreciate the long slog of democratic change that occurs through the political journey.

AVOIDING THE EASY SOLUTION

The tendency to remain at the top of the Advocacy Hourglass can lead to searching for silver-bullet solutions to our problems. This can result in half-baked, insufficient answers. It can also result in unintended negative consequences.

On April 30, 2006, I helped to organize a nationwide rally on the Mall in Washington, D.C., to bring attention to the atrocities in Darfur and call for increased governmental action. Over fifty thousand people came to attend one of the country's biggest rallies of the year. George Clooney, then Senator Barack Obama, and Holocaust survivor Elie Wiesel all spoke. Students came by bus from across the country to attend (including two overnight buses from Brown University that our team helped to organize).

As I stood near the front of the stage, I could not believe the energy the movement now possessed. The air was abuzz with youth activists, excited to be part of one of the largest student movements of our time.

"If we care, the world will care," Obama said at the rally. "If we act, then the world will follow."

Yes! I thought, in the moment.

But how should we act? How should the world follow?

Whereas many of the policy requests in the Darfur movement, including the divestment campaign, were highly targeted and informed, the rally had purposefully vague objectives. We wanted to draw attention to the atrocities, but we also intentionally created a message that appealed to a broad coalition of stakeholders. Indeed, the *New York Times* story the day after the rally noted that the thousands on the Mall "urged the American people and the Bush administration to do more to help end the ethnic and political conflict in the Darfur region of Sudan." Pretty ambiguous. We deliberately did not get into specifics, in order to mobilize as many people as possible.

I had spent years learning about the situation in Darfur, but it was an exceedingly complex conflict. The situation involved a number of different militia groups and a centuries-long conflict that implicated everything from divergent ethnicities to oil-revenue sharing to the lack of water and scarcity of resources in the region. In other words, the root cause of the problem, which we often failed to even attempt to analyze, was convoluted. It wasn't just people killing others because of their ethnicity, which was often the simplistic message we relayed to galvanize support.

Regardless of these complexities, we threw the word *genocide* about frequently because it was the ultimate moral threshold for action. We always pointed out that over four hundred thousand Darfurians had lost their lives.

Most of the fifty thousand people at the rally did not hold a deep understanding of the crisis in Darfur. They wanted to do what they could to draw attention to a genocide occurring on America's watch and ensure that we actually adhered to the slogan we often uttered after genocides but never actually abided by: never again. They wanted to play their small part in making a difference to people suffering thousands of miles away. And, to some extent, honestly, they probably wanted to feel engaged at a rally in which George Clooney and Barack Obama spoke.

To an extent, the pressure of mobilizing the masses worked. The night after the rallies, the Bush administration sent its chief envoy to the region, Robert Zoellick, to Abuja, Nigeria, to help negotiate a peace treaty in Darfur. After a week of negotiations, the Darfur Peace Agreement was signed—with multiple rebel groups in the region agreeing to a cessation of hostilities.

The immediate international press was favorable—we held a rally! A week later, a peace agreement was signed! Advocacy worked! The Bush administration and the media alike played on this narrative, demonstrating activists had taken real action and they, in turn, had effectively responded.

In reality, the agreement did not address any of the root causes of the conflict. Those who were perhaps the best experts, Darfurians themselves, were immediately skeptical.

One Darfurian refugee knowingly articulated in the wake of the agreement's signing, "This will lead nowhere."

The U.S. government seemed to press for the agreement to be signed mostly to demonstrate that they were doing *something*. They showed little interest in implementation, and Zoellick resigned from the U.S. government within one month of the agreement being signed. Many previous advocacy efforts had focused on the deployment of United Nations peacekeepers in the region, noting a root cause of not enough stability and security in Darfur. The agreement made no mention of peacekeepers.

Unsurprisingly, within a year, the agreement was essentially rendered meaningless as strife began anew in the region. Even worse, the rebel groups in Darfur disagreed on next steps. The dissolution of the agreement meant that a more rigorous future peace treaty was less likely, as trust had dissipated.

It was powerful to see fifty thousand people in Washington, D.C., advocating for change because most of us there were not experts, and we wanted something, anything, done. But in the process, we may have unwittingly contributed to a completely inadequate and potentially harmful solution that did not address the root cause of the issue. Most did not educate themselves after the rally either, meaning their activism stopped at the poles of the Hourglass: at action for a broad issue. Human-rights attorney Rebecca Hamilton, who wrote a postmortem book on the Darfur movement, sums up this tension well:

> If you want to build a mass movement you must, by definition, attract people who are not already specialists in the issue you are advocating. When your issue is complex, like Darfur, you have to simplify the issue to make it accessible to people who have no background knowledge ...
>
> For those who believed that building a mass constituency of regular citizens was the way to build political will, there was no good alternative to simplification at the beginning. But 18 months into their organizing, it was reasonable to expect the movement's leaders to have started educating their constituents on the way that the conflict was changing over time.

Hindsight is always twenty-twenty; in retrospect, I wish our movement had intentionally brought in more Sudanese to lead. People directly affected by the issue are always the best reality checks when it comes to assessing whether a movement is doing what needs to be done. We should have done a better job developing the expertise of our supporters and honing in on the root causes of why the crisis in Darfur occurred and how it was worsening.

Accepting the inevitability of hindsight, however, there are lessons here for our own political journeys. The message is not to avoid rallies or call-in days or any sort of political action unless you know everything about the issue at hand. That approach can be alienating; it's almost a form of elite activism. "Only participate if you know everything"—that's not what we ultimately want.

But as you select the issue you want to focus on, and dedicate yourself to living a political life, it is crucial to develop expertise and dig into the roots of the problems you're tackling.

WE CAN ALL DEVELOP EXPERTISE

A key way to becoming an expert is to determine the underlying reasons a problem may exist, or the *root cause*. There are two specific types of root causes—individual root causes and systemic root causes.

Individual root causes refer to an issue existing because a person has failed to do something. For example, the individual root cause of why a student might be late arriving at school could be forgetting to set an alarm or consistently staying up late.

Systemic root causes refer to the systems that prevent an issue from happening or contribute to the problem. The systemic root cause of why a student might be late arriving to school could be a lack of public transportation in the neighborhood or not enough buses on a route.

Real systems change derives from a focus on systemic root causes. The graphic on the facing page shows all the different types of systems that may contribute to the types of problems we can tackle.

Darius's story demonstrates the importance of developing expertise and assessing root causes. Darius has become an

LEVELS OF COMMUNITY

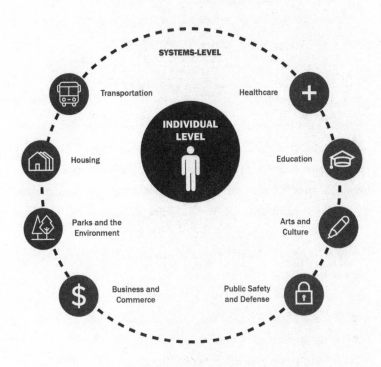

www.generationcitizen.org

expert, using his lived experiences and compelling data to analyze why inequity in Baltimore has become so entrenched. As he begins his life as a young elected official on his local county board, he is beginning to speak truth to power.

"You're not going to silence me because I'm twenty," he told me. "I found my calling when I got involved in politics. At the same time, I'm never going to forget where I came from. That's where I developed my expertise."

Here are some tips to keep in mind as you find your own issue and develop expertise on its root causes:

TALK TO PEOPLE WHO HAVE BEEN AFFECTED BY THE ISSUE

Oftentimes, this might be you. But in order to develop expertise, make sure you're talking to folks most affected by the issue you care about. If you want to take action on homelessness, spend time talking to people who have been forced to live in the streets. If you've selected racial justice, like Darius, make sure that those most affected inform your own thoughts and are leading the movement itself even as you offer solidarity.

READ, READ, AND READ SOME MORE

It's critical to educate yourself on the issue. Read any pertinent and relevant news articles. Find studies that have come out that dissect the issue in its entirety. Find organizations that are focusing on the issue, and get to know their analysis of the problems and potential solutions.

This research and advocacy cannot be a one-time thing. You need to remain up-to-date on the issue. One of the challenges with Darfur activism is that we continued to use an antiquated analysis of the situation to inform our own advocacy. Be aware of the changing dynamics of the problem.

While you're reading, make sure that you're looking at and

analyzing counterarguments as well. Try to determine why gun rights advocates are against gun control. Learn why some people want to ensure that the police are able to use even more force. This will help you strengthen your own argument and your own analysis.

GET AT THE ROOT CAUSE

After surrounding yourself with folks who understand the issue, try to determine one of its systemic root causes. There are many root causes to any given challenge, but the more specific you can get in determining why an issue occurs, the better advocate you'll become.

These questions can help you in examining the issue and determining the root cause:

- Is there a lack of something contributing to the issue? For example, a lack of homeless shelters may be contributing to homelessness.
- Is there too much or too many of something? For example, individuals having too much access to guns may lead to more gun violence.
- Does something need to be better in quality? For example, certain school buildings are falling apart, causing a lack of learning.
- Is something unequal? For example, many transit options in low-income areas are limited, making it challenging for individuals to get to work or school.

This work all takes time. Becoming an expert on your issue will not occur overnight. But the more you know, the better prepared you will be as you continue your political journey—the better you'll be able to articulate your goals, and the more you'll be able to convince others to join your cause. As with all elements of the political journey, the work is arduous but rewarding.

9

"THEY WERE MOVED BY MY STORY"

Changing Hearts and Minds Through Narrative

On the morning of November 14, 1960, Ruby Bridges walked down North Galvez Street in the Ninth Ward in New Orleans, Louisiana. Armed with a determined resolve, expressed by the steeled look on her young face, she took a right turn down the street and then walked through the yard of William Frantz Elementary School.

That day, like all six-year-olds across the country, Ruby was walking to school. But this morning was a little different. On this morning, Ruby was challenging entrenched segregationist school policies, and she was on the way to permanently changing public education in this country.

Ruby was not alone. She walked cautiously with her mother by her side, tightly gripping her hand. Four federal marshals escorted them through the schoolyard. Crowds attempted to burst through the ropes that had been erected as protective barriers along their path. The protestors screamed vicious slurs and hurled bananas; they were objecting to the very fact that this six-year-old was about to enter a public school. Ruby walked forward, becoming stronger and more resolute with each step, only growing nervous when she saw a woman holding a black baby doll in a coffin. The doll gave her nightmares for the rest of her childhood.

She braved the crowds, and entered William Frantz Elementary. The moment she did so, Ruby became the first African American in the entire southern region of the United States to enter a previously all-white elementary school.

A six-year-old was playing a major role in breaking barriers and blazing a path for the entire civil rights movement. Ruby's personal story demonstrated the value and importance of racial equality beyond talking points and policies. Her buoyancy, natural innocence, and energy drove home the very personal way that the civil rights movement could affect real lives. Ruby's journey began to provoke a sentiment of empathy that would soon pervade society.

She was only six years old, but she was facing down a country built on generations of racism.

CHANGING THE STATUS QUO

We have chosen our issue. And we have begun to develop expertise through effective policy and research. Our next step in our political journey is to tell the story of why we started the journey in the first place.

Compelling personal stories are indispensable to changing and transforming hearts and minds, and they are a crucial component to a political journey that leads to lasting and systemic change. Ruby's personal journey, which began after policy change mandated integration, inspired millions of people across the United States. Ruby put a face to the challenges of school segregation.

Ruby was born in 1954 in Tylertown, Mississippi, the oldest of five children. Her birth year coincided with the U.S. Supreme Court's *Brown v. Board of Education* ruling, which established the legal precedent for effectively ending racial segregation in schools. Despite the legally binding decision requiring schools to open their doors to students of all races, Southern states continued to resist integration, arguing that whites and African Americans should receive different schooling. This continued a policy of "separate but equal," which implicitly, and even sometimes explicitly, argued that white children deserved a more advanced form of education solely based on the color of their skin. Segregation became a national spark plug, with Southern governors and states rebuking the federal government and refusing to follow the law of the land. The Eisenhower and Kennedy presidential administrations were forced to continually, and often times ineffectively, grapple with their role of enforcing the Supreme Court decision at the local level and effectively ensuring Southern states were compliant.

Amid this national turmoil, Ruby's parents left Mississippi. In 1956, they attempted to find more lucrative employment and better educational opportunities for their children in Louisiana. While Ruby had attended a segregated kindergarten in Mississippi, her parents hoped that would not be the case in New Orleans. A 1960 federal follow-up ruling to *Brown v. Board* ordered Louisiana schools to desegregate immediately.

In their persistent resistance to legal compliance, the New

Orleans school district created another work-around. The district created biased entrance exams specifically administered to African American students in order to assess whether they could compete at the same academic standard at all-white schools. Hundreds of students took the test. Ruby, along with five other students, passed. Technically speaking, Ruby was now free to attend the school of her choosing.

Ruby's parents, however, were not in agreement on the decision for Ruby to attend the all-white William Frantz Elementary School, located just a few blocks from their home in New Orleans. Having witnessed the challenges of navigating a white-dominated society for his entire life, Ruby's father resisted his daughter's matriculation, asserting that it would be too dangerous for a six-year-old to fight against the historical oppression that had held him and his family back for so long. He did not want Ruby to face racism every single day she went to school.

Ruby's mother, however, was adamant that her daughter should attend William Frantz. She wanted Ruby to have the educational opportunities that her parents had never been afforded, even if she would have to fight every single day for that right.

The state legislature, meanwhile, continued to drag its feet, passing numerous anti-integration bills in the late summer and early fall. The Louisiana governor, Jimmie Davis, indicated that he would go to jail before allowing black children to attend all-white schools. He went as far as to threaten to close down all public schools in the state if the federal law was implemented.

Finally, the federal district court struck down the state's anti-integration laws as unconstitutional. United States district court judge J. Skelly Wright ordered the Orleans Parish School Board to put in a formal plan to desegregate, and President Eisenhower ordered the federal government to send federal marshals to New Orleans to protect the students.

And so came the fateful November day. Ruby was excited to attend her new school, but she was largely unaware of her looming role in a moment of national reckoning.

Ruby resisted the protesters and ignored the slurs as she entered the school. She recalled that her six-year-old self thought that it must be Mardi Gras. "I'm in a parade because that's what happens in New Orleans," she said in a recent interview. "We have Mardi Gras and the street is blocked off and people are standing there and there's police officers everywhere and they're throwing things, it's a huge celebration. So in my six-year-old mind, we stumbled into a Mardi Gras parade."

But after she passed through her "parade" and walked through the school doors, the unrelenting storm of racism continued. She spent her entire first day in the principal's office, attempting to outlast the bedlam. But chaos ensued throughout the school, with many white parents pulling their children from school for the day. Some parents ultimately forced their kids to leave the elementary school permanently, unwilling to allow them to attend class with an African American girl.

Ruby was unable to understand the racism exhibited in the halls around her. She was confused as to why she was being treated differently solely because of the color of her skin. She said her parents did not even try to explain racism to her. "The only thing they said to me is, 'You're gonna go to the new school today and you better behave.' That is what I was concentrating on."

Only one educator in the entire school, Barbara Henry, a white Bostonian, was willing to teach Ruby. And so Ruby attended a class of one for the entire year. Her solitary education led to a gradual understanding of the fact that she was treated differently because of her skin color. Ruby ate lunch alone and attended class alone. But she did not miss a day of class the entire year.

Ultimately, neither Ruby's determination nor her performance in school was enough to end the tensions surrounding the fall of segregation. Protests continued outside of the school building for months. Ruby's father lost his job: his employer was unwilling to tolerate the hatred the Bridges family now engendered throughout the community. Stores refused to sell food and clothing to Ruby's mom. Her grandparents were evicted from the farm where they had lived as sharecroppers for over twenty years. All because a six-year-old girl had torn down the artificially imposed walls that had come to define education in the United States.

But Ruby kept attending school, and ceilings kept shattering. Other African American students enrolled in public schools—in New Orleans and eventually across the entire South. Ruby ended up graduating from a desegregated school and became a national civil rights icon. Her journey through the school gates was memorialized in a Norman Rockwell painting entitled *The Problem We All Live With*. Decades later, she was awarded a Presidential Citizens Medal by President Clinton.

Although Ruby's political journey was prominently featured in the news, it would be wrong to declare that Ruby's story singularly changed the course of the civil rights movement. It's critical, as we learned from Anthony's story, that we don't simplify individual stories into broad success narratives.

Ruby's political journey, however, demonstrates the importance of storytelling, and the personal narrative, in creating change. When Ruby started school, morally just governmental policies were already in place. The ruling to desegregate schools had granted African Americans the educational equality they had long sought. Doing its part to enforce the law, the federal government sent in the National Guard to protect Ruby and fellow classmates as they entered school under extreme duress.

But in this case, policy was insufficient. Popular culture needed to change, and citizens needed to change their minds. Fair and just policy is critical to lasting social change, but a culture supporting the policies is just as important. Telling effective stories is vital in helping to persuade people of the validity of the cause.

Simply put, stories can change the status quo. Stories are a critical component to all political journeys.

THE PUBLIC NARRATIVE

Stories have been creating change since the dawn of personhood. *The Epic of Gilgamesh*, often regarded as one of the earliest surviving forms of literature, dates to 2100 BC, over four thousand years ago, and focuses on themes like the importance of wisdom and kindness that remain relevant in modern times. Homer's *Odyssey* and *Iliad* are masterpieces created over two millenia ago; these texts contain stories about loyalty, family, and vengeance that we can still relate to and learn from.

Since before humans could write, we have inspired our brethren through stories. We grow to understand and appreciate our shared values through stories that inspire, teach, and entertain. Stories also inspire necessary empathy on the long road to political change.

Change in a democracy is ostensibly dependent on the will of the people. Thus, in order to enact real change, citizens must be able to convince one another to alter opinions and to adopt causes. To achieve progress, it is important not only to select an issue and develop expertise, but also to engage in the art of persuasion, influencing others to agree with your issue and join the cause.

Harvard professor Marshall Ganz learned the importance of persuasion through effective political storytelling while working with Cesar Chavez and the United Farm Workers in the 1970s. Ganz and Chavez helped to revolutionize rights for workers in this country through organizing, unionizing, and fighting for farmers' rights. Storytelling was critical in the effort to persuade the American public that the farm workers were worthy of equal rights. Many Americans believed that the lives of migrant workers were worth less than ordinary citizens, and thought that they could carry out only the most menial of tasks. Americans did not consider that these humble migrants were worthy of receiving the same rights as the majority of American workers.

Using the art of storytelling, Ganz and Chavez helped to tell the real story of the migrant workers, ensuring that the American people saw them as laudable individuals who merited equal treatment under the law. Storytelling helped spur a national movement to unionize, which changed how farm workers were treated and how employees organized in the face of oppression in the workplace.

Ganz used his observations to develop a technique he has called the art of public narrative. For Ganz, "Stories not only teach us how to act—they inspire us to act. Stories communicate our values through the language of the heart, our emotions. And it is what we feel—our hopes, our cares, our obligations—not simply what we know that can inspire us with the courage to act."

This rhetoric, while inspiring, is not just Ganz's philosophy—it is empirical truth. Scholars at one point believed that people process messages in two fundamental ways. The first is "centrally," in which we critically examine a message. The second is "peripherally," in which we do not pay substantive attention to the message and focus more on the speaker or our mood.

If they are to be convinced to care about an issue, audiences must process information centrally. For people to viscerally understand the importance of desegregating schools, they must examine why such a change is warranted—they cannot reluctantly or passively engage with the issue.

The problem, however, is that people engage centrally only if they have a personal stake in the issue. This truth becomes a challenge. How can you convince people to engage centrally in an issue like racial equality if they do not have anything at stake? Relatedly, how can you convince white people to allow an African American girl to attend their school if they feel like their own well-being is at risk, as irrational as that might be?

An answer (not necessarily *the* answer) is public narrative. Researchers have found that we actually process stories not centrally or peripherally, but through a third route. When we hear powerful narratives, like that of Ruby Bridges's travails, we personally empathize with the subject, and, in a way, we process the actual events and emotions that the narrator experiences. This type of visceral immersion can lend itself to persuasion and the changing of opinions, even when people are not personally invested in the subject. The brain itself processes stories empathetically, relating to the narrator and diving to a level deeper than solely connecting to the facts at hand.

Politicians buy into this reasoning. Listen to any political speech, and you'll see this logic at work as elected officials use stories to engage in the art of persuasion as they attempt to solidify support. At any given State of the Union, the president will (quite literally) point to people present to illustrate broader points. This is exactly why Anthony was in Michelle Obama's box—his rags-to-riches story illuminated the potential of any young person in this country to emerge from a challenging past, achieve success, and attend college.

Telling Anthony's narrative is more powerful than regurgitating statistics. Stories persuade where statistics exhaust. This is why nonprofit organizations plaster stories of kids like Anthony on their promotional materials; they create an emotional connection with the audience that can lead to real change.

But of course, compelling stories don't always work.

Stories can become overly didactic and high-minded. Research has also demonstrated that stories actually have no effect if the message is too explicit. People want to come to their own conclusions—they do not want to be beaten over the head with a moral argument. They do not want to be told that they are a bad person, or less than, if they do not empathize with the protagonist. They do not want to be shamed into a specific position. We can see this play out with Ruby's predicament in the desegregation of schools. Citizens did not want to be thought of as deplorable humans because they did not immediately buy into the moral argument about the importance of diversity and inclusion.

Often, political messages play to the lowest common denominator and apply guilt to force agreement with a certain position. Politicians will play on either-or narratives, simplifying complex stories into dichotomies in an attempt to achieve marginal political gains. For example, politicians can sometimes blame the entirety of a family's financial challenges on the greed of Wall Street. This story can be overly simplistic and can lead to mobilizing a base more than it effectively convinces others to join a particular side.

Nonprofits can engage in similarly deceptive and moralistic behavior: simplifying their narrative in a way that implies their intervention quite literally transforms the lives of their constituents. Go to any nonprofit gala—the organization will parade its stakeholders (oftentimes brown and black young people) in front of wealthy individuals (usually white older people) in an attempt to dictate the moral argument that the nonprofit has unilaterally changed their lives. This simplistic act is demeaning to constituents and can (and should) come across as shallow to the audience. To an extent, GC did this through our telling of Anthony's story.

Along these lines, it can be easy to oversimplify a story and suggest that it is the *only* story. Chimamanda Ngozi Adichie, a Nigerian American writer, calls this "the danger of the single story." In a 2009 TED Talk, Adichie used her complex personal history as a woman from Nigeria who grew up in the United States to make the case for the richness of individual human stories, and she warned about the danger of reducing nuance into a single narrative. Adichie declares that, "The single story creates stereotypes, and the problem with stereotypes is not that they are untrue, but that they are incomplete. They make one story become the only story."

Adichie argues that Africans are much more than poor starving children with flies on their faces—even if this narrative may motivate a donor to give more upon seeing a nonprofit annual report. When using narrative to persuade, Adichie argues, we cannot reduce people to one single story and essentially take away their humanity. Thus, we need to engage in narrative storytelling that captures the essence and complexity of the protagonist and does not hit the audience over the head with an overt morality tale.

As Adichie concludes, "Stories matter. Stories have been used to dispossess and to malign, but stories can also be used to empower and to humanize. Stories can break the dignity of a people, but stories can also repair that broken dignity."

One way to tell personal stories that persuade others while respecting the humanity of the subject is to engage in the narrative framework that Ganz has attempted to perfect and popularize over time, which includes three elements: story of self, story of us, and story of now. This method of storytelling is a critical component to any political journey. It allows us to explain why we care about a specific issue, relate how this issue affects a community, and provide specific action items that relate to the current moment. This form of storytelling can inspire, inform, persuade, and eventually lead to action. The framework also builds upon the first steps of our political journey, utilizing the issues we have chosen and the expertise we have developed in a compelling, accessible format.

The *story of self* involves articulating why you have been called to the work, or why the issue affects you. In a sense, you're articulating the elements discussed in chapter 7: explaining, on a personal level, why the issue matters so much to you.

We can look to Cristina's staunch advocacy for immigrant rights through the lens of her own family background as an example of the story of self.

The *story of us* incorporates elements to explain how the issue affects the broader community and describes the shared purposes and values related to the issue. Effectively articulating a story of us ensures that the issue becomes about more than a story of self and appeals to a broader segment of the population. We are all part of multiple communities, so it becomes critical to determine the identity you wish to call upon in this story of now. It could be a family, a school environment, a city, or even the state and country.

The *story of now* relates to the specific action that we can take in this moment to further the issue and make a difference. Here we can call upon the expertise we've developed on the issue. This part of the narrative ensures that the people you've inspired can take concrete action in the moment.

Ruby's story fits into this narrative framework. Her story of self is that of a six-year-old girl fighting to enter an elementary-school building and receive an education. But her story of self is more than this simple narrative. Her family suffered tremendously while standing up for Ruby's right to go to a white school. And Ruby herself spent much of her childhood being scrutinized by the media. We celebrate Ruby's story now, but her story of self, in 1960, was not necessarily a cause for celebration. She was a six-year-old subjected to daily abuse because of the color of her skin. Ruby's story of self has had zigs and zags, like any political journey. She encountered many setbacks on the road to real change.

For Ruby, the story of us focuses on a society, largely, and a community, specifically, forced to grapple with whether the words our founders once memorialized—that all of us are created equal, with certain inalienable rights—are just a creed or are a reality. The story of us compels us to ask if a true democratic and equitable society can hold if it causes a forced separation of young people from public institutions of education.

Ruby's story touched multiple communities: the school, which was forced to decide whether it would actually work to educate all young people; New Orleans, which unwittingly became ground zero for the desegregation fight in the South; and the United States, which, through the civil rights movement, continued to reckon with the entrenched, racist institutions and policies that accompanied the white supremacy and legacy of slavery upon which this country was founded.

Ruby's story of now called for concrete action: desegregating schools and ensuring that African American children had the same educational opportunities as their white counterparts. Ruby was a model and a catalyst for change, demonstrating to other children and their families that they too could begin the process of desegregation.

Ultimately, this led to a cultural shift in which Ruby's journey became seen not as the exception but as the norm. While the courts and the federal government had mandated desegregation, Ruby's political journey, which is memorialized through her personal narrative, played a pivotal role in making the policy a reality.

Ruby herself may not have articulated this personal narrative when she was going through her political journey. But the facts of her story, which fit into Ganz's public narrative framework, did play an integral role in persuading others of the validity and importance of desegregating schools.

SEGREGATION REEMERGES

Ruby's story is powerful. But just like any story on the political journey, it is incomplete.

Segregation continues to be a rampant problem in public education. Today, schools are actually resegregating; they have become as separated as they were about fifty years ago when *Brown v. Board* was first ruled on by the Supreme Court. We cannot reduce the story of segregation into a single story, as the reality is much more complex.

In the mid 1980s, after significant progress, 40 percent of African American students in the South attended a formerly all-white school, while less than a third of all African American students attended African American–only schools. Since the 1990s, however, the trend has almost completely reversed. In the South, more than 75 percent of African American students attend majority-minority schools, and 38 percent attend schools with a white population of 10 percent or less. In other words, schools are becoming segregated by race anew. And the issue is not particular to the South—school resegregation is happening across the country.

Despite an American public that can sometimes claim racial enlightenment, a more perverse, soft form of racism has led to some of the resegregation of our schools today. Many communities say one thing about diversity in schools but act in another way when the issue hits them personally. Many white families claim to support policies that integrate schools and provide more diversity, but their actions speak louder than words. Too often they opt to put their children in predominantly white schools with better funding, rather than promoting fully diverse schools that actually statistically can produce better academic outcomes.

Writer Nikole Hannah-Jones offers her personal narrative to shine light on this hypocrisy. Hannah-Jones engages in the art of persuasion in a 2016 *New York Times Magazine* article entitled "Choosing a School for My Daughter in a Segregated City." As her African American daughter came of age in a predominantly black, low-income neighborhood in Brooklyn, Hannah-Jones noticed that, "In one of the most diverse cities in the world, the children who attend these schools learn in classrooms where all of their classmates—and I mean, in most cases, every single one—are black and Latino, and nearly every student is poor."

Hannah-Jones and her spouse were doing well financially and interacted with neighbors and peers of a similar economic status. None of Hannah-Jones's middle-class neighbors sent their kids to lesser-resourced schools. Instead, they found more prominent magnet schools, which require admissions tests, or even private, progressive schools with a majority white student body.

Hannah-Jones's story of us demonstrates that this school segregation reality is not just germane to her neighborhood: New York City has one of the most segregated school districts in the United States. According to a report released by the Civil Rights Project at UCLA, 85 percent of black students and 75 percent of Latino students attend "intensely" segregated schools in New York City, which are less than 10 percent white. This self-segregation occurs despite study after study demonstrating that more diverse schools lead to better learning outcomes. The city, while claiming to be a beacon of progressivism, has become increasingly segregated in recent years precisely because concerned parents voice one opinion about supporting and wanting diversity in schools and then act in a divergent manner.

Hannah-Jones and her husband intentionally fought against this new reality by sending their daughter to a neighborhood public school. They did this despite the fact that their economic status would have allowed them to send her elsewhere. Their story of now encourages families to abide by their own philosophies and rhetoric, bucking current trends to fight for a more equitable education system by speaking truth to power.

By publishing this piece in the *New York Times Magazine*, Hannah-Jones hoped to use her story, just like Ruby did, to persuade others to adopt her cause. She wasn't only trying to create policy change. In New York City, some of the right policies already exist to encourage school integration. More than pushing for a policy, Hannah-Jones was trying to use her narrative to cause a culture shift: she wanted to convince parents to send their children to neighborhood schools to desegregate the system.

It is a rich personal narrative when contrasted with Ruby's. Ruby's family had her attend a majority-white school in order to begin to desegregate the United States' schools. Hannah-Jones and her husband sent their daughter away from a majority-white school in order to fight against the increasing ability for wealthier parents to send their students wherever they wanted.

Of course, no single story is adequate. We must tell many personal narratives. The constant with both Hannah-Jones and

Ruby, despite the fact that their narratives occur decades apart, is the power of story.

Approaching the challenge of segregation with open eyes, and as an ongoing conflict, is not meant to denigrate or dismiss Ruby's efforts. It is also worth noting that although Ruby embraced her role in the national racial justice efforts, her family did not ask to be the national face of desegregation. They simply wanted Ruby to receive a high-quality education. Oftentimes, because of the power of personal narrative, we put all of our hopes and dreams on one story, without recognizing the players' own agency in the story or others who may have helped pave the way.

Ruby's narrative made a real impact in terms of convincing the rest of the United States of the merits of desegregation. But just like so much progress we see on the political journey, the path to change is not linear. Rather, the journey, pushed forward by Ruby Bridges, continues today.

EXPERIENCE TO ACTION

Lexie Tesch, a Berkeley High School student, used personal narrative to motivate others to care about an issue close to her heart—homelessness.

Lexie grew up in a single-mother household. Her mother worked in the catering industry, and, according to Lexie, she saw politics as "one giant mess." But Lexie ran for student council in fourth grade, though she lost by one vote. She ran again in fifth grade, and she lost by two votes. She began to doubt that the whole notion of youth change would lead anywhere. After her second heartbreaking loss in two years, she decided her days in politics were over. Who could blame her?

Disappointment at school turned to even more disappointment at home. Lexie's mom lost her job and was unable to afford rent. Before long, Lexie and her mom were evicted from their house. Lexie spent the next three years floating around the homes of family and friends, effectively homeless. At the time, Lexie could not comprehend why they had been evicted in the first place.

"I did not understand why," she told me. "Why would they take my home from me and my family? I was really confused. I was upset at the system."

Lexie, like so many of her young peers, was disenchanted with politics. The public system had consistently told Lexie that she could not do anything to change her situation. She could not do anything to secure housing. Politics and government became defined as nameless but malevolent institutions that had forced her and her mom away from her childhood home without any reason.

In eighth grade, Lexie's home life finally became more stable—her mom found employment and was able to rent a new house. At school, in one of her classes, Generation Citizen entered, and she began an Action Civics project, embarking on her political journey through the Advocacy Hourglass.

When it became time to choose a focus issue, Lexie's classmates wanted to explore homelessness. Lexie did not want to go along with the issue: she was embarrassed and ashamed by her past. She felt that if her class chose the issue, she would be forced to talk about her experiences.

"I just felt really weird about it," she admitted.

Against Lexie's protests, the class did select homelessness as their issue. Soon after, in front of the entire class, Lexie found the strength to talk about her experience being temporarily homeless. She admitted how challenging it was as a young person, moving from home to home, devoid of stability. She admitted she was ashamed. She thought being homeless was partially her fault, since she did not think many other young people were homeless.

This was the first time she had told others about her family situation. Talking through the experience was liberating. Opening up allowed Lexie to feel like her voice really mattered. She began to appreciate that her personal experience also gave her valuable expertise that she could use.

As her class engaged in research on the issue, developing their expertise, Lexie recognized she was not the only young person in such a situation, especially with rising housing costs and an unemployment crisis in the Bay Area.

"I realized that I was not the only one who had been homeless," she told me. "Eventually, I felt a sense of closure. I wasn't alone; there were so many people like me in my situation." In fact, thousands of youth were homeless in the area, despite the fact that the Bay Area is a paragon of immense wealth. It has become an epitome of the realities of massive economic inequality that have come to define the modern United States.

She began to recognize that her experience was a way to elicit empathy. "People never would have suspected that I used to be homeless," she said. "It allowed me to connect to other people. They were moved by my story."

The class realized that Berkeley had only one homeless shelter, and it was open for only half of the year because of a lack of funds. The class decided to focus on convincing the city council to fund the shelter year-round. While this would obviously not solve the homeless problem in its entirety, it was a necessary step to helping young people throughout the region.

The class met with the city council, and Lexie put her expertise to work. She used her story and public narrative to make the case:

> The issue is particularly personal for me because I was homeless for about three years. If it wasn't for my family, I would have needed to stay in that shelter. But where would I have gone during the time it was closed? This is what other real youth have to go through.
>
> We need to fix it. As a community, we need to ensure that all young people are cared for and valued. We can take a step in the right direction by making sure that this shelter is funded year-round.

Lexie's storytelling did more than guilt the council members through a moral imperative. She helped them to empathize with her plight. Here she was, an eloquent and compelling young woman standing before them who had been homeless only a year earlier.

Additionally, rather than focusing only on her story, she told a story of the entire community. She then gave a specific way that the council could take action.

The city council was startled that these middle school students were advocating so forcefully for the measure. "People were shocked that we were trying to do these things," Lexie said. "We showed how young we were, but how much we cared about the issue, and how much we wanted the shelter for those who needed it."

Largely because of the work of the young people, the city council ended up passing legislation to increase funding for the homeless shelter, which is now open year-round.

Still, youth homelessness continues to be a problem. As the Bay Area continues to develop with a presence of wealthy technology entrepreneurs, this wealth is not trickling down to the majority of citizens, and economic inequality is worsening. Many are struggling to afford basic housing. As a result, in 2017, more than fifteen hundred young people in the Bay Area were homeless, one of the worst per capita rates in the entire country. Lexie's work made a difference, but the political journey continues, both for her and for homeless youth across the area.

TELLING STORIES IN A POLARIZED WORLD

While stories matter and can change minds, and ultimately, policy, it is increasingly complicated to use stories in a country in which we often are not even able to agree on the same facts. Personal narrative, rather than being a persuasive storytelling technique, can sometimes alienate and divide people.

We can look to NFL player Colin Kaepernick's story as an example. A successful quarterback who led the San Francisco 49ers to the Super Bowl in 2014, Kaepernick began sitting during the National Anthem in the lead-up to the 2016 NFL season. Kaepernick stated that his intention was to bring attention to racial inequality in this country through his action.

After the first game in which his sitting was noticed, he remarked, "I am not going to stand up to show pride in a flag for a country that oppresses black people and people of color. To me, this is bigger than football and it would be selfish on my part to look the other way. There are bodies in the street and people getting paid leave and getting away with murder."

Kaepernick was, perhaps without realizing it, telling his personal narrative. His story of self, growing up as a mixed-race athlete in a divided country, worked as a window that displayed racial tensions across the United States. His story of us focused on the community of people of color, shining light on the police shootings of African Americans. And his story of now demanded concrete action: sitting for the anthem and making specific policy demands of law enforcement. Kaepernick soon began to work more extensively with different racial justice groups and to direct his personal philanthropy to community groups across the country.

Kaepernick's story inspired millions—other NFL players began to sit or kneel, and Kaepernick became a racial justice icon, with many young people pointing to him as their reason for engaging in activism. At the same time, many believed that sitting for the National Anthem was blasphemous and that Kaepernick had committed the equivalent of treason. During the 2016 presidential election, then candidate Donald Trump urged NFL owners to never sign Kaepernick and to keep him on the streets. Trump's rhetoric may mark a principal reason that Kaepernick remained unsigned for the duration of the 2017 NFL season while much less skilled players were picked up by franchises week after week.

Kaepernick demonstrates that while having a personal narrative is critical, it can be challenging to deploy effectively. It does not always work. Kaepernick, like Ruby Bridges before him, shows that when you are engaging in your political journey and telling your story of self, us, and now, there is no guarantee that everyone will find it persuasive. Indeed, some might push back and tell completely different stories.

It is challenging to promote individual narratives that inspire action without alienating fellow citizens. But storytelling remains an incredibly important and powerful method of persuading citizens to care about your issue.

DEVELOPING YOUR PERSONAL NARRATIVE

Here are some potential questions you can ask when developing your story of self, your story of us, and your story of now:

TELL WHY YOU HAVE BEEN CALLED TO SERVE

To begin your story of self, recall your own moments of political awakening. Focus on moments in your life when you had to choose values in the face of uncertainty. Consider potentially including the answers to the following questions in your story of self:

- When did you first care about being heard?
- When did you first care about the issue you're tackling?
- When did you first feel like you had to do something?

Answering these specific questions will allow you to relate your story and tell people why you care passionately about the issue. To relay my story of self, I began this book with my story of starting Generation Citizen and my story of becoming inspired to engage politically through observing elections in Kenya.

DEFINE THE COMMUNITY IN "US"

As you define the story of us, it's critical to define the specific community you want to care about the issue. Tell a narrative that focuses on specific people—the folks that have shaped your community—and ensure that your story invites others to join you. This could be your school. It could be your larger neighborhood. It could be your city or even your state.

For Hannah-Jones, this community was New York City parents. For Lexie, this community was her city of Berkeley.

Ensuring that you concretely define your community will allow you to tailor your story to motivate a specific segment of society.

FOCUS ON CONCRETE ACTION

As you close with your story of now, focus on the choice you are asking others to make. Incorporate a concrete invitation to action in your story, like Lexie did in asking for funding for the youth homeless shelter.

You'll be able to draw upon your developed expertise to think about the concrete action. It should relate to the root cause you've determined for your issue. The more specific the action, the more effective your request will be. Don't ask to end climate change. Ask people to support the specific carbon bill that your state is considering. The more specificity you're able to provide, the more people will be able to join in your journey.

An effective political journey requires that you engage in real persuasion. Using the personal-narrative framework to tell your story is an indispensable tool in ensuring that others are compelled by the same issue and expertise that drives your work.

10

"LET OPPRESSION SHRUG HER SHOULDERS"

Collective Political Action

The individual often reigns supreme in the political journey. Just as we are apt to celebrate individual athletes like Michael Jordan and Stephen Curry over the collective efforts of their teammates, we have a tendency to glamorize solitary leaders in the political arena. We behave as if individual leaders can bring about change entirely on their own.

Uplifting the individual can be powerful and motivational to any journey. There's no doubt that Jordan and Curry single-handedly won more than a few games through their other-worldly skills. And while not many of us can profess to have the same talent as Curry, young people across the country have begun to emulate his unique three-point shot. We practice in our backyards, counting down the clock, before launching a Curry-like quick-release shot to win the game, running through the yard in mock celebration. Curry, as an individual, inspires our game. Similarly, learning about other change makers can inspire our action.

Ruby Bridges's individual story motivates us to persist through our own struggles to ultimately achieve social change. Lexie and Anthony are two individuals from Generation Citizen classrooms who have demonstrated the potential of young people to take effective political action. We look to these individuals and strive to emulate their journeys, thinking that we'll be able to celebrate our own, just as we do with Curry's three-point shots. Their ability to push forward to achieve positive change, in the face of seemingly insurmountable obstacles, is the embodiment of political inspiration.

Individual achievement, however, is always more complicated than it looks. Jordan did not win a championship until Phil Jackson came to coach the Bulls and Scottie Pippen became his wingman. Curry didn't win championships without Klay Thompson, Draymond Green, Kevin Durant, and an entire team of all-stars. They both were transcendent players. They also needed teams.

Politics is the same. Successful political change always stems from the collective. Singular political journeys are never sufficient to bring about real change. Going beyond the individual and recognizing the importance of building and collaborating within a team is crucial. Our individual political journeys must become collective political journeys.

THE ORIGINAL WOMEN'S MARCH

Lowell, Massachusetts, located about fifty miles outside of Boston, was founded as a municipality in 1820, primarily to usher in the new age of the Industrial Revolution. The town was named after American businessman Francis Cabot Lowell, who, after learning about textiles and the emerging mill-factory industry through his travels across Europe, became one of the leaders of bringing the manufacturing industry into the American economy.

Lowell soon transformed into the national epicenter for the Industrial Revolution. Creating a foundation for the entire country, the city developed and utilized new, heavyset, and efficient machinery to mass-produce cloth while simultaneously organizing workers en masse to work in the factories. The new technology, coupled with an expanded labor force, led to an exponential growth in manufacturing.

Just in Lowell, between 1840 and 1860, the number of spindles in use increased from 2.25 million to more than 5.25 million. During the same time period, the bales of cotton produced annually increased from three hundred thousand to more than a million. This production directly translated into increased revenues for factory owners—profits increased at an average of 14 percent per year for textile-related investors between 1840 and 1850.

As the town transformed, so did its workforce. In an unprecedented move for the time period, the new factories employed a large number of women workers, commonly known at the time as Mill Girls.

The rationale for the factories' employment of women instead of men was not driven by avant-garde visionary dreams of gender quality. Instead, the shift was provoked largely by economic principles: basic supply and demand. When the Industrial Revolution first began in the United States, many traditional workers were simply unwilling to leave their agrarian lifestyles to work in the harsh conditions of factories. They did not have sufficient training to engage in factories and refused to change with the times (a frequent occurrence in transforming economies).

Because few men wanted to shift into factory jobs, wages for these jobs could ostensibly be driven high. Factory owners were confronted with this challenge: they desired heightened production, but they did not want to pay high salaries in their quest to maximize profit. The (often-cruel) realities of capitalism were present even in the mid-nineteenth century.

Hiring women, who did have experience spinning and weaving, helped to mitigate these complications. Women were willing to work, and because they were principally new participants in the workforce, they were willing to be employed for lower salaries. The factories were not hiring women to break the proverbial glass ceiling; rather, they were hiring women because they were cheaper.

It is estimated that by 1840, more than eight thousand women were employed at Lowell factories, comprising more than 75 percent of all the workers. The women, primarily daughters of farmers from the region, were also young: mostly between the ages of fifteen and twenty-five. A small number of workers even migrated from Canada, eager to take part in the emerging industry.

Despite the unsavory reasons for bringing the women into the workforce, the situation did afford some advantages for the new employees. Often for the first time, women were collecting paychecks, which provided them with money for previously unavailable educational opportunities. The factories also led to a new independence that had eluded women in their male-dominated agrarian lifestyles. Some saw this increased employment as a threat to the traditional American lifestyle, in which women stayed at home and took care of the family.

At the same time, others saw the entire factory system as a form of indentured slavery. Women were forced into menial roles in oppressive work environments by domineering male bosses for marginal pay. This reality caused the Mill Girls to criticize, and eventually organize against, the harsh conditions and limited independence that defined their employment.

Harriet Robinson, a factory worker who began her tenure in 1832 at the age of ten, penned an autobiography in 1898, describing the conditions of the factory vividly:

> At the time the Lowell cotton mills were started, the caste of the factory girl was the lowest among the employments of women ... She was represented as subjected to influences that must destroy her purity and self-respect. In the eyes of her overseer she was but a brute, a slave, to be beaten, pinched, and pushed about.

Other historical accounts largely confirm Harriet's analysis, providing a gaudy glimpse into the severe hardships imposed upon the women workers. Most women received contracts for only one year at a time and were paid a fixed daily wage. The Mill Girls usually worked fourteen-hour days, from 5:00 a.m. to 7:00 p.m., without a real break. Each textile room in the factory held approximately eighty women, with a small number of males overseeing the entire operation.

Because the machinery was so new, it did not operate at

peak safety or efficiency. The machines were exceedingly loud; one worker described them as "something frightful and infernal." The air inside the factories was filled with loose particles and thread. Even during the harsh, hot, and humid weather of the summer, windows remained closed to ensure optimal conditions, at the risk of the safety and well-being of the workers themselves. As one girl, Amelia, noted of the conditions, it was worse than "the poor peasant of Ireland or the Russian serf who labors from sun to sun."

After work ended for the day, the women all boarded together, in extremely tight quarters. A worker-run newspaper from 1845 entitled *The Voice of Industry* recounts the living realities:

> Then too, when she is at last released from her wearisome day's toil, still may she not depart in peace. No! her footsteps must be dogged to see that they do not stray beyond the corporation limits, and she must, whether she will or no, be subjected to the manifold inconveniences of a large crowded boarding-house, where too, the price paid for her accommodation is so utterly insignificant, that it will not ensure to her the common comforts of life; she is obliged to sleep in a small comfortless, half ventilated apartment containing some half a dozen occupants each.

The tension between the women workforce in the factories and the conditions imposed by their male supervisors was not sustainable. However, just as there was little precedent for a women workforce, there was essentially no history of women in the country organizing to improve their working conditions.

Instead, the women were told to be grateful for the very opportunity to work.

In 1834, using the same exploitative logic that they deployed when starting the factories, the owners unilaterally decided to cut the wages for the women by 15 percent. The economy was booming, but why not cut costs to further maximize profits? The Mill Girls had had enough. They decided to advocate for themselves, beginning their political journeys.

But they could not act on their own. If only a few women insisted they would not continue to work under such harsh conditions, the mill managers would not take their complaints seriously. Or, worse, management might cast them aside and hire different workers. In order to take substantive action, the young women would have to act collectively.

In the 1830s, the idea that a group of women could retain any amount of political power was completely ludicrous. Especially crazy was the notion of younger women taking political action. But the Lowell women persisted, adopting a collective-action framework and acting as a team.

Immediately after hearing about the wage cuts, the Mill Girls held a series of meetings, or caucuses as they called them, subverting their rigid schedules and convening during the workday, or sometimes late into the night, to discuss ways to organize. They decided to "turn out"—essentially go on strike—to protest the wage cuts and refuse to work until their salaries were reinstated. Additionally, they collectively withdrew their money from area banks, understanding how they could apply economic pressure onto a venerable and critical institution in their local community. Approximately eight hundred women decided to participate in the strike, representing nearly a sixth of the workforce in the Lowell factories in 1834.

After agreeing to strike, the women decided to march into the town of Lowell and appeal to the community for support. Risking their reputations, and their jobs, they made a public display of their demands. They left the factories during work hours, stunning crowds who had never before witnessed a group of women marching together. According to a *Boston Transcript* article from the time,

> A procession was formed, and they marched about the town, to the amusement of a mob of idlers and boys. We are told that one of the leaders mounted a stump and made a flaming speech on the rights of women and the iniquities of the "monied aristocracy," which produced a powerful effect on her auditors, and they determined to "have their way if they died for it."

The protesters continued their march past the town. They walked miles to other factories, enlisting other young women in their pursuits. The women organized a formal petition stating that they would not go back to the factories until their wages were increased.

In a sense, the Lowell Mill Girls' efforts formed the original Women's March.

Attempting to appeal to the masses and gain more political power, the women directly appropriated the language of the Revolutionary War. They understood that in order to successfully mobilize and attract others to their effort, they needed to convince the broader Lowell community that their cause

mattered on a deeper level and that their fight was more systemic in nature than solely a battle for higher wages for women.
Lobbying for women's rights unfortunately would probably not
resonate for men unaccustomed to women working in the first
place. An argument for freedom, however, could reverberate
among the masses.

Having developed expertise on their issue, the Mill Girls
recognized that the root cause they wished to address was not
simply an increase in wages. The change they wanted to push
for was independence and equal rights for women. The women
argued that the conditions in the factories served to essentially
enslave women workers. Their rhetoric conveyed a deep understanding of the root causes of their plight. The broader community might not care about wages for women. They would,
however, care about the subject of independence and freedom—
the very issue on which the United States was founded.

Their mass petition concluded with the following poem that
borrows heavily from Revolutionary language:

> Let oppression shrug her shoulders,
> And a haughty tyrant frown,
> And little upstart Ignorance,
> In mockery look down.
> Yet I value not the feeble threats
> Of Tories in disguise,
> While the flag of Independence
> O'er our noble nation flies.

The coordinated efforts of the Mill Girls infuriated the male
managers and owners. The men declared the protests to be "an

Amazonian display" and noted that "a spirit of evil omen has prevailed," chauvinistic language that may not be unfamiliar to women's rights activists today.

Unmoved by the protests, management outlasted the strikes and refused to take action. The women were back at the mills within a week, without having made progress on the wage issue. They felt that they had no real choice but to return, as they were at risk of losing their jobs.

The first leg of their political journey was not completely successful, but they did not give up. The workers had demonstrated that women could organize and bring others to their cause. They had also begun to form and utilize a collective activist voice.

In 1836, management once again lowered wages for the Mill Girls. This time, faced with a local economy in decline as more and more factories emerged throughout the region, indicating that both the demand and supply for Lowell goods had decreased, the men coupled the reduction in salary with an additional rent hike for all the women boarders. Again, their goal was to maximize profits for themselves, without heeding the needs of the women.

The Mill Girls decided to take the next step and form an official union: the Factory Girls' Association. The Association was the first women-only workers union in the country. The ability to better coordinate efforts across the region led to increased action: this time, over fifteen hundred workers decided to strike, almost double the amount from 1834. The women shut down the mills and marched again to downtown Lowell.

Harriet Robinson remembered the event clearly in her autobiography. On the first day of the strike, the women gathered to decide whether they would leave the factory and march out. At just eleven years old, Robinson helped to lead the charge:

> As I looked back at the long line that followed me, I was more proud than I have ever been since at any success I may have achieved, and more proud than I shall ever be again until my own beloved State gives to its women citizens the right of suffrage.

Robinson declared that when the women finished marching, "one of the girls stood on a pump and gave vent to the feelings of her companions in a neat speech, declaring that it was their duty to resist all attempts at cutting down the wages." When she finished her impromptu remarks, the crowd cheered. It was not dissimilar to A'Niya's speech in front of her school in Oakland.

This time around, the strike continued for weeks, and the women garnered more support from the Lowell community. The collective action represented a movement with which community members could empathize. Neighbors began to recognize the validity of the women's grievances, in particular because the rent hike was seen as a direct violation of the contract between the Mill Girls and the factory owners. Harkening back to their usage of Revolutionary language, this time, their very freedom was at stake.

In the end, by holding out and threatening to fire all offenders, management was able to squash the protests without a rise in wages. The Mill Girls did experience some success though: their rent did not increase.

The Mill Girls again refused to give up. In the 1840s, they continued to flex their political muscle. Wishing to address the root causes of their atrocious working and living conditions, they began to push for a state law that would legally reduce the workday to ten hours. Even though women could not vote, they organized massive petition campaigns, convincing thousands of individuals to ask the Massachusetts state legislature to pass a bill to cap the workday. They testified before a state legislative committee. They also began to organize union associations in other mill towns throughout the Northeast; these groups published pamphlets and organized to defeat state representatives who opposed their efforts.

This new legislation took decades to pass, even though the women were highly organized. While it took them longer than they would have liked, ultimately, they prevailed. They ended up being among the first women in the country to successfully push back against an oppressive system that did not treat them as equals.

As one of the Mill Girls noted, "[the men] have at last learnt the lesson which a bitter experience teaches, not to those who style themselves their 'natural protectors' are they to look for the needful help, but to the strong and resolute of their own sex."

The Mill Girls' groundbreaking movement can teach us much about effective political organizing. The Mill Girls chose an issue close to their hearts, developed expertise on the root causes of their own economic and labor injustice, and told powerful narratives to ensure that they inspired others to join their cause. They followed all the steps of the political journey we've been talking about.

Perhaps most crucially, though, the women acted collectively, working as a team to make political progress. As we continue on our political journeys, the importance of enlisting others, and creating a team, which can ultimately turn into a movement, cannot be understated. The Lowell Mill Girls recognized that their individual plights could be best addressed through a collective. This is perhaps their most enduring legacy.

THE COLLECTIVE ABOVE THE INDIVIDUAL

A democracy is defined as a system in which citizens participate in their own governance. Thus, laws, institutions, and culture are meant to reflect the opinion of the masses, all in an attempt to give credence to the visionary preamble "government of the people, by the people, and for the people." Politics becomes a process through which the will of the people is solidified.

But while democracy relies on a collective vision, we have a tendency to elevate individual achievements. Herein lies a tension of democracy, especially in a place like the United States. We celebrate individual freedom, citing it as one of the principal reasons that the country has become the global economic and entrepreneurial power it is today. We are proud of the right to express our opinions, start our businesses, and lead our lives, devoid of significant government interference. We celebrate the best individuals in every industry—the Currys and Jordans—superior musicians, athletes, and writers, offering them awards each year at fancy ceremonies. The entire creed of the American dream, as fleeting as it may currently be, is that any individual can amount to anything.

And so, despite the fact that we live in a democracy defined by the collective, the individual is paramount. In this world, problematically, the role of government, and the overall collective, becomes downplayed. Success is due to individual work, not due to the public systems around us that incubate and promote our very talents.

Even our politics, or perhaps especially our politics, ostensibly designed for collective decision-making, has become focused on the individual. People look to savior politicians, like Barack Obama or even Donald Trump, to articulate all of our hopes and dreams. We sometimes count on them alone to enact all of the laws and reforms we feel our country needs. Despite the reality that a democracy is defined by the fact that a citizen holds unique power, we have increasingly embraced white-knight politicians.

Similarly, we glamorize the journey of the individual change maker. The "follow your dreams and embrace your passion" language that we so often hear in inspirational books and commencement speeches validates an individualistic pathway to change. At the extreme, we are told to focus on our happiness, and our success, rather than thinking and caring about the journey of the broader collective.

As a society, we're focused inward rather than outward. We are digesting and affirming our political viewpoints on social media rather than collaborating with our fellow citizens. We are focusing on our own political journeys, rather than the journey of the collective. Regardless of the glamorization of the individual in American society, the reality is that our democracy won't move forward unless we learn to play as a team.

Our national education system mirrors, and perhaps sets, this trend. Schools have become focused on the success of the individual rather than promoting the collective endeavor. Nationally, the success of any given school is measured primarily through the educational attainment of individual students, assessed through personalized scores on high-stakes exams. This shift, which has drastically accelerated in recent years, requires schools to focus on teaching to the test, rather than engaging their students in holistic, collaborative pursuits. Naturally, and logically, students focus on their own studies, rarely collaborating with their peers.

A 2015 Council of the Great City Schools study found that a student takes approximately 112 mandated standardized tests between prekindergarten classes and twelfth grade. That averages out to over eight tests per year for each student. In eighth grade specifically, the same study found that students spend an average of 23.5 hours during the school year simply taking standardized tests. This does not include, of course, the amount of time spent on test prep. Our educational system has become focused on producing the best individuals, rather than empowering and training the most effective team.

This focus on the individual, which runs contrary to the entire ethos of democratic change as exhibited by the Lowell Mill Girls, illuminates the uniquely American tension between the proclivity to highlight individual progress and the collective efforts required to achieve change. Indeed, in other democracies like India and Japan, talking and drawing attention to the individual can be seen as socially inappropriate. Individuals, regardless of their lot in life, shy away from sharing their life stories. Even historic Indian activist Mahatma Gandhi, who led India's movement for independence, had to be convinced to write his autobiography (by folks in the West, of course).

Qi Wang, a professor of psychology at Cornell, asserts that the uniquely American focus on the individual narrative occurs because of our country's distinctive emphasis on the combination of rugged individualism and storytelling. American society has, both implicitly and explicitly, according to Wang, created the model of the heroic individual, who happens to pull him or herself up by his or her own bootstraps.

Wang provides Steve Jobs, the founder of Apple, as an example of this dynamic. Popular culture continues to promote the narrative that Jobs was a completely self-made American hero. Yet, while Jobs obviously worked hard to get where he landed, he also had the benefit of an incredibly supportive family who adopted him as a baby and made sure he had all the resources he needed to succeed. Additionally, the success of Apple was not due solely to Jobs—there were so many other individuals involved in the journey to computer superiority. The collective of Apple includes cofounder Steve Wozniak, who developed the first hardware and systems for the first Apple computer; Ronald Wayne, who designed the original Apple logo; and the thousands of employees that provided input on hardware, design, and distribution. It also includes the government itself, which provided the public infrastructure and research necessary for Apple to take off.

But even today, when people think of Apple, they think of a single individual: Jobs. They discount the role of his fellow entrepreneurs. And equally problematic, they discount the role of government.

Real change in a democracy does not happen solely through individual action. It requires the type of collective (and often anonymous) action that the Lowell Mill Girls exemplified. We know only the names of the Mill Girls who were able to get published when, in fact, thousands of women whose names we will never know contributed to the effort. Their action was so inspiring and trailblazing precisely because of its communal nature.

The Mill Girls were impactful not because of any individual, but because they walked out of the factory en masse and showcased the extent to which the factories were dependent on female workers. Ultimately, they were able to enlist others throughout the entire region in their cause, and, in doing so, they began to create a community in which young females were seen as individuals deserving of workers' rights.

Derek Sivers, an American entrepreneur, discusses the phenomenon of the collective above the individual in a 2010 TED talk. As he begins, Sivers shows a video of a shirtless man crazily dancing by himself at a large party. The lone entrepreneur with an inspiring vision. Curry. Or Jordan.

Before long, someone else comes forward and begins to dance with him. As Sivers says, this "first follower transforms the lone nut into a leader." They become equals, and before long, a large crowd has formed around them.

One way to interpret this awkward dance is to say that the first actor helped to start an entire movement. He should be glorified and revered. He is the individual change maker we love to write about. But Sivers pushes back on this narrative. His thesis is that solitary leadership is, in fact, overrated.

Sivers recounts, "Yes, it was the shirtless guy who was first, and he'll get all the credit, but it was really the first follower that transformed the lone nut into a leader. So, as we're told that we should all be leaders, that would be really ineffective. If you really care about starting a movement, have the courage to follow and show others how to follow."

As you think about your political journey, the key to success is not necessarily to focus on starting your own movement. Instead, you may need to follow others. As important as it is to pick your issue, become an expert, and develop your own narrative, it is perhaps equally critical that you ensure you've formed a collaborative. Immersive teams and coalitions play pivotal roles in our political journeys. We can't just dance alone at the party. We must invite others in to grow our political power and build our movement.

A NEW ACTIVISM IN A NEW LOWELL

Nearly 180 years after the Mill Girls spearheaded the labor rights movement in Lowell, fourteen-year-old Julian Viviescas immigrated to Lowell with his family from Colombia. After proceeding through the official immigration process, Julian and his family were able to obtain a residency visa to join extended family. And so, Julian moved away from the only country he had ever known, taking with him just a rudimentary knowledge of English.

The Lowell that Julian arrived at in 2012 looked much different than the town that ushered in the Industrial Revolution. As the industry that defined the town became antiquated, the town became a relic of the time period. Lowell transformed from a bustling industrial town to, as *Harper's* magazine called it in 1931, "a depressed industrial desert." Its last textile factories shut down after World War II, followed by a period of economic depression and population loss.

In recent years, however, Lowell has grown once again. This time, the city has become an epicenter of new immigrants. The racial makeup of the city, long a bastion of the white working class, is now majority nonwhite, a dramatic shift from just two decades ago. Latinos, like Julian and his family, comprise 17 percent of the population. The economy has also modernized, becoming a hub for higher education, with two colleges in the town, and new and emerging industries, like mixed-use facilities built in the former factories. The city of Lowell revitalized its waterfront area by building a stadium, which is now home to a minor-league baseball team (in a nod to the city's history, the team is called the Spinners) and a popular summer music festival.

But despite economic gains and increasing diversity in the region, Lowell is still led by predominantly white leaders: as of this writing in 2018, the mayor and nine of ten city council members are white. This demonstrates a power imbalance that harkens back to the days of the Lowell Mill Girls. The city is increasingly diverse, but the white power brokers do not necessarily understand the needs or concerns of the new Americans that now call Lowell home.

Julian observed this power imbalance in real time in a town's leadership structure that did not look like him and so many of his peers, and interpreted it as a reality that government did not value him or his family. Accordingly, as a new American, he did not believe that he could affect serious change.

"I was not interested in politics," he said. "As a nonvoter, and a Colombian, I did not think that my voice could matter."

Lowell High School brought Generation Citizen and our Action Civics curriculum through its school doors to empower the city's young people to begin to change the negative power dynamics that afflicted the town. The school wanted students to feel that they had a voice, could take effective action, and, in the long run, become the new, more representative power brokers in the city. Teachers at Lowell High School recognized the only way to rebalance power in the long-term was through collective action led by young people.

Julian and his fellow students began their political journeys by discussing various challenges in Lowell. They expressed concern about the lack of jobs, depressed economic development, and skyrocketing housing costs. The class decided to focus on gun control, an issue that was becoming a spark plug in the national consciousness and increasingly a problem in Lowell itself.

Julian provided his rationale for focusing on the issue in an op-ed published in the *Lowell Sun*:

> This past October a third-grader here in Lowell brought a gun to school. He thought it was a toy gun. It was in fact a loaded .25 caliber pistol. After school the boy brought the gun out on the school bus, passing it around to show to his classmates. What would have happened if a child pulled the trigger?

To ensure that such an incident would never happen again, the students contacted local officials, from city council members to the chief of the police department. They decided to start a gun buy-back program, offering community members the opportunity to sell their guns for money.

"At the beginning," Julian asserted, "no one took us seriously. They didn't think we'd actually get anything done." It was not lost on Julian that his entirely nonwhite class was contacting an entirely white group of power brokers.

But the students kept at it. They ensured that they were able to show the community the power and strength of their collective voice. They reached out to and met with the super-intendent of police in Lowell, and contacted and ultimately secured as partners more than forty local houses of faith (including Buddhist temples, churches, synagogues, and mosques), local businesses, and local nonprofits—all which helped spread the word and raise more than $4,000 for the buy-back gift certificates. Jessica Lander, the teacher of the class, told me that the class separated into four teams focused on communication, fundraising, outreach, and logistics.

"Over time, the whole class had a change in confidence. They believed they could make a difference," she said proudly.

The project was effectively collaborative, and, in the end, the collective efforts paid off. The class worked with the Lowell Police Department, the Middlesex Sheriff's Office, the Lowell Health Department, more than thirty local houses of faith, and more than ten local nonprofits and local businesses, in addition to the school itself. Working with each entity, Julian admitted, was challenging. Each power broker required different conversations, and each needed convincing that the students were serious. But Julian and his twenty-five classmates (and all of their other peers who engaged in the process) demonstrated to the community that they were serious about taking action. Carla Duran, another student in the class, told me how challenging it was to get the adults to pay attention to them, especially with the majority of them being immigrants.

"I felt hidden in the shadows. I was an immigrant—they would not pay attention to me. I realized though, that we could change those dynamics," she told me.

Indeed, they successfully held the gun buy-back event and bought back over forty guns from local community members in exchange for gift cards they fundraised for in the community. Just as Lowell was flabbergasted when women took to the streets and organized their own union, the community was shocked that the students started fighting for gun control.

"'Wow, teenagers are doing this kind of stuff?'" Julian quoted while he described the city's response. "No one actually believed that we could do anything. We were able to because we worked together. As one team."

This is what real change requires: Not the glamorization of individuals. The messy work of the team. Obviously Julian, Carla, and their fellow students did not singlehandedly solve the ever-challenging gun control issue. But, perhaps more importantly, just as the Mill Girls demonstrated decades earlier the power of the collective in a changing Lowell, Julian, Carla, and their team gave voice to the beginning of a new, necessary, more representative power structure in Lowell.

Here are some tips to keep in mind as you build your collective power through forming a team:

FIND OTHERS WHO CARE ABOUT YOUR ISSUE
As you set out on your political journey, be sure to find other folks who care about the issue you've selected. They might be your peers and best friends; they might be folks you've never talked to before. But undoubtedly, there are other people out there who want to mobilize and work with you.

ENSURE EACH TEAM MEMBER HAS A TASK
Every person has to know how they can participate in the collective activity to help win the game. Similarly, when taking collective political action, it's necessary to spread out the responsibilities.

The Lowell Mill Girls organized to ensure that some women wrote pamphlets, some held meetings with decision-makers, and others led the rallies. Julian and his classmates had to contact several different city departments and officials while organizing an entire gun buy-back program. In any movement, each player has to take on diverse roles to make a real impact.

DON'T BE AFRAID TO FOLLOW

As Derek Sivers said, we don't all need to be leaders. Movements are often formed when followers back powerful ideas. The Lowell Mill Girls needed some women at the forefront, leading the rallies through the town center. They also needed the thousands of women who joined in, with anonymity, to achieve a cumulative voice. Let's not glamorize the role of the individual in change, but rather recognize that every person in a movement plays an integral role.

CELEBRATE THE TEAM

While it's distinctly American to celebrate the individual, perhaps the best action we can take is to celebrate the team. We can celebrate the Lowell Mill Girls instead of the individual women who helped lead the charge. We can celebrate all of the young people at Lowell High School who are shifting the dynamics in the town.

Lowell is a microcosm for a changing country—a community that saw the emergence and downfall of the Industrial Revolution and that now is grappling with the necessary effects of a changing population on an entrenched power structure. The city has changed, and will continue to change, through the collective efforts of all of its citizens. Let's remember that as we engage in our political journeys.

11

"MORE PROVOCATIVE, MORE IRREVERENT, AND MORE CONFRONTATIONAL"

Becoming Powerful

By this point, you're well on your way. You've selected an issue you're passionate about. You've studied the issue and developed expertise. You've searched within yourself to develop an authentic narrative, and, in doing so, you've persuaded others to join your cause. The political journey is full speed ahead.

But now, what do you do with this momentum? How do you actually enact change?

Here's the simple, but never-ending, answer: you need to become powerful.

Perhaps the most vital and challenging step in any political journey is building and consolidating power. As young people, this political power is essential as we engage in the process of moving from words to action. Power then allows us to move from action to change.

I admit that my word choice might seem like a radical shift. *Power*, indeed, has become a bit of a filthy term. Power suggests authority. Oppression. Wielding harmful influence over others.

This definition of power is not the most egalitarian. Those who do obtain influence over others frequently seem to be inattentive to the needs of those around them, breeding a sense of powerlessness within the rest of us. Oftentimes, those in control are apt to take advantage of those they control.

Naturally, many of us have felt taken advantage of. We feel powerless. Subsequently, we lose faith in our elected officials and our democratic institutions. We sense that out-of-touch leaders who possess control, authority, and influence don't use it in the best of ways.

Our powerlessness is both amplified and confirmed when we see overt abuses of power and corruption, explicit displays of opulence and privilege and policies that favor those with means over those without. We see wealthy individuals articulating methods and models of transformative change without doing anything that would actually result in their having fewer resources or less power.

People across the political spectrum are disgusted by and fed up with these hypocritical abuses of power. Citizens become frustrated when they see President Donald Trump opining about the forgotten in Middle America and pledging to restore coal and manufacturing jobs before flying away for a weekend of banquets and golf in Mar-a-Lago, far removed from all the problems he pledges to solve. He has the power to talk about change while acting in a way that's utterly incongruous to his rhetoric.

At the same time, in New York City, Mayor Bill de Blasio, a Democrat, often talks about the small actions that individual citizens can take to cut their carbon footprint and benefit the environment. But almost every morning, he takes a convoy of high-emission SUV vehicles from his home on the Upper East Side to Brooklyn, to go to his former neighborhood gym, an approximately ten-mile trip in morning New York City traffic. When a call-in guest on the Brian Lehrer radio show pointed out this discrepancy in his words and actions, de Blasio insisted that this was a different situation. "It doesn't really have anything to do with how we change the world," de Blasio said of his frequent gym jaunts. "We change the world with policies that affect people."

In other words, *you* should curb your carbon footprint, but *I'm* above that because I'm powerful.

It is this blatant hypocrisy that has come to define power in the modern lexicon: leaders do whatever they please while they consolidate and exploit their control.

But that's not what power has to be. Power can also mean the ability to produce an effect. In this meaning, anyone can hold power. We can redefine it. It's not just held by those who are rich. Or malevolent.

We can be powerful.

We need to be powerful.

We, as citizens and as young people, possess the ability to hold power. Because it's possible for any of us to act and produce an effect.

Eric Liu, a former Clinton administration official and the founder and CEO of an organization called Citizen University, wrote a book on citizens harnessing power entitled *You're More*

Powerful Than You Think. Defining power as a concept that anyone can practice, Liu presents three principles of using power that are relevant to our political journeys.

Liu's first rule is that power concentrates: those with more of it tend to continue to obtain more, and those with less of it continue to influence less. This is one of the reasons why we continually observe the corrosive effects of power—the concentration at the top drains influence and resources away from some while perpetually building up those who then reap its benefits. This unequal distribution of power is especially true for young people, who recognize how difficult it is to get a fair shot in the destructive political environment we live in today.

Consider how our society addresses issues that affect older voters as opposed to policies that pertain to our youngest populations. Older populations vote at disproportionately high levels and typically have more money to contribute to politicians. This gives them more power to influence elected officials.

On a policy level, this means that despite budgetary deficit levels that continue to skyrocket as our country borrows more than it brings in, politicians rarely touch issues like social security, which provides benefits and income to Americans over the age of sixty-five, or Medicare, which provides health care for elderly Americans. Older Americans have gained, and consolidated, political power.

Another related example is the corrosive influence of money in politics. Those with resources, like corporations, and those in the top 1 percent, or even 0.1 percent, spend hundreds of millions of dollars in campaign contributions to their favorite politicians. Our elected officials then pass legislation that largely helps those donors become even wealthier. They then have more money to give to politicians. The destructive cycle continues: the power consolidates and concentrates.

On the opposite side of the spectrum, issues pertaining to young people, like the soaring student-loan rates and long-term issues related to climate change, largely remain unaddressed. Young people do not vote at the same rate as older Americans, and they have less money to give to campaigns, so they wield less power.

Liu's second law is that "power justifies itself." This means we create narratives to explain why certain people have power and why some do not. Mayor de Blasio is allowed to drive his SUV to his gym miles away because he is powerful—and that power justifies itself.

For example, our society has created a narrative in which young people know less about politics and therefore their opinions are less valid. It makes sense, the narrative concludes, that older Americans should have more power because they possess more wisdom.

This same narrative applies to those who are wealthy. If you have earned money, you know more. I know this narrative intimately from working in the nonprofit sector. Running an organization, I often must bow down to those with more money, who tell me, based on their years of experience during which they've made much more money than I'll ever make, how to do my job. Because they have money, they know more than me— despite the fact that they have no experience in nonprofits or, often, little knowledge of our educational system. The narrative follows that younger, less wealthy people should wait their turn until they gain power. Or until they become rich.

Combined, these two laws can be a little depressing. If those who have power consolidate more power, and we simultaneously perpetuate narratives that justify this imbalance, then how can we break this cycle? If we accept this logic, then, as young people, we're hopeless. Our political journeys have become bridges to nowhere.

Liu's third rule is that power is infinite. As he writes, "There is no inherent cap on the amount of power citizens can generate." People generally assume that because power tips in favor of one entity, then the other naturally possesses less. Liu argues that it's necessary to reimagine this equation. His argument is that power, and politics, is not a zero-sum game.

But I don't 100 percent agree with Liu here—I'm not sure how the world would work if everyone was powerful. It might be a little challenging to get things done. Certain people do have more power than others, and it seems that this is slightly inevitable. The necessary intersectionality of issues means that public challenges like the college-debt crisis, or massively increasing and pervading inequality, is not divorced from segments of the population that have systematically gained and consolidated power.

The challenge in politics today is that older, wealthier, and whiter individuals and corporations have too much power. Young people, and people of color, do not have enough power. Regardless of whether you believe that power is infinite, or that the current contours of power are unjust, the logical conclusion is the same: in order to affect change on issues we care about, young people need to become more powerful.

THE STEPS TO BECOMING POWERFUL

So how do we become powerful? There isn't a concrete equation. Rather, there are a variety of action steps, all of which can be deployed in different ways.

In Generation Citizen, we call this accumulation of power the Tactic Toolkit. Each "power" tool in our political arsenal provides us with a wide array of methods we can use to accumulate power and influence those in leadership.

These tactics lead us to the bottom half of Generation Citizen's Advocacy Hourglass. Once we have selected our issue, developed expertise, determined the root cause of the issue, articulated a concrete goal, and built our team, we can, and must, use tools to influence our targets.

The fact that the tactics are on the bottom of Hourglass is purposeful—it's big and wide. Whereas our root cause and goal are very specific, we have a limitless array of means to take action.

We can make phone calls to legislators to express our opinions on the issues of the day and make requests of how we'd like them to take action. The more people that call, the more powerful we become—and the more pressure legislators feel. We can similarly start email campaigns to lobby for legislation. If they receive email after email, they can be forced to act.

We can convince thousands of our peers to sign a petition. We can write an opinion article in our local paper. We can organize a rally. It's about showing how many people care about the issues that define our political journeys.

The list of tactics in our arsenal goes on and on: there are more creative measures than your standard civic demonstrations. You can start a social media campaign to get your issue trending and put pressure on elected officials and corporations alike.

You can hold a lobbying day at your city council or state legislature, where you meet with elected officials to convince them to support your issue.

You can host your own town hall meeting, bringing together community members with public officials.

It's important to note that all of these tactics should still follow the steps we've taken in our political journey as we go through the Hourglass. If you're meeting with a legislator, you should be speaking about your specific issue, deploying your expertise, and demonstrating that you are part of a larger team that cares about the issue. Advocating for a specific goal is a more effective approach than lobbying for a very broad issue.

Sometimes, our action itself can be sufficient to persuade elected officials. But our action can be greatly aided by influencers who can persuade decision-makers. These influencers can run the gamut: if you're taking action on an issue related to education, teachers can help. If you're trying to change the actions of a harmful company, consumers can play a role. If you're trying to take action on housing, constituents who live in affordable housing units can be powerful influencers. In any issue, convincing the media to cover your campaign can play a pivotal role—they are always vital influencers.

If we, as young people, are able to mobilize influential stakeholders, and ultimately persuade decision-makers to adopt our cause, we have created power outside the typical channels and beyond conventional expectation. Doing so makes us powerful political actors.

HISTORICALLY POWERFUL

Throughout history, youth movements from all across the political spectrum have utilized a variety of tactics to become powerful and achieve real change. These movements, which follow the trajectory of the political journey we've begun, illustrate the necessity of being creative in order to subvert the status quo.

The campaign to lower the voting age to eighteen from twenty-one is an example of young people becoming powerful and enacting sweeping and lasting systemic reform. We now interpret it is as a given that eighteen-year-olds can vote. But the critical reform did not happen until 1971.

Despite initial hesitancy, there was some limited local support for this idea. In 1942, West Virginia Democratic congressman Jennings Randolph introduced federal legislation to lower the voting age, the first time such an effort emerged on the national scene. Randolph based his support on a belief in the power and abilities of the country's youth, declaring upon introducing legislation that young people "possess a great social conscience, are perplexed by the injustices in the world, and are anxious to rectify those ills."

A year later, in 1943, Georgia became the first state in the country to lower the voting age to eighteen, but only for state and local elections. In Congress, Randolph did not have the widespread support needed to enact a national reform: Georgia remained an isolated event. Indeed, most people thought the idea was ludicrous and that eighteen-year-olds were not smart enough, or mature enough, to help decide the future of our democracy.

The legislative action required to lower the voting age was daunting: it meant changing established law in every state in the country and ultimately amending the U.S. Constitution itself. How in the world could that ever happen?

After these initial successes, the campaign to lower the voting age began to gain real steam during the Vietnam War. The key difference between this moment and earlier pushes for change was that young people began to lead the movement.

Young people expressed fury that eighteen-year-olds could go off to war to be killed but could not vote for the very public officials who were sending them to war through the mandatory draft. In 1968, more than twenty-five thousand U.S. soldiers killed in Vietnam were under the age of twenty. Not one of them could vote.

"Old enough to fight, old enough to vote" became the movement's rallying cry. A national campaign started by young people, called Project 18, aimed to catalyze the newly found momentum and messaging into a national movement.

But the young people leading the movement were often written off as naive youth, incapable of producing real change. The *Washington Post* wrote that the youth activists were politically inexperienced and looked decidedly "un-hip" in their earnest "gray-flannel suits." *The Christian Science Monitor* reported that political operatives cast them as "another children's crusade enlisting volunteers." Conservatives worried that lowering the voting age would hand over government to "impetuous, long-haired kids who lacked adult judgment and experience."

This is rhetoric we see utilized today in describing any youth-led movement. "Seasoned" experts discounting youth activists is nothing new (and probably will never go away). That these young people pushed forward despite vehement opposition is also nothing new.

They deployed their own tactic toolkit to take effective action. Some youth engaged in wide petition drives in their states, encouraging state legislatures to pass laws giving eighteen-year-olds the right to vote. Others gathered en masse in the street, holding marches and demonstrations to alert lawmakers to the hypocrisy of drafting young people into the war while simultaneously restricting their right to vote.

Other young people wrote opinion articles in local and national newspapers in which they pointed out the moral urgency of lowering the voting age. Before long, the issue began to transform from an absurdity into a potential reality.

The activism began to produce a necessary change of opinion as the youth tactics began to persuade people of the validity of their cause. In June 1939, before the movement had really taken off, only 17 percent of the American public was in favor of lowering the voting age. By 1967, this had changed dramatically: 64 percent of Americans were in favor of the change.

You don't need to be a mathematician to understand the dramatic shift in public opinion. The shift wasn't led by legislators or think tanks or journalists. The shift in opinion was led by young people. It also took a long time, and a lot of activism.

We know that power justifies itself. In this case, young people changed this power justification, and the broader narrative, by convincing the public that they deserved the right to vote, and that our democracy would be better off with their participation.

The youth also enlisted allies and political leaders in their cause to create power. President Dwight Eisenhower first gave his voice to the cause in his 1954 State of the Union, arguing that eighteen-year-olds should have the right to vote. He used the same justification that the young people had brought to the forefront:

> For years our citizens between the ages of eighteen and twenty-one have, in time of peril, been summoned to fight for America. They should participate in the political process

that produces this fateful summons. I urge Congress to propose to the States a constitutional amendment permitting
citizens to vote when they reach the age of eighteen.

But he did not use his own political capital to help the cause;
he just gave lip service to the issue without attempting to push
it forward.

In 1963, a report issued to President Johnson by the President's Commission on Registration and Voting Participation
encouraged the policy change as well—citing that the move
would bolster overall voter participation. Similarly to Eisenhower, however, Johnson did not expend his own political capital to push the issue forward.

Recognizing that empty words from politicians would not
lead to real change, young people focused on the grassroots:
Project 18 formed partnerships with local and national organizations across the country. Persuading groups of the urgency
of the moment and demonstrating its appeal to young people,
Project 18 teamed with a wide array of diverse youth-serving
organizations like the YMCA, the union group AFL-CIO,
and the racial justice–focused NAACP to create the Youth
Franchise Coalition to lobby for a constitutional amendment.
Groups across the country, from all over the political spectrum,
mobilized in favor of the cause after listening to their young
constituents.

On March 10, 1971, the Senate voted 94 to 0 in favor of pro-
posing a constitutional amendment to lower the voting age. Just
thirteen days later, on March 23, the House of Representatives
voted 401 to 19 in favor of the amendment. Per law, the amendment was then sent to state legislatures for their consideration.

The ratification was completed on July 1, 1971, after the amendment had officially been ratified by thirty-eight states.

President Nixon spoke at a ceremony on July 5, 1971, to mark the occasion. He talked about the potential of youth activism as part of the United States' cumulative political journey and the country's democratic fabric:

> As I meet with this group today, I sense that we can have confidence that America's new voters, America's young generation, will provide what America needs as we approach our two hundredth birthday, not just strength and not just wealth but the "Spirit of '76," a spirit of moral courage, a spirit of high idealism in which we believe in the American dream, but in which we realize that the American dream can never be fulfilled until every American has an equal chance to fulfill it in his own life.

It is sometimes claimed that the Twenty-Sixth Amendment was ratified at a historically fast pace. Indeed, it was less than four months from the Senate first voting on it to its ultimate ratification. That speed is unprecedented for a change to our constitution, given the fact that the move requires a two-thirds majority in the Senate and ratification by the same percentage of states in the union.

But this analysis does not take into account that the first efforts really started in the 1940s: the actual campaign for ratification took over thirty years. The speed of the final efforts was only possible because of all the momentum that had accumulated.

Simply put, the expansion of suffrage would not have

happened without young people, who deployed their complete tactic toolkit to take action.

They became powerful.

And this power changed the very electorate of the United States.

YOUNG CONSERVATIVES ARE POWERFUL TOO

There is sometimes a perception that young people tend to be more liberal and focus on more radical causes. Statistics do demonstrate that, on the aggregate, young people gravitate to causes on the progressive end of the political spectrum. While this book has definitively focused more on young people adopting and participating in liberal movements, it is critical to address youth power holistically. And there are numerous examples of young people on the conservative side of politics gaining power and influencing more right-leaning policy platforms.

One such example of youth conservative power is evident through the efforts of the Young Americans for Freedom (YAF), a student movement founded in September of 1960. The group was first conceived of through a convening of youth activist leaders in the Sharon, Connecticut, home of conservative folk hero William Buckley. These young people were frustrated with conventional conservative politics and leaders who they felt had stopped listening to the concerns of regular citizens throughout the country. Just like young people who wanted to lower the voting age to eighteen, the young conservatives behind YAF wanted to fundamentally transform the conservative ideology that had grown to define and govern the country.

Accordingly, YAF perspectives were more conservative than most Republicans' at the time. Republicans, on the aggregate, believed in some government intervention in the free market and were increasingly gravitating toward a more nationalistic, rather than federalist, worldview, in which more power would be concentrated with the federal government, rather than the states. The young people in YAF, idealistic about their own orthodoxy, felt that the modern Republican Party had become too complacent, overly bureaucratic, and nationally focused. To that end, YAF supported free-market economics, extreme and total states' rights, and extremely limited federal government.

They also advocated for staunchly defeating communism rather than coexisting with the governmental philosophy. Consequently, YAF supported robust military action in Vietnam as a critical component to stopping the spread of communism. These young people were pro-war, and they wanted to make their voices, which they felt were in the minority, heard.

In a *National Review* article published on September 24, 1960, Buckley provided the rationale for founding YAF:

> What is so striking in the students who met at Sharon is their appetite for power . . . It is quixotic to say that they or their elders have seized the reins of history. But the difference in psychological attitude is tremendous. They talk about affecting history; we have talked about educating people to want to affect history.

This language is compelling to liberal and conservative young people alike. We can all agree on the importance of young people affecting history, rather than just being affected by it. Youth power, despite connotations as a left-leaning idea, is a formidable and nonpartisan concept.

When YAF was first founded, its young members were seen as overly radical and out of touch with the mainstream. Liberals derided their efforts, and moderate Republicans approached them with trepidation. But YAF's youngest members were able to deploy a variety of tactics that allowed them to gain power and affect the very terms of the conservative debate. These young people changed the face of the Republican Party in this country.

YAF gained its power primarily through organizing chapters on college campuses across the country. Students circulated petitions to gather public support and spread awareness on key issues, like support for the war in Vietnam or opposition to communism. Chapters were adept at exploiting media interest to spread their message, utilizing Buckley's prestigious *National Review*, as well as campus newspapers, to ensure that their conservative orthodoxy entered mainstream debates.

By organizing at the campus level, YAF students were able to gain real power, which they quickly unleashed, demonstrating the breadth of their support by holding massive rallies across the country. In March 1962, less than two years after their founding, they spearheaded a "Rally for World Liberation from Communism," hosting almost twenty thousand young conservatives at Madison Square Garden in New York City. At the time, the event was one of the largest conservative gatherings in the history of the country. That same summer, YAF held its first annual National Conservative Student Conference, effectively utilizing and harnessing all the energy and momentum they had inspired to continue to build youth power for their agenda. At the conference, the youth activists adopted a slogan to define their efforts: "We have not been heard because we were study-ing. Now we must be heard!"

This could have been the motto of any youth movement in the country. It actually reminds me of my response to President Simmons's convocation at Brown—I did not want to just study; I wanted to take action. YAF activists took this motto to heart and forced their agenda on conservatives across the country.

YAF also encouraged their university chapters to stage "Stop Red Trade" boycotts against national corporations—such as the American Motors Company, IBM, and Firestone Tire and Rubber—that were actively trading with communist coun-tries. These strategies proved effective; the YAF successfully convinced Firestone to terminate a contract with the commu-nist government of Romania. The policy change came after the YAF threatened to distribute five hundred thousand flyers at the Indy 500 and to pay for a small plane to fly over the race with a banner reading "The Vietcong ride on Firestone," a play on Firestone's then-rival company's slogan "More people ride on Goodyear tires than on any other kind." Similarly, American Motors Company broke a contract with the Soviets because of YAF pressure.

The YAF also engaged in the electoral process, focusing their initial efforts primarily on local elections. They were key back-ers behind Ronald Reagan's initial long-shot 1966 campaign for California governor. When Reagan galvanized grassroots sup-port and a message of a new conservatism to earn a surprise vic-tory, YAF experienced massive growth in chapter membership. People started to recognize their appeal and power.

Again upsetting Republican orthodoxy, the YAF broke the party line and endorsed the more conservative Reagan for president in 1968 over the establishment's choice of Richard Nixon. While Nixon proved victorious, Regan's (again) unexpected momentum afforded more influence to the youth activists. They continued to organize, playing a central role in the successful 1970 New York senate campaign of James Buckley, brother of William, who ran on the platform of the previously miniscule Conservative Party.

The members of the YAF demonstrated the power of living full and complete political journeys. They selected key issues they cared about and composed a concrete policy agenda. They developed expertise on the issues they cared about. They told powerful narratives about the importance of free-market economics and fighting against communism. And they formed a movement across the country.

They then used this movement to create power through tactics that included everything from circulating petitions to holding rallies to organizing boycotts. In this process, they demonstrated that not all youth voices organize on the left.

The YAF's newfound power was truly unleashed when their efforts helped Ronald Reagan become president in 1980. Just like when he was elected governor of California in 1966, Reagan rode the wave of the young people, through YAF, to power.

Today, young people vote overwhelmingly Democrat. But this was not really the case during Reagan's rise. In the 1980 election, he and Jimmy Carter split the eighteen- to twenty-nine-year-old vote 45 percent to 45 percent. In 1984, Reagan won 62 percent of the youth vote, with only 39 percent going to Walter Mondale. Young people liked the Gipper (Reagan's infamous nickname) helped partially by the fact that YAF members put him forward as their inspiration and leader.

All of a sudden, YAF members were not just influencing decision-makers; they *were* decision-makers. When Reagan was inaugurated, at least fifty graduates or members of YAF were appointed to the White House staff, with others sprinkled throughout outer layers of the administration. They weren't just talking about change. They were leading it from the most powerful perch in the world. YAF's extreme conservative and federalist ideology formed the framework of Reagan's entire presidency, which changed the course of the Republican Party. When we hear Republicans idolizing Reagan's presidency, or pledging to be an incarnate of the thirty-ninth president himself, it is critical to keep in mind, for better or worse, that he would not have been elected president without the support of young people.

Just like they promised they would in the 1960 *National Review* article, the Young Americans for Freedom movement demonstrated the ability of young people to affect the political agenda for the entire country. They became powerful.

They, as young people, changed what it meant to be a conservative in the United States of America.

RUNNING FOR OFFICE

Pushing for political change is one way to become powerful. Another way is to become a political leader yourself.

We could stand to ensure more young people join the ranks of our politicians. Right now, our elected officials are, well, pretty old.

The 115th Congress, which began in 2017, is one of the oldest in American history. The average age of a representative is fifty-seven. The average age of a senator is sixty-one. Compare this to 1981: the respective average ages were forty-nine and fifty-three.

We see this same pattern at the state level. The average age of the approximately 7,383 state legislators in the country is fifty-six: a whopping one year younger than the federal congressional average.

While our elected representatives have slowly become more diverse along gender and racial lines (although not fast enough), age has not followed suit. We do not need research to tell us that an older Congress is less capable of relating to, or understanding, the issues that young people care about. An older electoral body will naturally be predisposed to focus less on issues important to young people.

In order to successfully carry out a political journey, and make a difference on the issues you care about, it is not necessary to run for political office. There are many ways to make a difference on these issues, influencing those in leadership and deploying a wide array of tactics to gain and wield power.

At the same time, if you want to run, you should: we do need more young people in office. And, in good news, there are a lot of different ways to become an elected official. According to American University professor Jennifer Lawless, as of 2012 there were over 519,000 elected officials in the United States, from the Senate and the House of Representatives to school boards and city councils. We need more young people to be among the ranks of those half a million citizens, speaking truth to the issues we care about.

EIGHTEEN AND ELECTED

When Saira Blair was first elected to the West Virginia House of Representatives, she became the youngest state representative in the country. Her story demonstrates how, regardless of your age, you can become really powerful really fast.

Saira first attended a summer program called Youth in Government when she was fifteen. Geared toward West Virginians from all walks of life, the program encouraged young people to write legislation, bring it to the floor, and then present it to the youth governor to be signed. It was a simulation, but one that provided the young people a sense of how politics could work.

"It was an awesome experience," Saira said. "It made me want to run for office myself."

The next summer, when she was just sixteen years old, she decided that she was going to run for state representative in the West Virginia legislature. Saira did not talk to anyone about her decision, including her parents.

This might sound ridiculous—a sixteen-year-old deciding to run for state office. She couldn't even vote. How in the world could she win?

"I was wildly frustrated with the system," she told me, justifying her decision. "I thought that the best way I could change it was to join it."

Saira takes heat for being a young Republican, which in our current climate sometimes seems like an oxymoron. To attempt to counteract this reality and wear her Republican badge proudly, she prefers to focus less on the hotbed social issues that define many political arguments of the moment. She said she ran because she is a fiscal conservative and wanted to address the never-ending budget issues in the state.

"We're fiftieth on every good list and first on any bad list," she said. "We needed new thinking to address our tax issues in the state. It sounds strange for a teenager to focus on taxes, but that's why I ran. To create a better tax system in the state."

In her quest to live a political journey, Saira chose an issue she cared about. She focused on a potentially idiosyncratic issue: West Virginian state taxes.

A few weeks after her cracker-barrel epiphany, having turned seventeen, she attended a West Virginia Federation of Young Republicans meeting. She decided to make her intentions public.

Saira stood up in front of the room of approximately one hundred activists. She was nervous as she began to address a roomful of people who barely knew who she was.

"My name is Saira Bair." She paused. "I'm going to run for state representative."

Chuckles rang out in the room. Was this a joke? A student project?

She still had not told her parents that she would run. The room was shocked. A seventeen-year-old was running for the West Virginia House of Representatives?

But Saira quickly silenced her doubters and put her campaign into action, traveling door to door throughout the district and convincing people that, even though she was young, her energy, enthusiasm, idealism, and conviction would allow her to make a difference in the legislature. She won the primary overwhelmingly.

"I was not a silly candidate anymore," she said. "I was *the* candidate."

In a heavily Republican district, Saira won the general election as well, becoming a state representative in West Virginia.

By this time, she was eighteen. She became the youngest state representative in the country.

Since her election, Saira has worked with her fellow legislators to attempt to deal with West Virginia's tax problems and address issues like a growing teacher wage gap, an unsustainable pension fund, and the loss of coal jobs throughout the state. She's trying her best to get West Virginia to rank a little higher than fiftieth on all those state surveys.

As she legislates, her age, she said, is becoming less of an issue. But she says she has a unique perspective because she is young.

"Every elected official is a human being," she said. "People are there because they want to do the right thing. People don't get elected solely to advance their political parties. Even if I disagree with my colleagues, I respect them for who they are and what they're doing."

This might seem idealistic, but it's also a welcome change of pace from the cynicism that defines so much of our politics today—which is largely led by older elected officials. Saira's no-nonsense attitude and ability to work across the aisle allows her to accomplish change on issues she cares about. We could stand to have more people like Saira in our elected bodies throughout the country, regardless of their party affiliation. Saira is showing that eighteen and elected isn't too young. Maybe it's exactly what we need.

WINE AND CANVASSING

New York city councilman Ritchie Torres grew up in a public-housing project in the East Bronx, alongside his mother, sister, and twin brother. The complex, isolated and a forty-minute walk from the nearest subway stop, was in terrible shape. In Ritchie's apartment, water leaked through the ceiling whenever it rained, mold grew on the bathroom walls, and the elevators broke down often. The elevators malfunctioning was such a common occurrence that whenever Ritchie visits public housing now, he takes the stairs. Housing access and affordability became the issue that defined his political journey.

"Your home is supposed to be a sanctuary," he said. "I didn't feel safe in mine."

Ritchie attended Lehman High School in the Bronx. Although he was bright and involved in extracurricular activities at a young age, he often skipped school—he did not find it challenging enough.

Ritchie did join the law team in tenth grade, and he led his school to the moot court championships, beating more well-resourced schools throughout New York City. He also helped to run a city council campaign for a mentor of his, James Vacca. Ritchie caught the political bug early, seeing it as a way to make a difference for the housing issues he so cared about.

Ritchie started at New York University as a freshman in the fall of 2006, excited to receive a college degree. Soon after starting, though, he quickly fell into depression. He decided to drop out. He initially struggled to obtain the antidepressants he needed, experiencing the lack of mental health care available, especially for low-income families.

Eventually he was able to receive the medicine he needed and was on the mend. But he decided not to return to college. Instead, he returned to his first love, politics, and he began his work with the city council.

Ritchie used his experience with substandard housing as motivation for his new city job, which was focused on improving public-housing conditions. He visited constituents' homes; took extensive documentation of neglect, including taking pictures and writing reports; and pressured landlords to make necessary repairs. He had found the issue he was passionate about and became an informed expert.

Despite the passion for the issue, and his developing expertise, Ritchie never thought he'd be in elected office. "I am too much of an introvert," he told me. He thought he'd stay focused on the inside game, documenting abuses of power and working directly with families to improve their housing conditions.

But, in 2013, a neighboring city council seat opened up. Despite the fact that Ritchie was only twenty-four years old and experienced anxiety when meeting voters, he decided to run. He felt that he'd be able to make a difference in elected office.

"There is nothing like lived experience to motivate you," he said of his desire to run despite his reclusive proclivities.

In order to fight back against the notion that he was too green and inexperienced to run for office, Ritchie engaged in old-fashioned retail politics. Over the course of his first campaign, he called or met more than six thousand voters in his district. To compartmentalize his anxiety, he drank a glass of wine every day before canvassing.

Despite an incredibly low-turnout primary, Ritchie received enough votes to win. Meeting voters one-by-one, and telling them about his passions and plans, allowed Ritchie to demonstrate that age was just a number. Just like Saira, he used his youthful energy and vitality to get stuff done. And he got his supporters to turn out to vote for him.

In his first months in office, Ritchie became the chair on the council's Committee on Public Housing. He used his new position to take immediate action. He convinced the federal government to spend more than $100 million to fix water boilers damaged by Hurricane Sandy. He introduced legislation that would reform the City of New York Police Department by requiring officers to inform those they stop of their constitutional rights before searching them. And he pushed for increased reforms from the New York City Housing Authority to ensure that all public-housing units received sufficient protections and resources. He furthered these efforts by lobbying for thousands of new public-housing developments.

Despite his age, or perhaps because of it, Ritchie has become one of the most influential members in the New York City Council. But every step of the way, he's had to fight against the perception that he's too young to get anything done.

"There is a persistent age bias among other elected officials. I actually think it's rooted in jealousy," Ritchie reflected to me, noting that other elected officials are resentful that such a young official is gaining power so quickly.

To push forward and combat these sentiments, he says that he has to act "more provocative, more irreverent, and more confrontational. I've had to be aggressive out of necessity."

This aggressiveness has allowed him to gain more power, significantly changing the maligned public-housing system that has defined his political journey. But, for Ritchie, getting small things done isn't enough.

"I'm in politics to transform systems and institutions," he says. Ritchie sees his role not as affecting small change but as fundamentally transforming the power structures that have too often defined American politics. He's well on his way to doing so.

It was power that enabled young people to lead on the movement to lower the voting age to eighteen, a quest that seemed quixotic and crazy at the beginning of the twentieth century. It was power that allowed the Young Americans for Freedom to change the direction of the Republican Party and gain real influence in the Reagan administration. And it was power, and a dose of idealism, that led to the elections of Saira Blair and Ritchie Torres.

As young people, we can redefine power as a way to mobilize, to influence, to change.

Our power can change our democracy. The pinnacle of our political journeys is becoming powerful.

12

"IT'S TOO HARD"

Remaining Resilient in the Face of Failure

ow you're making progress. You're enlisting a host of tactics to make headway on solving your previously intractable issue. You have momentum. You're becoming powerful. It's exciting, exhilarating, everything that political participation in our democracy can be.

But then there's this.

At some point, you will fail.

There is no way to sugarcoat the inevitable struggles that will accompany the political journey. Part of engaging in the long slog of democratic change is realizing that the work is hard. Really damn hard. As much as we would like it to, change does not come overnight. Rights are not wronged with the flip of a switch. There is no app that can bring change by swiping to the right.

You are going to be railroaded. You are going to meet

powerful individuals that fundamentally do not believe that your voice, or youth voice in general, matters. You are going to encounter systemic oppression that runs counter to the cause you are attempting to fight for. You are going to recognize and experience the tyranny that has pushed down so many in our democracy for so long. You are going to, in some way, shape, or form, lose battles along the way.

There is no way to avoid these inevitable losses. In a sense, our democracy is built to ensure that change is difficult. Our founders intentionally constructed a system in which the long road to change is purposeful and ensures that unstable or despotic leaders cannot move mountains autonomously. While recent presidents, on both sides of the aisle, have used executive orders in an attempt to bypass Congress, our founders intended to promote a system in which no single individual could create drastic and systemic change on their own. Democracy is composed to be durable and slow-moving.

Accordingly, the best antidote is to be steady for the failures, embrace them, and learn from them.

To live political lives, we need to learn to love political failure.

The political journey, as described in this book, is not a recipe for success. I can't tell you that by picking an issue, developing expertise, creating a narrative, and becoming powerful that your issue will be solved. Rather, the journey is a roadmap that ideally will lead to change. And a key component of this roadmap is recognizing that failure is inevitably part of it.

The first time I attempted to pass Sudan divestment legislation, I failed wildly. We were told we were too young to push a bill in the legislature. In retrospect, I learned more from this first attempt than I did with any success I've had.

Our failure taught me that we did not embrace the right supporters. We did not enlist the ideal allies. Our messaging was not tailored to our Rhode Island audience. We moved too quickly without obtaining buy-in from key constituents. We were too confident that our moral cause would carry the way to victory. So, we lost.

The next time around, we mobilized the right people in our efforts, we were deliberate and thoughtful in our outreach, and we became more powerful. We passed the bill unanimously through both chambers and the governor signed the bill in a public ceremony.

The road to Generation Citizen, a key component of my political journey, has also been rife with failure. Every single day, I screw up. I don't prepare enough for a meeting, and receive a rejection from a donor. I am too harsh with an employee, and fail as a boss. I provide coaching to teachers that is not adequate, and don't do right by our students. Every day, I expect perfection, but know that I will never, ever reach it.

Sometimes, these failures stack up. There have been so many times when I thought that the organization would not succeed. So many times when I thought I should close up shop and try something else.

But each failure moves us forward. Every time I fail, I learn more than any accomplishment or successful grant application ever could teach me.

Just two months after graduating from college, my mom came to visit me. At the time, my parents were living in Zimbabwe, and I had moved to Somerville, just outside of Boston.

My first few months running Generation Citizen were challenging, to say the least. I did not have a team. I had no idea how to fundraise. I woke up every morning with a pang in my stomach and no real agenda, no one telling me what to do, and no idea how to build an organization.

I was spending my days running around schools, crafting organizational bylaws out of nothing, and writing grant applications that would likely go nowhere. I did not even have a formal entity to receive donations. At least once a day someone older than me would tell me that I was too young to start an organization. That I had no idea what I was doing.

So I was looking forward to my mom's visit. And I was dreading it.

I put on a brave face: it had been my choice to stick with Generation Citizen. I was beyond privileged to have $50,000 at my disposal to pilot our programming. I knew many folks would not be able to count on that support when working for a cause they loved.

But I was really lonely. Every single day, I felt like I was failing. The first thing I would do every morning when I woke up would be to check out the blog for the teaching corps in New Orleans—the one I had rejected just days after graduating from college. New teachers would write posts about their successes, their travails, their first days with their students. They'd write about the power of being part of a teaching corps. The camaraderie. Sometimes, when reading them, I'd cry.

I was really feeling sorry for myself.

My mom arrived, and she and I went to a movie in Harvard Square—it was a nice reprieve from my self-inflicted sorrow.

But I needed to tell her I was having serious doubts about sticking with GC.

After the movie, we headed to a generic Italian chain restaurant a few blocks away. The appetizers and wine arrived, and we stopped our small talk about the movie and my life in Cambridge.

"Mom, I'm not sure I can do this anymore," I confessed.

She paused.

"I could tell that you were having trouble," she said. "What's wrong?"

I could barely look up at her and began to sniffle, attempting, badly, to stifle my tears.

"It's just too hard! I have no idea what the fuck I'm doing. No one is helping me out."

The tears were now flowing.

"Scott, I had no idea. I thought things were going so well. But I can tell you've been distracted." My mom was always supportive, and I could tell she felt guilty that she lived thousands of miles away.

"No one thinks I can do it. I should just close up before I get going with schools in the fall." I could barely get the words out.

My mom looked at me, lovingly but firmly, in the way that only mothers can.

"Just stick with it for two more months. See what happens. If it doesn't work out, it really is fine. But give it a fair shot."

My mom's comments comforted me, largely because I assumed that two months later I would close up GC.

"Deal," I agreed.

The rest of the summer, I stopped reading the blog entries so much. I put energy into work. I did everything I could to make GC succeed.

I kept going for two months. And then for four more. Six months after my mom's speech, though, I met another breaking point.

As the end of the first semester of GC approached, I felt like I was hitting my groove. I raised some money. I built a board to govern the organization. I hired my first staff person. We launched successful programming in both Providence and Boston.

The program was working: I loved getting into classrooms in Boston, where we had not launched previously, and seeing students take action on teen jobs, gang violence, and gun reform. Every day, I could see the program at work at a different class in one of the two cities. I was getting my hands dirty: when I went into classrooms, I helped to facilitate the dynamic conversations that helped to spark that first political interest in our students. It was fun.

As the semester concluded, I set to work organizing my first Civics Day in Rhode Island. I wanted to make it a big one. Students would present on the issues, and we would showcase their work to the world. I hoped the event would succeed beyond our wildest expectations: Partially because the students were awesome and I wanted them to exhibit their projects to the community. And partially because I wanted to show people I had made this thing work against all obstacles.

I invited big political players: members of Congress, the governor, the superintendent of the Providence Public School District (PPSD). Somehow, they all said yes to attending and speaking; it would be a real rolling-out party. I invited everyone

I knew in Rhode Island. This day would show how far GC had come in just a few months.

Five days before Civics Day, I received a call from PPSD. I assumed that they wanted to go over final logistics.

"Scott, we need you to come in right away. Please don't delay." It was the chief of staff for the district. She was obviously not expressing praise for all we had accomplished.

I took the first train from Boston to Providence. I didn't quite know what to expect.

But when I got there, I realized it quickly: they were pissed off. I had not followed field-trip protocol or gathered all the necessary permission-slip forms from the students. To me, the oversight seemed incredibly menial. But the district felt that by bypassing protocol, I was putting them at legal risk. In retrospect, they were definitely right.

The director of high schools for the district was not shy about chastising me.

"We're not sure this event can still happen. How hard would it be to shut down Civics Day? It's pretty ridiculous you haven't followed any of our protocol," she said sternly.

I was in shock.

"I'll make it work! We'll pay for the buses! Whatever you need," I offered. Personally, I thought the notion they'd cancel Civics Day over a bureaucratic snafu was absurd. I also had no idea where we'd find the money to pay for the buses. Our cash flow was perilously low.

"Fine. Go get the permission slips now. Don't mess around with us anymore," the director scolded.

They were frustrated with me, tired of a twenty-two-year-old pretending he knew how to run an education program for the entire district.

I ran around the city and picked up the permission slips at each participating school. We paid for the buses with our limited budget. The event went on, and the students all arrived. It went pretty well. All the luminaries spoke and were impressed by the students.

But the district did not calm down. They thought I had demonstrated disrespect for their guidelines, and through my arrogance, I had put them at risk for liability if anything had happened to any of the students attending Civics Day.

In hindsight, I acted childishly. I thought I should not have had to deal with their guidelines and processes. I thought I knew more than they did. The day after the event, I received an email from the head of social studies for the district. It read:

> Do not make any more attempts to circumvent and disrespect our guidelines . . . You have repeatedly demonstrated a lack of respect for the Superintendent who is at the helm of the District and my office.

Two days later, they called in staff members from Brown University, who had helped to get Generation Citizen off the ground. They chastised me and asked Brown to divorce itself from Generation Citizen.

I was humbled. I knew I had screwed up. Once again, I contemplated shutting it all down. Days later, I was visiting my college roommate Dave for Christmas break.

"I don't know if I can do this anymore," I said. "It's too hard."

"Give it another six months," he said, not knowing he was echoing my mom.

I took his advice to heart, and I gave it another six months. And then another eight years.

Ten years after graduating from college, I'm still here, and so is GC.

My political journey has been full of failures. For every grant we receive, or for every successful student project, there's a rejection or upset teacher around the corner. I still worry, almost every day, that GC won't make it.

But I've learned, or tried to learn, not to get too high with the successes or too low with the failures—both will be present every single day. I've learned that the meaning of failure is totally misconstrued. Because it is inevitable, we shouldn't run from it. We should embrace the lessons failure teaches us and appreciate it when it makes our efforts stronger.

THE FIRST TO SIT AT THE FRONT OF THE BUS

We all know the story of Rosa Parks and her momentous role in the civil rights movement. On December 1, 1955, at the age of forty-two, Rosa paid her bus fare in Montgomery, Alabama, and refused to sit at the back of the bus like all African American passengers were supposed to do. She was arrested for her refusal to obey orders.

Rosa's action galvanized a nationwide boycott of public buses. It ultimately led to a change in nationwide bus laws, as well as a critical discussion, and eventual revocation, of racist Jim Crow laws throughout the South, which called for blacks and whites to receive different services from public and private institutions. Rosa became a powerful and lasting symbol for the civil rights movement. She is known by all Americans today as a hero for her efforts.

Rosa, though, was not the first African American to refuse to head to the back of the bus.

Nine months earlier, on March 2, 1955, fifteen-year-old Claudette Colvin was returning home from school in the same town of Montgomery. Negro History Month, which occurred throughout the month of February, had just concluded, and her still-segregated school had been studying the history of black leaders like Sojourner Truth, a former slave turned abolitionist, and Harriet Tubman, the founder and facilitator of the Underground Railroad.

Claudette reflected on the injustices she was learning about in class and the prejudices she faced every day because of the color of her skin. She could not eat at the same lunch counter as her white peers. She could not sit at the front of the bus. She could not attend the same school as her white neighbors.

"Can you imagine all of that in my head? My head was just too full of black history, the oppression we went through," she reflected in a recent interview.

When she got on the bus after school, she decided that she would take action against the legacy of oppression. She decided to start her political journey.

She paid her fare, like she always did. But this time, she sat at the front of the bus.

The white driver ordered her to the back of the bus. She did not move. She claimed it was her constitutional right to sit where she wanted. She had, after all, paid her fare.

The driver left the bus. He flagged down a nearby police car.

Two police officers climbed aboard the bus and put Claudette in handcuffs. She resisted, attempting to stay in her seat. They dragged her up, and her backpack went flying. The officers finally put her in the back of their car, leaving her backpack behind. They drove her to the city adult jail and took her straight to her cell, not even allowing her to make a phone call.

"He opened the door and told me to get inside," she reflected. "He shut it hard behind me and turned the key. The lock fell into place with a heavy sound. It was the worst sound I ever heard. It sounded final. It said I was trapped."

She started crying.

Claudette was bailed out a day later by her reverend, H. H. Johnson, who drove her home. She expressed concern during the drive. She wasn't certain she had done the right thing. She was still terrified and thought she might be ostracized.

"Claudette," Johnson said at the time, "I'm so proud of you. Everyone prays for freedom. We've all been praying and praying. But you're different—you want your answer the next morning. And I think you just brought the revolution to Montgomery."

Like so many revolutions we see in society, this one was started by a young person.

But unlike Rosa Parks, Claudette did not receive widespread acclaim. We rarely read about her in history books. She is not seen as the inspiration for a countrywide bus boycott. Her political journey is not well known.

After her arrest, Claudette, rather than being celebrated, was shunned by her community. "Everything changed," she said. "I lost most of my friends. Their parents had told them to stay away from me because they said I was crazy, I was an extremist."

Soon after the arrest, she became pregnant. Civil rights leaders felt that an expecting teenager should not be the face of the movement. They looked to the elderly, more acceptable Rosa Parks instead.

"I didn't fit the image either of, you know, someone they would want to show off," she suggested.

Claudette ended up dropping out of college and moving to New York City. She worked as a nurse's aide in Manhattan for thirty-five years. Until recently, few people had any idea who she was—she did not frequently tell her story. She rarely receives the same amount of adulation as Rosa Parks, and museums and books have largely ignored her contributions to the movement.

Claudette's political journey could have been defined by failure. She did choose the issue she cared about, and she took effective action. But she was not able to mobilize others. She did not become powerful in the long run. Her journey seems to have entered a void—she sacrificed so much of her livelihood and well-being for a vision of change that was actually articulated and realized, but with Rosa Parks as the protagonist instead of her.

In a cruel irony, Claudette's political journey itself was oppressed, just like the figures she studied in class: the same leaders that inspired Claudette to take the unprecedented step of sitting at the front of the bus and resisting orders to move back.

But Claudette's failure was crucial to the movement to end segregation on buses. She should have received more attention for her actions. She still should today. But she helped provide momentum to Rosa Parks months later. She instigated the spark.

Claudette demonstrated that young people can lead the way on social change. That Claudette's original efforts did not immediately spark a movement should be a lesson for all of us. We should prop up those who lead, especially when they are young. Especially when they come from diverse backgrounds and do not necessarily fit the prototype of leaders we expect to see in social and political movements.

Yes, Claudette experienced failure, but her journey has not been defined by it. She recognized this in a recent interview:

> Most of the young children, they have this takeaway, that the civil rights movement was a failure. But I tell them, it wasn't a complete failure. Yes, we had our tragedies, but we also had our triumphs. The young group now has a different attitude than the old group, than we veterans. You don't understand, we had never been accepted before! America as a society, as a country, had never accepted black people. We were still second-class citizens.
>
> So now, I hope [my story] inspires the young groups, that they should use every resource available to them so they can reach their fullest potential and become very productive in this so-called—well, America isn't flawless, but I still love America—this democratic society that we live in.

Claudette is still alive today, pushing for change. Rather than being bitter about the fact that history failed to put her first, she uses her journey as inspiration. Her failures to be the public leader of a movement illuminate a road forward for all of us.

THE NECESSITY OF FAILURE

In Generation Citizen, despite the specificity of the goals our students choose, many times our students are not as successful at accomplishing these goals as we would hope. Sometimes local officials refuse to support their work. Sometimes politicians refuse to take their calls or stand them up at meetings.

Our students become understandably frustrated.

"We did everything right," one student once told me. "We followed the Hourglass perfectly. We sent our councilman's office hundreds of letters and circulated a petition that almost our entire school signed. And he won't even meet with us?"

"We put hundreds of hours of work into lowering the voting age," said another student who worked on a campaign in San Francisco to lower the voting age to sixteen. "We contacted thousands of voters. And we lost by three points! I feel like it was all a waste. What do we do next?"

There is no easy answer. Failure can be frustrating. Disorienting. Demotivating.

It also is unavoidable. Because democracy is about an exchange of ideas, and not a dogmatic allocation of power, there will inevitably be many times when our ideas do not carry through and do not resonate. Perhaps we are, like Claudette, slightly ahead of our time. Perhaps our messaging wasn't quite right. Perhaps there are structural barriers at play, preventing our voices from being heard to the extent that they deserve to be. Regardless of the reason, failure provides an opportunity to step back and reassess our efforts.

If we look at any successful movement throughout history, the road to success is paved with many failures.

Today, gay marriage is the law of the land. Individuals can marry partners of the same gender. This was not always the case.

The movement endured a multitude of challenges along the way to passing the law that allowed same-sex couples to wed.

The struggles of the movement include the centuries-long oppression that gay people in this country have suffered. The failures also include the often-violent retaliation that activists have faced for their efforts.

On June 28, 1969, young activists in New York City met an existential challenge to their fight for equal rights. Back in 1969, there were few safe places for lesbian, gay, bisexual, transgender, and queer (LGBTQ) Americans to gather. Public laws outlawed holding hands, kissing, or dancing with someone of the same sex. Bars became safe havens, areas to congregate without fear of repercussions. Stonewall, a bar located in Greenwich Village, was such an establishment.

During this time period, police often raided bars to crack down on unlawful activity. Usually, in a sort of truce, the police ignored LGBTQ establishments, or, at the worst, tipped off owners before a raid. They did not want to cause trouble in places where individuals congregated to feel safe.

But in the early morning hours of June 28, the police did not follow their usual protocol. They entered the Stonewall Inn without notice. Upon witnessing technically illegal homosexual behavior, they beat up patrons with their batons. They arrested thirteen people for violating New York's gender-appropriate clothing laws. At one point, an officer hit a woman on the head with a baton as he forced her into his car.

The egregious police activity triggered widespread protests in the streets that continued for five days unabated. The protests were largely led by youth activists, who'd had enough of being treated unfairly because of their sexual orientation.

To call Stonewall a failure would be disrespectful to the movement. But it's fair to call the Stonewall incident a setback.

After police disrupted the peace, Stonewall was no longer a refuge. Activists did not feel safe. It seemed like their previous refuges for safety would no longer be such.

This obstacle, however, became one of the most galvanizing moments of the LGBTQ movement: many activists and organizations were born out of the Stonewall riots, along with a desire to change the status quo. Young people specifically led the way. They realized that fighting for clandestine bars as refuge would no longer be sufficient. They needed to fight for true equality.

As historian Michael Bronski noted, in the wake of Stonewall, "gay liberation was a youth movement whose sense of history was defined to a large degree by rejection of the past." Stonewall inspired a generation of youth LGBTQ activists, who engaged in organizing, partially motivated by a sense of failure of past activism efforts.

Almost forty years later, the LGBTQ movement propelled itself forward to a much more ambitious goal: ensuring that marriage became a right, an expectation, and a law. This is asking for a lot more than a safe bar. And because of the enormity of the goal, the path to success has been full of zigs and zags.

On the same day as Barack Obama's monumental election win in 2008, the people of California voted in favor of Proposition 8, which outlawed same-sex marriage in the state. The fact that liberal California would vote, by ten percentage points, to restrict marriage was unfathomable for activists, who had essentially pinned the future of the marriage debate on a positive result in California.

Indeed, the day after the election, while many in the liberal parts of the United States were celebrating Obama's win, groups of determined Californians took to the streets.

But rather than lamenting Prop 8's passing as a failure of the movement, activists, led by young people, recognized that this was just *one* failure. And it was one to learn from.

Young people mobilized and organized, more than they ever had—introducing lawsuits across the country, starting other state referendums, and refining their message. The result: within eight years, largely because of the activism of young people, same-sex marriage became part of the law of the land.

While it's important to note that there is still work to be done to ensure equality for LGBTQ people across the country, we can be hopeful because of the lessons and actions taken after Stonewall and the failure of Proposition 8. Yes, these failures initially discouraged people. But they also spurred them to action. And that action led, ultimately, to success.

LEARNING THROUGH FAILURE

Failure is inevitable, but it provides an opportunity to learn. The majority of our recent presidents lost their first election: Barack Obama lost his first congressional bid. George W. Bush lost his first congressional bid. Bill Clinton lost his first congressional bid. George H. W. Bush lost his first senatorial bid. Sense a pattern?

One might argue that their initial losses paved the way for ultimate political success; they learned from their early mistakes.

The civil rights movement is another example of a youth-led movement that was forced to learn from its early pitfalls.

Four years before the famous March on Washington, where Martin Luther King Jr. gave his famous "I Have a Dream" speech, youth organizer Bayard Rustin planned a march in

Washington called the Youth March for Integrated Schools. Rustin was a gay man, and due to the stigma associated with homosexuality at the time, he is not widely known as a leader in the movement. Like Claudette Colvin, Rustin and his role in the movement has too often been marginalized.

On April 18, 1959, Rustin brought together more than twenty-five thousand young people in the nation's capital for the March for Integrated Schools. They marched through the streets, exposing the reality that, five years after the seminal *Brown v. Board of Education* Supreme Court decision, schools were still segregated. (It's worth noting that this rally took place more than a year before Ruby Bridges began the process of desegregating the South.) The rally was quickly put together, without an attempt to mobilize other groups and ensure a large presence in D.C.

After the march through the streets, Rustin led a delegation of students to the White House to meet with President Eisenhower to force his hand on the ruling. They were promptly turned away. Eisenhower had no interest in meeting with them. At the time, the protest did not receive significant attention, locally or nationally, and the organizers were slammed for not being sufficiently prepared. Leaders in the movement felt the rally had actually set them back: the students came across as muddled and unprofessional, with disparate messages. Relatedly, they felt, the march had been completely organized by youth activists, who wanted to share the power of their own voices. The adults in the civil rights movement felt that they were not adequately consulted on the strategy behind the tactics of the march. They felt that young people should not be at the forefront.

Perhaps frustrated by Rustin's role in planning the rally,

leaders in the movement pushed back on his leadership, and Rustin experienced his low point in his activism a year later. Fellow activist leader Adam Clayton Powell Jr. was concerned that Rustin was planning another rally, this time outside the Democratic National Convention in Los Angeles. He warned Martin Luther King Jr. that if he did not disavow himself from Rustin, Powell would assert that King and Rustin were lovers. King called off the march and publicly distanced himself from Rustin. For three years, Rustin was largely ostracized from the movement.

But when it came time to organize the large, critical March on Washington four years later, activists knew they needed Rustin back in the fold. He was one of the best pure organizers the movement had. Despite the fact that he had been exiled from activists and was targeted by the CIA, King appointed Rustin as the chief organizer for the march.

Following the March for Integrated Schools, Rustin knew he had to focus on the details. No stone could go unturned. He wanted to learn from his past mistakes.

Rustin organized everything from the logistics to the messaging, from the selection of speakers to their placement on the stage. He wrote a pamphlet that described how to transport two hundred thousand people to Washington, D.C., organized the speaking order, and determined the number of bathrooms that would be needed. He also led the messaging, taking the stage to read the ten "demands for the revolution," which were later delivered to President Kennedy.

The march captured the country's attention. And this time, the activists were able to meet with President Kennedy after the rally concluded. The sheer volume and power of the rally assisted the eventual passage of the Civil Rights Act of 1964.

Again, the Civil Rights Act did not end all racial oppression in the country. And many today criticize the goals and tactics of the civil rights movement as being not radical enough, and too focused on white acquiescence.

Indisputably, however, the youth activists learned from their smaller rally of 1959, and they came back in full force. Rather than lamenting their losses, they organized successfully, with Rustin at the helm. Rustin, once seen as a pariah in the movement, should be seen as one of the architects of its ultimate success.

Failure is inevitable in the political journey. Rather than running away from it, we can accept it. It is as valuable as selecting an issue or developing expertise. Regardless of the strength of your plan, weaknesses will emerge. Failures will occur. People will doubt your ability to bring about change.

Every single successful political movement has had failures along the way to progress. Every single successful political leader has lost campaigns and races and made mistakes in his or her journey.

Yours will be the same. Along your path to political change, you will fail. I guarantee it.

So let's embrace failure.

13

THE PEACEFUL PLAY OF POWER

Trying to Work Through Our Differences

The morning after the 2016 presidential election, I found myself at LaGuardia Airport, preparing to fly to Texas to celebrate the opening of GC's newest office in Austin. The day after that, we planned to open in Oklahoma City. These would be our first two non-coastal offices—we were eager to prove that educating young people with our Action Civics programming was something all Americans could agree is important and was a concept that could and should work everywhere.

I was excited for this new frontier in our programming. I was conscious, however, that our timing wasn't great. The flight to Texas was at 7:00 a.m., and I had fallen asleep on my couch at 3:00 a.m., not in the greatest of moods, and not the most sober, taking in the last of the election returns.

LaGuardia, already a decrepit airport, felt like a funeral home. People stumbled past me as if they were sleepwalking, suitcases in tow, attempting to stifle tears. Some wore sunglasses to cover up the damage.

I could barely gather my thoughts. I felt the world as I knew it was coming to an end.

My cloudy eyes met the TSA security guard as I gave him my ticket.

"How are you doing this morning?"

"Shitty. You?" I think it was the first time in my life I swore in front of a TSA agent. I was fairly confident that I wouldn't be arrested on this particular morning.

"I don't know, man," he responded. He was, after all, a federal employee.

"Yeah."

"Keep your head up. And laptop out of the bag."

"Right."

I met up with Sarah, our director of programming, and Jessicah, our director of development, who were flying to Texas with me. We couldn't even mouth out greetings. We just had to get through the day.

I want this book to be nonpartisan and to appeal to all young people in this country. So while I believe in democracy, and I do think that Donald Trump won the Electoral College legitimately (albeit with a little, or a lot, of help from the Russians and James Comey), I was personally crushed and thought that his victory was a harmful event for the long-term prospects of our country's democracy. I may still think that.

Like me, many Americans on November 9, 2016, were haunted by questions. How could our country ever be the same? How had we elected an objectively incredibly unqualified person to become the most powerful person in the free world?

What did it say about our country that we went from Obama to Trump?

But not everyone shared those beliefs. Walking through Will Rogers Airport in Oklahoma City just two days after the election, we encountered considerably more optimism than we had seen in New York. The televisions in the terminal showed President Obama and President-elect Donald Trump shaking hands, greeting the press after their first-ever meeting together. It was jarring, to say the least.

"I can't believe this," I groaned to Sarah and Jessicah. "This is our new reality."

A man next to us offered a contrasting perspective, gesturing at the TV. "Our national nightmare is over! President Trump will make America great again!"

Over the next few days, we realized the extent to which we lived in a seemingly different country. We met people throughout Oklahoma who thoroughly celebrated the election of Trump, thinking a new dawn had finally arrived. Some were more blasé, but they did tell us they thought our fatalistic behavior was absurd. The United States would still be the United States, they assured us (though one could interpret this as the United States would still continue its policy of upholding rich white people and repressing minorities, but whatever). They didn't love Trump, but they hated Hillary, and they thought our country would be fine.

Some Oklahomans told us that the way we felt in the election's aftermath was exactly how they felt after Barack Obama was elected president. Despite our opinions that Trump's ascendancy was an unparalleled stain on the country's history, we did try to hold conversations with some of his supporters.

"I understand that you all feel like the world is falling apart. And look, I don't like the guy personally. But I wanted something new. We need to kick-start the economy and get the corruption out of Washington. We didn't need more of the same. Trump is going to be different," an avowed Trump supporter in Oklahoma told me.

On that last point, we could agree. Having largely been in a New York bubble for the last few months, we had rarely, if ever, talked to Trump supporters. This made us, in a way, like most of the country. A 2016 poll in Virginia, a contested purple state, found that 54 percent of Trump supporters said they didn't know any Clinton supporters. Sixty percent of Clinton supporters had not talked to any Trump supporters. I am not sure I had a real conversation with a Trump supporter during the 2016 election cycle.

That Friday night, just three days after the election, we held our launch party in the cavernous Will Rogers Theater in Oklahoma City (the native son's name is all over Oklahoma). I knew going in that we would have a mix of Trump and Clinton supporters. Crafting a speech that emphasized youth civic engagement while catering to both sides of the aisle was anxiety-inducing. Could I avoid the topic completely? Would I start crying mid-speech? Who the hell knew.

Jack Funk, one of our Oklahoma supporters, had grown up in a conservative household but now lived in New York City (and was admittedly more liberal than he once was). He walked to the front of the stage to introduce Generation Citizen.

"We're gathered here in incredibly divisive times," he began. "We're upset—we still can't believe how this ever happened, how our community will ever be the same. Really, it's totally unconscionable that this happened."

The room became visibly tense. I looked around: folks were frowning, clutching their drinks a little tighter.

I'm screwed, I thought. The event is ruined. Why was Jack being so divisive and alienating? He had messed up our launch.

"I'm talking, of course, about Kevin Durant, and his decision to leave the Oklahoma City Thunder," Jack said with a mischievous smile.

The crowd burst into laughter. It felt like a giant weight had been lifted. I smiled for the first time since Tuesday.

(Kevin Durant had been a beloved member of the Oklahoma City Thunder basketball team, and months earlier, had left the team for the Golden State Warriors. Six months later, the city was still upset. Despite all their differences, everyone in the city was, in my opinion, justifiably united in their antipathy for Durant.)

"Damn you, Jack! I thought you were really going for it," Jeff Cloud, an avowed Trump supporter, bellowed from the back of the room.

The room agreed on something. Maybe sports really are the great political equalizer.

But, despite the night's success, there was no way to avoid a larger, more existential question facing our country.

In the face of such wildly different reactions to the election, how can our democracy remain functional if we do not know how to talk to fellow citizens who disagree with us?

DISAGREEING EQUALS DEMOCRACY

At this point in your political journey, you've selected the issue that you care most about. You've done your research, developed expertise, and determined the root cause of why the challenge persists. You've developed a personal narrative that convincingly inspires others to care about the issue as well. You've mobilized a team, and together you are ready to move forward to affect change. You're gaining power. You're even embracing failure. You're ready to engage in the hard work required for true systems transformation.

But what if not everyone agrees with your stance on the issue? What happens when people disagree with the premise that you can embark on a political journey?

Should you steamroll through the obstacles, doing everything you can to build power and defeat the opposition? Or is there an imperative to work for compromise, attempting to find common ground that may lead to more progress?

The process of developing a plan to move forward on your political journey when not everyone agrees with your end goal, or that you should even be on the journey itself, may be one of the most critical components to living a political life.

Democracy functions best when people can disagree, at times deeply and fundamentally. A governance system that does not welcome dissent runs the risk of transforming into an authoritarian dictatorship, in which rulers set the direction of the country unilaterally, without taking into account the diverse will of the people. Thus, ensuring that we, as citizens, can openly and productively engage in disagreement is more than the capacity to laugh at a sports joke at a party: it becomes an existential question about our ability to thrive as a robust democracy.

Many countries throughout the world experience the type of dictatorial reign that discourages dialogue and dissent among its citizens. The democratic watchdog organization Freedom

House estimates that 26 percent of countries across the world today are "not free." An example of such a country is Turkey, in which President Recep Tayyip Erdoğan has consolidated unilateral power and recently engaged in a flawed constitutional referendum that provided his office with expanded authority. Erdoğan replaced elected mayors with his own appointees and purged unfriendly state employees from government. The result is a country in which citizens are increasingly hesitant to express their views. The government's opinion has become the only one that matters. A dictatorship, not a democracy.

Turkey's descent into an authoritarian regime is unfortunately not an isolated incident in our modern times. According to Freedom House's *Freedom in the World* report, which uses hundreds of experts to assess metrics on basic democratic functions like an independent press and freedom of speech, the world has witnessed twelve straight years during which the number of countries who suffered democratic setbacks outnumbered those who registered gains.

The United States itself has seen a recent serious erosion of democratic standards, primarily stemming from a continued decline in the behavior and values vital to an effective democracy. A key component of this decay is an unprecedented political polarization and an inability for citizens to engage with each other across differences of opinion.

There are many reasons for this recent broader decline in democracy, and many of these problems do start at the top, with leaders seemingly more interested in their own well-being than the protection of the rights and opinions of all citizens. But, we, as citizens, are also partially to blame. We jeopardize our political engagement when we, as a people, are divided and self-segregating in our living styles and habits. If we are unable to interact with our fellow citizens, or even agree on a set of facts, our democratic center cannot hold. This lack of communication can lead to a demonization of those who do not hold our same beliefs.

George Washington predicted this democratic threat in his farewell address. Warning against the possibility of one segment of society suppressing another and not allowing for open dialogue, he stated, "The alternate domination of one faction over another, sharpened by the spirit of revenge, natural to party dissension, which in different ages and countries has perpetrated the most horrid enormities, is itself a frightful despotism."

Washington was articulating that history has time and again demonstrated that conflict inevitably occurs when one side unilaterally imposes its beliefs on another. A democracy cannot hold if dissent is not welcome, tolerated, or even encouraged.

The challenge, then, is actually not creating a democracy in which all of our individual desires, or those of our preferred party, are always implemented. That type of governance system goes against the very definition of a democracy. Opposition, or, in current terms, resistance, is completely necessary in a functioning democracy. The critical test becomes working with others who inhabit our communities to formulate responses to societal problems. This, in a sense, is functional politics. A functional politics that we, on the aggregate, no longer practice.

In order for a democracy to work, we need multiple ideas at the table. Political sociologist Seymour Martin Lipset puts it another way in his 1959 book *Political Man*: "A stable democracy requires the manifestation of conflict or cleavage so that there will be struggle over ruling positions, challenges to parties in power, and shifts of parties in office."

He also added that the system must allow "the peaceful 'play' of power," and "the adherence by the 'outs' to the decisions made by the 'ins.'" In a democracy, no one side can claim to have the universal moral authority.

But problematically, Washington's alarming warning is now becoming closer to a reality. When New York City wakes up feeling one way about an election and Oklahoma wakes up with a completely opposite reaction, our democracy begins to fracture. When those two sides do not even talk to each other, the rupture increases exponentially.

As I've written, I am a Democrat, and I believe strongly in my values: I think that government can and should play a strong role in curbing the social, racial, and political inequality that plagues our country. But am I exacerbating the very polarization that threatens our democracy by highlighting the stories of young people that largely affirm my worldview? When I emphasize the efficacy and expertise of Black Lives Matter activists and focus on the problems inherent with an education system that continues to promote segregationist policies, am I alienating citizens who agree with engaging in a democracy through political journeys but do not agree with my stance on those issues? Fair questions.

The counternarrative is that we should all work together to make a difference on the issues we care about. This, candidly, in our current times, can seem remarkably quaint. Do we even have common issues or values as a society anymore? In a country grappling with profound economic and social challenges, the plea to get past our differences and work together can come across as stemming from a privileged position. Those pleading for common ground usually do not have their own rights at risk.

Indeed, what if there are explicit moral rights and wrongs? Should you listen to someone who questions your very right to be in this country? If you are an immigrant, are you supposed to productively engage with someone who questions whether you should stay in the country? Or who wants to build a literal wall to keep more immigrants outside the country? If you are a person of color, should you be forced to engage with racist white supremacists?

As a comparison, should we have worked out our differences with slave owners during the time of slavery? The issue of slavery had a clear moral right and wrong, and it literally drove the country to war.

Challenges in the modern-day United States sometimes follow this clear moral right and wrong, where this is no gray zone. But I am aware that not everyone agrees with these sentiments. Therein lies our collective challenge: learning to embrace dissent when perspectives threaten our values or even our existence.

This is not as easy as just sitting down with people who disagree with our viewpoints. Achieving disagreement productively becomes even more difficult if some individuals fundamentally impinge on the rights of others. If someone holds explicitly racist, sexist, or homophobic viewpoints, it is difficult to expect that an interaction will change their mind. Engaging with people who value other citizens as less than them similarly seems an exercise in futility. As the United States becomes a more diverse country, this debate becomes more pressing. It is challenging to achieve progress on issues like immigration or racial justice if certain Americans feel that those who do not look like them are worth less. Or more fundamentally, that they are not American.

In our current times, white America may be attempting to

hold on to its last vestiges of power, as the United States will soon become a minority-majority country. As Steven Levitsky and Daniel Ziblatt argue in their book, *How Democracies Die*, "The simple fact of the matter is that the world has never built a multiethnic democracy in which no particular ethnic group is in the majority and where political equality, social equality, and economies that empower all have been achieved."

The unprecedented polarization that has accompanied our self-segregation as a society amid increasing amounts of diversity is an existential threat to our democracy. It's both comforting and terrifying to note, as Levitsky and Ziblatt do, that a democracy as diverse as the United States has never survived.

Indeed, herein lies the challenge and the potential. We can create the first diverse democracy that actually survives, and thrives. We, as young people, have the opportunity, and potentially the obligation, to work beyond our differences. Young people, on the aggregate, are much more tolerant and open to diversity than previous generations. So our ability to bridge these gaps may define the future of our democracy.

IT'S NEVER BEEN THIS BAD

Statistic after statistic demonstrates the extent to which political polarization in this country is at unprecedented levels. Over the last few decades, Democrats and Republicans have begun to view the other party with complete disdain. Historical surveys have used a hundred-point meter to assess how voters feel about the opposite party—with higher numbers equating to warmer feelings. In 2008, the average rating for members of the opposite party was thirty.

By 2016, that rating had dropped five points, mostly because the most common answer given in the survey was zero. On the aggregate, citizens feel downright antipathy toward citizens of the opposite party.

A similar 2016 Pew poll demonstrated that 45 percent of Republicans and 41 percent of Democrats felt that the other party's policies and politics posed an existential threat to the nation itself.

A 2017 Stanford study demonstrated that partisan hatred and prejudice now exceeds racial hostility in this country, as measured by implicit-association group tests. Democrats and Republicans now frequently associate the other party with words and traits like *awful* and *evil*. In a country whose initial economic success was dependent on slavery, and where racial attitudes have become ingrained over time, the fact that party affiliation now matters more than race is nothing short of re-markable. It has now become acceptable and commonplace to demonstrate partisan hatred and prejudice.

This partisan antipathy has ramifications. University of Maryland political scientist Lilliana Mason argues that "the more sorted we become, the more emotionally we react to nor-mal political events." Thus, everyday events become a threat to our own status, and politics becomes about anger. Mason warns that "the angrier the electorate, the less capable we are of finding common ground on policies, or even of treating our opponents like human beings." This is not to say that certain unjust policies should not provoke anger. Rather, it is challenging to move for-ward as a democracy if anger, rather than inspiration for a better future, guides us forward.

Unsurprisingly, or perhaps correspondingly, Americans have

begun to concentrate their residential choices, living close to people who share their political beliefs. Democrats are increasingly inhabiting urban cities, while Republicans remain in more rural, smaller towns.

In the 1992 presidential election, 38 percent of voters lived in a "landslide county," defined as an area that voted for one of the presidential candidates by twenty percentage points or more.

In the 2016 presidential election, that number had increased to more than 60 percent. This is not purely accidental: a 2014 Pew survey indicated that 50 percent of conservatives and 35 percent of liberals agree that "it's important to me to live in a place where most people share my political views."

This segregation of political perspectives does not just happen where we live but is now manifesting in our online networks as well. In a phenomenon known as "filter bubbles," we seek out online content that confirms our beliefs and worldviews rather than challenges our principles. In a 2016 paper entitled "Echo Chambers on Facebook," social scientists used a variety of tests to confirm that online users promote their favorite narratives, form and belong to polarized groups, and reject information that does not neatly fit into their preexisting beliefs. The paper found that users interacted only with like-minded friends and that confirmation bias played a significant role in users' individual decisions to share content.

These realities created closed, non-interacting communities, or "echo chambers." Whenever we post an article or share our opinion, statistics demonstrate that the vast majority of time we are looking for people to agree with our perspective rather than challenge our beliefs. This closed behavior, while potentially making us feel better through an actual dopamine release every time someone likes one of our posts, does not promote true democratic values of discourse and dialogue.

Just as we live in communities that promote our worldviews and limit our exposure to other political philosophies, we interact online in social networks that do the same. This can prove just as significant as our residential choices. According to Pew Research, 61 percent of millennials use Facebook as their primary source for news about politics and government, a number that is only increasing.

The result of this stratification goes beyond disagreement on issues: it runs the risk of dividing the United States into two separate countries. Despite all of the flaws associated with the United States, this country is unique in that it was founded on ideas rather than a sense of identity. The ideal that we are all created equal is a premise that we continue to strive for, despite the fact that we have never actually succeeded in achieving that goal.

Our increasing self-segregation and inability to talk to one another indisputably threatens this unifying American premise. Our disagreements have increasingly become centered not on policy issues and discussing how to address public challenges but rather about what it means to be an American. Questioning the founding ideals threatens the fabric that holds together our democracy. We have "othered" complete swaths of the population. We fundamentally do not think that our fellow citizens represent our country. In some cases, we do not think they should actually be citizens.

We cannot embark on our path to change without working with people who disagree with us. We cannot assume that the way we felt about the 2016 election is the way that all good people felt, and that all others are fundamentally evil. And we cannot continue to remain in our echo chambers.

There may not be a more challenging political issue than determining how to work with others who do not agree with our beliefs. The good news, if there is any, is that we, as the youngest generation, can guide a way forward to rebuilding the American ethos: a society that productively disagrees but does not question the motivations of its opponents. Indeed, our democracy may depend on it.

DISAGREEMENT IN ACTION

We at Generation Citizen are always trying to answer the question of how to create productive political dialogue without dogmatism. We want to ensure that young people do not think in political absolutes, but rather respect the rights and opinions of others, even in times of intensive disagreement. One of the defining principles of the program is that each class can choose only one issue to focus on, despite the fact that the students will always hold differing opinions. Some students will want to focus on housing. Others argue for homelessness. Others on police brutality. But each class can select only one issue. This forces agreement through disagreement. Productive disagreement, or so we hope.

Kealing Middle School, which operates in the Austin Independent School District, houses a magnet program within its public school. In order to receive admittance into the magnet program, students must pass a series of tests. At the magnet program, 60 percent of students are white, 15 percent are Latino, and 1 percent are African American. Fewer than 12 percent of the students come from low-income backgrounds. The demographics are much different in the non-magnet side of the school: 29 percent of students are Latino, 13 percent are African American, and 32 percent come from low-income backgrounds.

Unsurprisingly, this leads to tensions—the magnet program and district school operate on the very same physical premises, but with totally different instructional priorities and resource allocation. In a sense, the divisions mirror American society—in which individuals can inhabit the same country and experience vastly different realities and material possessions through the lens of political and economic inequality.

Upon adopting Generation Citizen, the Kealing teachers decided to create a class in which 50 percent magnet-school students and 50 percent non-magnet-school students participated—the first class at the school that had such an equitable proportion.

As the students began to debate the issue they would take action on, divisions emerged. The magnet-school students wanted to focus on either LGBTQ or women's rights issues—both important subjects. The non-magnet-school students wanted to address issues they felt were more urgent and relevant to their everyday lives, like poverty and immigration.

The debate started with tension, with each side accusing the other of not understanding the severity of the issues at hand. But before long, the conversation turned respectful, deliberate, and thoughtful. Students asked the other side for their opinion. They brought in their personal expertise and shared their beliefs, generated by their struggles with each of the issues.

In the end, the class decided to focus on supporting immigrant families experiencing domestic violence, who they found were less likely to seek out legal support because of a fear of deportation. It was a compromise, but one that all the students became excited about. The students decided to support Texas Senate Bill 918, which would require cosmetology-license holders to take a mandated course on identifying domestic violence in their clients, with the goal of providing women with options when experiencing abusive situations without going through the legal system.

It would be naive to assert that students working through their disagreements to take action on issues can solve the nation's deep-seated political polarization. But, as young people, we do have the opportunity to construct a better, more accepting form of democracy that may begin to repair the deep ruptures that have emerged in our political discourse. While the problem did not start with our generation, the solution can.

CHANGE MY VIEW

Another surprising source of engagement in these polarized times comes from something that causes so many of our disagreements in the first place: the internet. In 2013, seventeen-year-old student Kal Turnbull created a sub-forum on the popular messaging site Reddit entitled "Change My View." Users come to the forum wanting to engage with others about an issue they care about, with the mind-set that they may change their opinions. The fact that this unique forum was created by a young person genuinely trying to bridge differences is unsurprising.

"I was generally surrounded by people that all think similarly," Turnbull said of the reason for creating the forum. "This led me to wonder, what does someone actually do when they want to hear a different perspective or change their mind?"

Whereas one might think that the forums would lead to bombastic statements and trolling, the result has been a respectful dialogue on a wide variety of issues. Users engage in discussions on everything from whether all forms of abortion should be illegal to whether Palestine should be completely annexed by Israel to whether we should reinstate the ban on assault weapons.

Users employ research, reason, and persuasion to make their case. Oftentimes commenters change their minds and admit when they do so. The ability to admit to a change in opinion showcases the best in human nature, and suggests how we might actually be predisposed to engaging with others in a productive manner.

As Turnbull said, "A view is just how you see something, it doesn't have to define you, and trying to detach from it to gain understanding can be a very good thing."

The GC class and the "Change My View" sub-forum are small but real examples that hope remains for a society in which we actually engage with one another. There are a few ways that we can begin to ensure that our political journeys involve communicating with people who disagree with our beliefs.

LEAN INTO THE CONVERSATION AND SEEK OUT DIFFERENCE

This may appear self-evident, but the first step toward engaging with folks who disagree with us is to recognize the importance of the act in itself. This is not to say that we should all move away from our existing echo chambers and into more diverse areas (although that could help). This is also not to encourage you to friend a whole host of people on Facebook with whom you disagree (although that might help as well, as might getting off of Facebook, honestly).

But it is to say that the obligation to engage with other people is a necessary component to a political journey that will lead to better arguments, more developed ideas, and a stronger, unified citizenry. This is not easy—facing someone who questions your ideas, or your very citizenship, is less than appealing. But if we agree that democracy is a marketplace, defined by the exchange of ideas and perspectives, we need to live our political journeys abiding by that principle.

DON'T START BY EDUCATING OR PREJUDGING

As you engage in these types of conversations, it may be tempting to start with the goal of educating the other person on how you feel about your issue. At another level, you may prejudge them, labeling them as less than because of the political beliefs that they hold. You may even be correct. But it's not going to get you to where you need to go.

Amaryllis Fox, a former undercover officer with the CIA, spent some of her job talking with extremists who had committed terrorist attacks against her country. But she listened to them, and her philosophy was revealing: "Everybody believes they are the good guy. The only way to disarm your enemy is to listen to them. If you hear them out, if you're brave enough to really listen to their story, you can see that more often than not, you might have made some of the same choices if you'd lived their life instead of yours."

There is power in empathizing with the person you are

talking with rather than demonizing them. Even if they hold contrary viewpoints, recognizing where they come from may help you make your point better.

Anand Giridharadas, author of the recent book *Winners Take All*, made this point eloquently at the opening of the inaugural Obama Foundation summit:

> The burden of citizenship is committing to your fellow citizens and accepting that what is not your fault may be your problem. And that, amid great change, it is in all of our interest to help people see who they will be on the other side of the mountaintop.
>
> When we accept these duties, we may begin to notice the ways in which our very different pains rhyme. The African American retiree in Brooklyn who fears gentrification is whitening her borough beyond recognition probably votes differently from the white foreman in Arizona who fears immigration is browning his state. Yet their worries echo.

We see the worries echo when we do not prejudge our neighbors and fellow citizens.

RECOGNIZE AND APPRECIATE DIFFERENCES

I once was working with a group of young Kenyans in Narok County, Kenya, leading a civic engagement training. We were going through an exercise entitled Four Corners that seeks out disagreement by encouraging participants to work through their opinions on certain issues by articulating and defending their beliefs. We started with a topic like "Dogs are better than cats" (extreme disagreement across the spectrum) and then explored issues like "My government cares what I think."

I decided to go a little deeper, knowing that the next topic would spark a broader conversation. I announced, "Gay marriage should be legal."

All the young people immediately dashed to the strongly disagree camp. The training happened to coincide with President Barack Obama, half-Kenyan himself, making his first trip as president to the country. While the country was ecstatic about his visit, there was much consternation about whether he would address the issue of gay rights. These young people, avowed fans of Obama, did not hesitate when I asked them to explain their position.

"We know you Americans are okay with the issue. But we are not. And we do not want to be lectured to."

"Obama can talk about anything, but he better not talk about the 'gay issue.'"

"You do not understand our culture. We are not okay with gay marriage here, and we never will be."

I struggled with knowing how to engage the young people. I was a white heterosexual American and did not want to lecture them on their perspective on the issue. I also appreciated the unique context here: they felt this way about sexuality partially because of their Catholic beliefs, which also dated to the religion imposed upon them by westerners during colonialism. So, ostensibly, I'd be doubling down on a form of colonialism by pushing the issue. Instead, we engaged in a short discussion in which I respectfully told them my position while hearing theirs out.

I do hope that they eventually change their minds. But recognizing the contextualization of others' beliefs, especially as they pertain to long-held power dynamics, is critical as you engage in these types of dialogues.

STICK IT OUT

Whenever you're engaging with someone who does not share your beliefs, frustration will inevitably mount. You'll think that they're insensitive, that they're unreasonable. It will be tempting to end the conversation and move on.

The best and most productive conversations take time. Whether online or in person, don't be afraid to work through the tension points. The most important discussions often entail conversing with people who are passionate, and therefore emotional, about the topics at hand. This passion inevitably leads to messiness and frustration. But working through this tension is necessary to finding the common ground that does exist.

There is beauty in the very exchange of ideas, and it may lead to you strengthening your argument or finding pockets of agreement. Even when the going gets tough, stick it out.

ACCEPT THAT AGREEMENT MAY NOT BE THE END GAME

The objective of having a discussion with people who may disagree with you is not necessarily to convince them to change their mind (although if that happens, great). More important, however, is a respectful exchange of ideas that allows us to strengthen our arguments, learn different perspectives, and, most importantly, recognize the humanity of people with whom we disagree.

This may be the most critical aspect of attempts to engage with others who may not espouse our beliefs. The polarization that has afflicted this country is perhaps most worrisome because of how we have demonized our opposition. Those who do not agree with us are seen as less than and as our enemies.

The process of engaging with others is a vital step in reestablishing the American creed of a country based on a shared set of values, even if we have different opinions on how best to achieve them. As we explore our own political journeys, taking action on issues we care about, engaging with those who disagree with us is a necessary step.

There are still going to be mornings when I wake up feeling like I did after Trump's election, and the areas I live in may mirror these emotions. But I can work to ensure that I'm having more conversations with those whose feelings are different. And more importantly, I can see them as passionate citizens who believe in a better country. And even if we have nothing to agree on politically, at the very least, we can all still laugh about sports.

14

"BY ANY MEANS NECESSARY"

A Global Democratic Movement

This book has focused on the importance of living a political journey in the context of the United States of America. This is logical and necessary: because I am an American, I have more expertise relating to our unique political system. Additionally, Generation Citizen's mission focuses on working with young people in the United States. It would be challenging for me to write about international democracies and suggest how citizens, and especially young people, could participate politically to help create a better society in their home countries.

The current crisis in democracy, however, is not purely American. Rather, all across the world, the concept of democracy is at risk, with authoritarian leaders usurping power and citizens tuning out of politics. Similarly, there are also young people across the world pushing back and taking action in their communities to fight for a better future. We shouldn't pretend we live in isolation from those young people. More importantly, we can learn from them in our own quest for power.

Indeed, we have the opportunity, and perhaps obligation, to become part of a larger movement to form youth power and create a new, positive narrative for democracy. Even as we engage with local issues, and as we become powerful as young people, we are part of something bigger—a global movement for a new, twenty-first-century democracy.

To participate in this new global movement, we must first recognize that the political journey is not strictly an American concept. Young people everywhere want to become powerful and lead change. Young people everywhere want their voices to matter.

Talking about democracy through the framework of other countries and cultures can be challenging. We do not want to impose our values internationally, and we can never fully understand political contexts abroad. A common critique following this logic argues that there are numerous problems in the United States—shouldn't we remain focused on tackling the issues occurring in our backyard?

Yes. It is important to focus on American problems. And we do not want to impose our Western belief structures internationally. Especially given the colonialist history that defines so much of our history with the rest of the world.

That said, it is both important and inspiring to learn about young people around the world currently creating a new democratic narrative. We have a lot to discover from their desire to participate in the political process and their recognition that democracy is not a given. The efforts of international youth activists demonstrate that democracy is something we have to fight for, every day.

I have spent almost a third of my life living internationally, and so to write a book about democracy without talking about global politics would fail to take into account to my own lived experience. More importantly, it would be incomplete and would fail to elevate certain lessons I've learned that can be applied to our political journeys, even if they center in the United States.

This book argues that young people in this country always lead us to a better future. But this reality extends past the United States. Indeed, young people around the world are always at the forefront of political change.

WE ARE NOT PERFECT

Despite frequent exhortations from our politicians, our American democracy is not exceptional. Period.

Our founders did have some good ideas. We generally do allow for a freedom of thought and expression that is not always common around the world. The local roots of our politics, formalized though our federalist system, allow for citizen input on everything from school policies to housing zoning laws to health care. And our history has demonstrated a general flow, or maybe a trickle, toward economic and social progress. We (most of the time) attempt to aspire to the values idealistically enshrined in the Constitution: namely that we are all created equal and endowed with certain unalienable rights.

But at the same time, as we've learned throughout this book, our democracy does not always work the way that it should. We too often restrict rights, especially those of minorities. We have become too polarized and are unable to talk to people who disagree with us. Our government is not as responsive as it can be to the needs of our most vulnerable populations. Money often talks more than individual citizens when it comes to having a voice in government. The list of challenges in our democracy goes on and on.

Despite these obvious challenges, sometimes our American democracy is considered sacrosanct. Admitting that our democracy isn't perfect is thus considered sacrilegious. Before running for president, 2012 Republican nominee Mitt Romney wrote a book called *No Apology: The Case for American Greatness*, focused solely on perpetuating the idea that President Obama had staged an apology tour around the world when he took office. Republicans often followed this line of attack during the Obama administration, arguing that the president continually admitted the United States' imperfections. In actuality, it was more of a tour to restore the United States' image throughout the rest of the world after the disastrous wars launched during the Bush administration by admitting that we, as Americans, do not always know best. A pretty powerful sentiment.

Regardless of Obama's motivations, the reality is that our democracy is not perfect. At all.

I think the fact that our American democracy is imperfect is a potent message to share with the world. I often visit other countries—to share Generation Citizen's best practices, and to try to learn from the efforts of other young people. I try to travel internationally at least once a year, and I always tack on some civic engagement panels and trainings during the trip. As part of this work, GC has begun to facilitate a Global Network for Youth Action, bringing youth civic engagement leaders from across the world together to learn from each other and begin to create a global movement.

To help start the Global Network for Youth Action, I recently visited the Democratic Republic of the Congo to speak to youth activists about civic engagement. I was inspired throughout the trip—Congolese youth are pushing for change in their country despite a government that has oppressed and marginalized the opposition and repeatedly acted in a fashion that demonstrates to young people that their voices do not matter. The Democratic Republic of the Congo suffered through decades of brutal authoritarian colonialism at the hands of Belgium, and its citizens have been trying to fight through the aftermath of their past since independence in 1960. It has been an arduous journey, with dictators clutching on to power and refusing to hold democratic elections.

I realized early in the trip that the Congolese youth presumed that the American form of democracy was the ideal. They assumed they could learn much from me, whereas I wanted to learn from their inspirational activism. So I decided to burst their bubble.

"What percentage of Americans do you think voted in the last presidential election?" I asked. I was speaking in front of more than fifty young people in a local library.

"Ninety-five percent!"

"All of them!"

"Maybe 92 percent to be specific!"

"Actually, less than 60 percent of eligible Americans voted in the 2016 presidential election," I said. "In fact, more Americans did not vote than voted for either Trump or Clinton. Do Not Vote would have won by a large margin over both of them."

"That cannot be true!" one student said, looking very upset. "America's democracy is the best!"

"We seek to follow your democracy! What are you telling us?"

This incident in the DRC was not singular: one of my favorite activities is to bust the myth that American voter participation rates are exceptional. By providing the real numbers—and showing that, of the thirty-five countries in the Organisation for Economic Co-operation and Development, the United States ranks thirty-first in terms of voter participation—young people realize that every democracy has challenges. While there are some lessons to be learned from the evolution of the United States' democracy, no one should copy our system in its entirety. The general chaotic political environment under President Trump has helped me make this point without my needing to articulate memorized statistics.

Instead of idealizing our American political system, we should focus on learning from other democracies around the world. We can learn how young people organize, mobilize, and create their own movements. Rather than exporting our brand of democracy, we can see ourselves, especially as young people, as part of a broader global movement to create a new narrative around what a twenty-first-century democracy should look like.

The challenges that we face in the United States, from income inequality to racial injustice to climate change to a workforce unprepared for a twenty-first-century economy, are global in nature. And the never-ending quest to ensure that citizen engagement is substantive and effective also occurs everywhere.

Perhaps the most enduring lesson I have learned from spending so much time abroad is that people, and young people specifically, possess a natural desire to have a voice in their own governance. We do not need, or want, to see a Western-style democracy all around the world, but we can acknowledge the deeply human desire to participate in self-governance. The longing to be heard is universal.

Again and again in countries around the world, I meet citizens who want to live political lives. But again and again, I meet individuals who feel constrained in their ability to do so.

This fight for power by our youth, even in the midst of seemingly insurmountable obstacles, provides the foundation for an aspirational global youth democracy movement. And it is this pursuit of democracy that we, as Americans, can learn from. Simply put, whenever I meet youth activists around the world, they do not take their participation in self-governance for granted. They do not take democracy for granted. And they will fight like hell to gain the ability to live political journeys.

ZIMBABWE

My job has provided me the opportunity to meet a wide array of people over the years, including executive directors and CEOs from other organizations, elected officials, and youth activists from across the country. I enjoy doing this as we build the Global Network for Youth Action. I also find the knowledge-gathering indispensable as we seek to improve GC's own programming.

I've learned the most about the importance and challenge of living a political life from the citizens and activists in Zimbabwe, where my parents lived while I was in college. I've visited the country six times and come away inspired and motivated after each trip.

After a long colonial rule under the United Kingdom, Zimbabwe received its independence in 1980. Robert Mugabe, a freedom fighter who helped to liberate the Zimbabwean people, became the country's ruler and was immediately hailed as a transformational leader. The early years of Zimbabwe's independence were defined by promise: the country transformed into the breadbasket of southern Africa, with a growing economy, natural resources, and a powerhouse agrarian-based financial system that contributed robust monetary development to the entire continent. Leaders throughout the world praised Mugabe as an ideal ruler: he was knighted by Queen Elizabeth in 1994, and he visited presidents Carter, Reagan, and Clinton in the United States. Mugabe was perceived as a leader who had endured endless hardship, vanquished colonialism, and led his country to greener pastures.

Despite this initial promise, before long Mugabe and his cronies cracked down, consolidating power and restricting the rights of citizens. The Zimbabwean economy was decimated through a perhaps well-intentioned but mismanaged attempt to take land from white settlers and return it to black Zimbabweans. Mugabe retained power through the chaos by continuously rigging elections. He attempted to demonstrate to the outside world that Zimbabwe was a democracy. In reality, he became one of the more autocratic rulers in the world. The Zimbabwean people lost their voices.

Themba Mzingwane is a Zimbabwean who was born in the early years of his nation's independence. He is not famous. He is not a politician. But he is passionate about working to create a better democracy for his country.

I first met Themba because his mother was my parents' housekeeper when they lived in the capital of Harare. (It is challenging to pause and explain to peers that this practice—whites employing black Zimbabweans—is incredibly common.

White foreigners can offer stable employment to Zimbabweans who might otherwise be jobless in a country with a 95 percent unemployment rate. The practice can also perpetuate colonialist behavior. Accordingly, does it make me uncomfortable? A very resounding yes.)

I met Themba when I visited my parents during a Christmas vacation from college. We became fast friends. He showed me Harare on bike and foot, describing the political and economic realities and anxieties and sharing local cultures and customs with me. After I returned to the United States, we exchanged emails back and forth. He consistently informed me on the latest political happenings in Zimbabwe.

Themba was raised by his grandmother in the poorest and most remote part of the countryside, an area called Chikwaka. His mother, Jane, was the sole breadwinner in the family; his father was never part of his life. At the end of every month, Jane took a bus from the capital and visited Themba and his sister with bags of vegetables to complement the harvest they worked to reap from their rural farm.

Themba finished his high school studies in 2001 and moved to Harare to begin college. His dream was to work in engineering and computers. His start of college coincided with the 2002 presidential election, the most violent and rigged in Zimbabwe's history.

Themba largely avoided politics during his childhood. This was partially due to the fact that his remote rural village had little access to news sources that could have kept him informed. But even when his mother brought him newspapers, he only used them to cut out pictures of soccer players from the sports pages. He did not think politics mattered. This changed when Themba moved to the urban capital.

"Suddenly, through watching the news and reading newspapers, my young rural mind started to make connections between the deteriorating conditions of living in Zimbabwe and how our government operated," Themba reflected to me. "I realized that politics mattered and affected my life."

At the close of the 2002 election, soon after Themba moved to Harare, Mugabe's regime did win, but by a closer margin than expected (with only 56 percent of the votes in an already-rigged race). The regime in power reacted by retaliating against the opposition, arresting many of their leaders, and further pursuing land-reform policies to satisfy Mugabe's political base. These actions continued to decimate the economy. Voices like Themba's began to matter even less.

While Zimbabwe plunged into a dictatorship, Themba struggled. This was not coincidental. Sending Themba to college was a huge financial sacrifice for Jane, who gave Themba almost all of her earnings. But after three years, Themba could no longer continue his studies. The already-exorbitant college fees skyrocketed as the hyperinflation plunged the Zimbabwean dollar into extinction. (At its peak, Zimbabwe's inflation reached 79.6 billion percent in November of 2008. It is one of the highest inflation rates in the history of the world.)

Themba dropped out of college, devastated. Despite being highly educated, it took him months to find a job. He started by working in a factory, stacking boxes to be shipped to other parts of Africa. But the hyperinflation showed no signs of slowing down, and the bus fares that Themba paid to travel to his job, an hour from his home, began to surpass his daily salary.

"It reached a point where I went to work just to occupy myself, not because there was an economic benefit. Eventually,

I was forced to quit," Themba said. "With a regime only concerned with keeping itself in power, the lives of many young men and women were ruined: our dreams turned into nightmares. As many companies closed, dejected young people left the country in droves into neighboring countries. Zimbabwe was ruined."

Themba ended up fleeing to neighboring South Africa, where he sought better financial opportunities. Two months after he left, his mother was killed in a car crash. He blames her death on an incompetent and corrupt state-run health care industry, which he asserts was unable to provide care quickly enough when she reached the hospital.

Themba found a day job the first day he arrived in Johannesburg. This gave him hope that perhaps this country would value his services more than his home country. As an undocumented migrant, stable employment would prove evasive at the onset, until he received his papers, but the odd handyman job he found on his first day in the country paid more than his daily rate in the formal sector in Zimbabwe.

The optimistic feelings, however, did not last. The next day, Themba's hopes were dashed.

A van screeched to a halt next to a street corner where he had begun to hawk his services for work as part of the informal economy. Two stern-looking policemen, hands on guns, anger etched on their faces, stepped out with an air that suggested the customary bribes would not help him.

The policemen began shouting at Themba and his friend, Valentine, in a language foreign to the Zimbabweans. The officers switched to English when they realized Themba could not understand them.

"Are you from Zimbabwe?" one officer asked.

Themba answered affirmatively, explaining that he possessed legal papers at home. The policemen laughed.

"You are lying," the officer said. "I know your people. You are a border jumper. Now we are going to send you back to your country."

The police forced Themba into the back of a van and then gave him a rough ride on the way to the infamously repressive deportation center in Lindela.

Themba remained in Lindela for two weeks alongside thousands of other immigrants awaiting deportation. He received two sparse meals a day and spent his time in a cramped shared cell. After two weeks, the legally mandated limit of stay, Themba headed home to Zimbabwe. He spent two days on a slow-moving train. After arriving in his hometown, Themba visited the immigration office to attempt to obtain another visa and go back. He returned to South Africa weeks later.

Themba does not want his story to provoke pity. The point is not that some Zimbabweans have really hard lives. Rather, his story demonstrates the real effects people feel when a government is not democratic and explicitly prevents its citizens from leading political journeys. Themba has not had a voice to express his opinions on the government: he would be punished if he spoke out. Instead, he was forced to flee to South Africa.

Life can improve for Themba, and the people in his country, with a more equitable democracy. Zimbabwe needs a government that cares more about its people and less about consolidating power. Anything less will fail to address the systemic reasons that Zimbabwean citizens continue to be unable to lead the type of productive lives they so desperately want.

I'm not trying to suggest that an American-style democracy can "fix" Zimbabwe. Rather, I'm attempting to emphasize the importance of citizen participation in government. Themba, like so many young people in this country, wants a voice. Themba wants to become powerful.

Themba deeply believes in the system of democracy. It is something he is willing to fight for. In his opinion, a more democratic Zimbabwe would lead to a better future for all:

> I believe democracy is a system of governance that allows its citizens to live, work, and pursue their personal and collective ambitions unhindered. A system that creates an enabling environment to allow citizens to reach their maximum potential individually and collectively as a nation. It is a system where everyone, regardless of race, tribe, and social class, is equal before the law and where there is zero tolerance on discrimination of any kind.
>
> It is a society where human rights, freedom of speech, and expression are respected and protected.

These are words that we could use here. These are words we can learn from.

A NEW ZIMBABWE?

I see this desire for power and representation everywhere in Zimbabwe. In August 2016, I traveled back to the country to meet with youth activists, civic-engagement groups, and political leaders.

Two days after I arrived, I spent time with Promise

Mkwananzi, the then president of the Zimbabwe National Students Union. Promise told me that he espouses the philosophy of "youth autonomy," which asserts that the young people of Zimbabwe should be at the forefront of the decision-making in any new regime.

On a Wednesday afternoon, Promise and his friend met me after a youth leaders' organizing session on the outskirts of Harare and drove me downtown. We got out of the car and stood on a sidewalk under a beaming afternoon sun that warmed an otherwise chilly day. August in the Southern Hemisphere means winter.

Across the street, next to a three-story furniture-and-electronics store draped with a poster advertising a couch-and-television-combination sale for $200 U.S. (the economic realities meant that the Zimbabwean government pegged their currency to U.S. dollars in an attempt to curb hyperinflation), hundreds of Zimbabweans gathered before Harvest House, the headquarters for the Movement for Democratic Change (MDC) opposition party. The protesters took up half of Nelson Mandela Avenue, congesting the ongoing traffic.

Cars drove on the single free lane of the two-lane street. I noticed a BMW straight out of the 1980s, emitting enough smoke to congest our view, and a brand-new Lexus that would have been at home on the streets of Manhattan. Inequality manifests itself everywhere.

The drivers honked—some out of solidarity as they smiled and raised their fists out of their windows and some out of annoyance, as they struggled to get by. The pedestrians on our side of the street walked on, barely paying attention, as if the weekday protest was now just part of everyday life in Harare.

The rally's ringleader must have been around thirty. He wore a Che Guevara camouflaged beret and matching faded baggy pants. He shouted into a bullhorn.

"We will no longer tolerate the police beating our people! Today, we start to take control of our own country!"

The agitator du jour transitioned into a rant criticizing the government's economic policies and bemoaning the country's unprecedented unemployment rates.

"Mugabe's government has turned graduates into street vendors!"

The bullhorn failed, and his voice struggled to rise above the sound of cars and buses passing by. The crowd began to disperse, and so he began a chant, which swiftly reconvened the masses. They shouted in unison:

"Mugabe must go! Mugabe must go!"

The protestors began marching away, following the Zimbabwean Che, en route to the Office of Home Affairs, five blocks to their west.

Promise, who was the leader of a new youth party called Tajamuka, or "We Have Rebelled," decided to look out for the safety of the *mzungu* in his midst: myself. He insisted that we duck inside a fast-food outlet, where we ordered fried chicken sandwiches and French fries.

As we entered, Promise remained perpetually tied to his phone, using WhatsApp to stay in touch with his youth comrades. He looked up as I asked questions, explaining that protests, once rare, were now becoming commonplace. People were fed up. He speculated that the upsurge in opposition activity signified that his movement was succeeding. Soon, he argued, President Robert Mugabe would be removed from his position.

Promise, a revolutionary at heart, or at least in training, explained to me how, in his opinion, the Zimbabwean government had legally delegitimized its right to rule. He pointed to the government's inability to provide economically for the population and the state's growing crackdown on protests. According to Promise, the people had an obligation to rise up against the oppressors by any means necessary.

Promise asserted that the Tajamuka youth movement, while refusing to be tied to any party or figure, was doing its part in the struggle. They attempted to use the lessons of civil disobedience from the American civil rights movement to refuse to abide by unjust laws. And they wanted to combine those tactics with the organizing capacity of the recent Arab Spring, whose young people had used social media to gather thousands in public spaces to push for change. He was unambiguously and effecively applying lessons from other youth activism movements, both historical and in the present, to propel his own work forward.

He passed his phone across the table and showed me the messages streaming through WhatsApp. I saw images of police brutality, batons beating down on civilians. And I saw pictures of Mugabe asleep during speeches. Both, Promise asserted, evidence that Zimbabwe needed change now.

Promise told me that the youth would go above and beyond peaceful protests if Mugabe refused to cede power: "We will use violence in response to the government if needed."

As we left the restaurant, the stench of tear gas suddenly filled the air. We shielded our eyes. Protesters ran in our direction, and cars anxiously reversed, driving the wrong way to flee the scene. Police used batons to beat the marchers and blasted water cannons to force others away. We fled the scene in Promise's Subaru.

"By any means necessary," Promise said under his breath, echoing the creed of one of his idols, Malcolm X.

A week later, back in the United States, I sent a WhatsApp message to Promise to check on a quote for an article I was working on. When he didn't reply, I Googled his name. He had been arrested; the government claimed he had set a police car on fire. He remained in jail for almost a month before the government granted him release on $100 bail.

Democracy meant that much to Promise. He would do anything—engage in subversive tactics, serve time in prison, put his own reputation at risk—all for a better democracy.

Finally, in April of 2018, both the activists and military had had enough of the ninety-four-year-old Mugabe continuing to decimate the country and formed an unlikely alliance that forced him out of power. The scenes in the news were both inspiring and a little strange: the military and activists celebrated in the streets together. The opportunity for a better, more democratic future was now, finally, a real possibility.

"IT'S DONE," Themba messaged me the day of the historic deed. "Mugabe has resigned."

"Wow! How do you feel?" I texted back.

"I'm so happy, man! Let's see if real change comes. For now, just grateful that an old man who was the face of Zimbabwe's failure is gone."

This feeling of optimism unfortunately did not last. An election in July 2018 demonstrated more of the same. After a peaceful day at the polls, officials took days to release the certified results. In the interim, as the opposition party protested in the streets, the government deployed the military to quash any sense of rebellion. Whereas just months earlier military and civilians had been celebrating together, a starkly different scene now emerged. Three people died in the streets of downtown Harare during the crackdown as the military shot into crowds to disperse the protests.

Days later, the official returns were released: Emmerson Mnangagwa, who took over for Mugabe, had received 50.8 percent of the vote, just over the 50 percent needed to prevent a runoff. Rigging was suspected once again. Mugabe the man might be gone, but the system itself remains the same. The new government is still run by Mugabe's cronies, and citizens fear that Mnangagwa will represent more of the same.

As Themba told me in the days following the results:

> Zimbabweans have not known peace for thirty-eight years. We have not known justice for thirty-eight years. We have not known freedom for thirty-eight years. In the last thirty-eight years, we have all been turned into vendors. Some of us forced to spend most of our adult lives stuck in hostile foreign cities scavenging for a livelihood. It is frightening to think we are doomed to endure five more years of this.

But Zimbabwe's young people are forcing a new conversation and are increasingly becoming a headache for the government. Eighty-five percent of the Zimbabwean population is under thirty-nine years of age, while more than 90 percent of government leadership is older than sixty-five. Young people are leading the charge forward. They must.

Young people propelled a movement called #ThisFlag,

advocating for a more democratic Zimbabwe through a national shutdown that crippled major cities. The head of the opposition party, the Movement for Democratic Change, is Nelson Chamisa. He is only forty and is the former secretary-general of the Zimbabwe National Students Union. Subverting official state-run media, the youth have used social media to reinvigorate a citizen's movement. A citizen's movement for democracy led by young people.

Hope might seem elusive for the people of Zimbabwe. But young people will not rest until a more democratic Zimbabwe exists. That, in itself, is inspiring, and a lesson we can all learn from.

Change is afoot in Zimbabwe. But, just like in this country, a better future depends on the action of young people like Themba and Promise. At the time of this writing, Zimbabwe's democracy is at the precipice.

A GROWING GLOBAL MOVEMENT

This type of relentless youth activism is surging around the globe as young people come of age in an era of political and cultural strife. With crisis comes opportunity, and the present day's extraordinary challenges may actually lead to the possibility of a renewed commitment to democracy. Srđa Popović, a Serbian political activist who, as a young person, led the student movement Otpor!, toppling then dictatorial president Slobodan Milošević, is optimistic about this future and the ability of young people to form a new, vibrant global democracy in the twenty-first century.

Noting that young people are always at the forefront of

political change because they "have less to lose," Popović told me that while young people may be disillusioned with democracy, they are continuously challenging authority structures in the current age. The idea of defying the status quo is foundationally democratic behavior, as citizens are questioning the system and striving to improve it. Despite this democratic action, young people might not define their actions as such, as democracy itself has become such a sullied term. Thus, for Popović, it's critical that we, as young people, rebrand democracy.

"You may be disillusioned with the Church but still believe in God," he explains. "The same is true for democracy—you can be disenchanted with the institutions but still believe in a government in which people are front and center at the push for change." For Popović, the surge of youth activism around the world demonstrates the universal desire for power and voice that intrinsically comprises democratic values and behavior. Mistrust in institutions, especially when they're not working for young people, can actually demonstrate a positive trend for the long-term prospects of democracy.

Popović points to the uprising of young people through the Arab Spring, a series of recent protests across the Middle East and North Africa, as evidence of the power of youth voice on the global stage. Frustrated with undemocratic institutions, young people have recognized that the best way to force change is not to divorce from the system. Rather, change stems from gaining power and changing the systems themselves.

Sparked by the Tunisian Revolution in December 2010, the Arab Spring was largely led by a young generation fighting against an oppressive authoritarianism. They took to the streets peacefully in an attempt to secure a more democratic political system, and young people were front and center in the movement, dissatisfied with the status quo and governments that did not take their opinions into account.

Experts cite two primary reasons for the outpouring of youth activism across the region—a rationale that could be used to explain the catalyst of innumerable youth movements around the world.

First, young people in the Middle East, especially in the growing urban centers, have been hit by increasingly depressive economic conditions, including low wages, high unemployment, and high commodity prices.

"Young people just want to live and not make trouble, but they are unable to break into the political, social, economic systems of their countries," says Rami Khouri, of the American University of Beirut, a journalist with joint Palestinian-Jordanian and United States citizenship. Like in the United States, the prevalence of economic and political inequality has burdened young people the most, provoking frustrations toward a system in which they cannot thrive.

Second, young people now recognize, due to the unprecedented interconnectivity of the world through technology, the possibility of a better future, even in the midst of pervasive inequality. Just through turning on their phones, young people can see the potential of a democracy in which their opinions matter. Like Promise, who was messaging with other young people across Zimbabwe, activists in the Arab Spring were communicating with each other, able to observe the possibility for a more open and democratic future occurring in countries around the world. The ability to experience other cultures, and organize online, is a new aspect in today's youth movements.

In the wake of the Tunisian Revolution, the youth did not turn violent, but they did show up in masses: in Tahrir Square in Egypt, in the capital of Sana'a in Yemen, in Tripoli, Libya. Gathering inspiration from iPhone videos and tweets from across the region, young people continued to press for change.

Demonstrators camped out in public squares, clashed with police, and risked arrest to combat their respective repressive regimes.

The youth of the Arab Spring did experience some immediate success. The autocratic president of Egypt, Mohamed Morsi, was removed from office, and the protests in Tunisia led to a full democratization of the country, ultimately resulting in free and fair elections. The leaders of Libya and Yemen were forced from office as well (albeit controversially, with the help of the international community).

But on the aggregate, change has been hard to come by and unsustainable. Even in Egypt, where the youth protests were arguably the strongest and most durable, the resulting governments, led by the Muslim Brotherhood, have been as oppressive as Morsi's regime. Instead of working with young people, many Arab governments have become even more tyrannical, seeing the youth as an existential threat to the consolidation of their rule. So now, in addition to continued high unemployment, young people face increasing political oppression.

Challenges have not weakened the resolve of the young people throughout the region. In Zimbabwe, in the Arab Spring, and throughout the world, young people want to create a more democratic future. In the midst of government crackdowns, inequality, a warming Earth, and many other issues, this unprecedented youth global political activism is both necessary and inspiring.

So what lessons can international activism hold for us as young people in the United States? How can we learn from the youth activists in Zimbabwe and the Arab Spring?

First, to repeat the point, we should not assume that our American democracy is better than any other. Our political movements or philosophies are not necessarily more radical or more effective. Instead of imposing our own values, we should seek to learn from others.

Second, and perhaps most important, we can learn from young people's fierce sense of urgency. Whenever I visit other countries, I am struck by the fact that young people are willing to risk it all to ensure that their voices are heard. They are willing to go to prison, to leave their country, to put their lives on the line—all to work for a better tomorrow.

Democracy, for them, is not a given. Rather, it is an ideal that they will spend their entire lives fighting to achieve.

As we look around the world, we realize that the fight for a more democratic future, in which young people are at the front and center of governmental priorities, is a global yearning.

The young people of Zimbabwe and the Arab Spring provide energy and motivation to me every day. They can do the same for all of us.

15

"OUR VOICES MUST BE TAKEN SERIOUSLY"

Elevating Youth Voices in Our Current Moment

On February 14, 2018, I was leaving my office after a typical day, a little frustrated with the slow pace of fundraising for the quarter—a bit of a perpetual sentiment when you run a nonprofit. As I waited for the elevator, my mind was elsewhere; I was thinking about how to add more momentum to our efforts to grow and raise money for Generation Citizen.

My phone buzzed in my pocket, bringing me back to Earth. It was a news alert.

Another school shooting.

I glanced at the story: seventeen had been killed in a school in Parkland, Florida. The shooter, a nineteen-year-old, had entered the school with an AR-15 assault weapon and gunned down his former classmates.

I was devastated, crushed that another shooting had

occurred. And yet, I was already thinking that nothing substantive would change in the aftermath of the tragedy. The shooting in Parkland would become just another chapter in a story we have read too many times before. Just months earlier, in Las Vegas, a middle-aged white male took deadly aim from his hotel room during a country music concert. Fifty-nine people died—the deadliest mass shooting in recent history. We heard a lot about proverbial thoughts and prayers. No real action followed.

In 2012, twenty kids, all between the ages of six and seven, were shot at an elementary school in Sandy Hook, Connecticut. Again, we heard thoughts and prayers. We saw no real action.

Two decades earlier, twelve students and a teacher were gunned down in a mass shooting at a school in Columbine, Colorado. The response? A lot of talk and outrage. Little real action.

In a conversation the next day with Sarah, our director of programming, we both acknowledged what we felt was inevitable—helplessness in the face of inaction.

"Nothing will change," I said. "This is pathetic. What does it say about our politics that we can't agree on policies that would save kids?"

"Yup, I'm numb at this point," Sarah agreed.

We were both numb.

It seemed the country was numb.

But young people were not.

The students at Stoneman Douglas High School refused to let the issue go away. Using mainstream news outlets and social media alike, the students, digital native activists, almost immediately became a political force to be reckoned with. They became eloquent and passionate spokespeople, using their personal experiences surviving the shooting, coupled with the rage of losing classmates, to keep a spotlight on the issue of the United States' continued gun violence.

Without hesitation, they started out on a political journey. In this case, an issue had chosen them, and as survivors of the shooting they held instant personal expertise. They cared deeply about this issue because seventeen of their fellow students had been killed.

Many of the Parkland kids had already learned about gun reform through their classes. They now dug deeper into the policy specifics around the types of guns the shooter was allowed to buy, the age and background-check requirements (or lack thereof) to purchase firearms, and the power of the Nationa Rifle Association. They did not question if they were too young to take action or if they were the correct messengers. The aftermath of the tragedy demanded urgency.

The youth activists developed incredibly compelling personal narratives to galvanize others to get behind their cause. When they spoke to the media, they were prepared and polished. Crucially, the students worked as a team. They recognized that their voices would be stronger together than they would be on their own.

They organized rallies, a TV town hall, and corporate boycotts, and they worked with other youth groups from Chicago to Baltimore, necessarily demonstrating the breadth and growing diversity of their movement. The young people began to accumulate real political power.

Some Republican politicians reversed some of their longheld positions on gun rights legislation. Florida governor Rick Scott and senator Marco Rubio indicated support for raising the age for gun purchases and universal background checks.

Within ten days of the shooting, companies across the country, like Delta Air Lines, withdrew their support for the NRA, and Dick's Sporting Goods halted all sales of assault weapons, largely because of the relentless pressure of the students.

The road ahead to enact change at the state and federal level is long, and disappointment will be inevitable for these students who, just days after the shooting, witnessed the Florida legislature refuse to even consider an assault-weapons ban. But there is no indication that the students are backing down; most recently they organized a nationwide youth voter registration drive in the summer of 2018, traveling via bus to cities across the country.

Many throughout the country have expressed surprise at both the aggressive student response and its effectiveness. But we shouldn't be surprised. These students are only the most recent proof that our country's history is the story of young people driving political progress.

If we are serious about ensuring that young people in this current generation propel us forward to a better democracy, we all need to live political journeys. We also need to enact structural reforms that will better ensure that all young people, irrespective of their background, are able to participate, and lead, in our current politics.

YOUNG PEOPLE AT THE CENTER

As we've seen, it is challenging to be hopeful in our current political moment. Our democracy has become a seemingly never-ending display of inaction, corruption, and name-calling from our elected officials. Political, social, and economic inequality is running rampant, and at historically unprecedented rates. We are incapable of talking to people who do not agree with us.

Politics sucks.

Seemingly, at every moment, another tragic issue defines the headlines. One week, our government is separating child immigrants from their parents. Another week, our politicians are slinging insults at each other rather than governing. And then we'll witness another police shooting, providing unabated evidence of the racial inequities that bedevil our current society.

The barrage of depressing headlines can cause hope for a better future to dissipate. Logically, it makes sense to stop paying attention to politics. And it makes sense to wonder if the center can still hold in our democracy.

The response by the Parkland students, however, demonstrates that hope still does exist. Rather than toiling in a democratic despair, we can all lead political lives. The response to our political moment cannot be to turn away. Rather, the response needs to be to turn to our young people.

There are two critical lessons to draw from the ongoing student response to the Parkland shooting and how these young activists were able to bring attention to an issue the government has been paralyzed to do anything about.

The first is that young people can be legitimate political actors. Young people can change the contours of the debate without needing to wait their turn. Indeed, especially in our current moment, we can no longer afford for young people to wait their turn.

In the week following the shooting, CNN hosted a town hall meeting in which the Stoneman Douglas students had the opportunity to engage with politicians and NRA officials over the issue of gun-law reform. In one particularly poignant moment, high school junior Cameron Kasky confronted U.S. Senator Marco Rubio.

Standing just five feet away from him, Kasky asked a question that went to the heart of the matter: "So, Senator Rubio, can you tell me right now that you will not accept a single donation from the NRA in the future?"

Rubio was flustered. He paused. And then he gave a typically evasive political response: "The answer to the question is that people buy into my agenda. And I do support the Second Amendment."

It was a patently absurd answer.

After some back-and-forth, Kasky asked an even more pointed question: "In the name of seventeen people, you cannot ask the NRA to keep their money out of your campaign?"

Another typical politician answer ensued: "I think in the name of seventeen people, I can pledge to you that I will support any law that will prevent a killer like this."

Rubio defended his position.

But Kasky did not back down: "So you're going to keep taking money from the NRA? All right, I get it."

Most adults in that situation would have been more respectful or more delicate in their questioning of a U.S. senator. Kasky didn't feel the need to bite his tongue. He and Rubio engaged in real political combat: his passion and conviction against a senator whose entire career has been defined by caution. In that moment, they were equals.

Watching the debate, I was moved. In some ways, I was seeing democracy at its best: a seventeen-year-old was publicly confronting a prominent politician. Rubio was clearly unfamiliar with this type of youth activism.

I often meet people who do not believe students are legitimate political actors. They think that the students need to wait their turn. They think students don't have enough experience, or knowledge, or maturity, or (insert quality here) to responsibly participate.

But as Emma Gonzalez, a seventeen-year-old from Parkland, said in the days after the shooting, "[People say] that us kids don't know what we're talking about, that we're too young to understand how the government works. We call BS."

"We call BS" became a rallying cry for the movement.

On March 14, the students held a National Walkout Day. Students across the country left their classrooms and rallied in the front of their school buildings demanding gun reform. Less than two weeks later, the national March for our Lives rallied in all fifty states, including the main rally in Washington, D.C. Across the country, millions of students came out. This was not just a few students railing against guns. This was a movement.

This type of youth activism is not just inspiring. It is not just impressive. It is completely necessary. We need young people to become active political citizens now. Older Americans are handing the next generation a democracy that is at a historic risk of failing.

It is not young people who have created an economy that no longer works for everyone. It is not young people unable to govern or compromise or legislate. It is not young people who are historically polarized and unable to talk to those who disagree with them.

But it is young people who can solve these problems. The idealism of young people, coupled with their powerful and real personal lived experiences, is a necessary antidote to our troubled political times. The challenge is to ensure that every young person in this country has their voices elevated and that they experience the same opportunities to participate in our civic debates as these students from Parkland.

And that leads us to the second critical lesson we can learn from the Stoneman Douglas students: we must acknowledge the inequitable nature of youth activism.

If we believe that we need the unique idealism of young people to repair our democracy, then we also must ensure that every single young person in this country is prepared to carry out a political journey. And that's not currently the case. Political activism, like everything else in this country, is increasingly unequal. We do not teach every young person to participate, and we do not equitably elevate their voices when they do engage.

It does not diminish the efforts of the students to acknowledge that Stoneman Douglas is an upper-middle-class majority-white school. The students have been prepared to hold power through their classes and an environment that has continually told them that their voices do matter. Census data shows that the median household income in the city is just over $128,000 and 84 percent is white, compared with less than $53,000 for the rest of Broward County, which is 63 percent white. Given the racial and economic oppression that has defined American history, the fact that these students accumulated power so quickly is not happenstance. Instead, this power accumulation is how American democracy has too often worked.

In her speech just days after the shooting, Emma Gonzalez explicitly thanked her AP government teacher, Jeffrey Foster, "for teaching us everything we learned. I could not have written that speech without you." Emma had a civics teacher that prepared her for the political journey of expertise, persuasion, and relentlessness. These students were primed to engage.

One of the other Parkland students noted that writing a fifty-page AP paper on gun control had enabled her to make her case to media outlets in the days after the shooting. Many of the students organizing the rally knew each other from a theater program, which had helped to give them the confidence to be on the national stage.

The fact that these more affluent students almost instantaneously gained political power is not a coincidence. Rather, the reality is that these young people were prepared for their role in the movement. Not all students feel so equipped to become activists. Not every student in the country has been given the same opportunities to develop the skills and acumen to organize.

This reality mirrors society at large. Political inequality has become a new normal that perpetuates the social and economic inequality worsening throughout the country. A 2004 report conducted by the American Political Science Association noted that "Citizens with low or moderate incomes speak with a whisper that is lost on the ears of inattentive government, while the advantaged roar with the clarity and consistency that policymakers readily heed." Wealthier citizens, and young people who come from more affluent backgrounds, have more power, and are more apt to engage fluently in power, than lower-income individuals. The same truth holds for racial demographics—white citizens have greater opportunities to influence government and public policy than people of color.

This political inequality starts in the classroom with how we teach our young people to engage politically. Despite the fact that lower-income and black teens are more than five times as likely to be killed from gun violence than their white counterparts, more affluent young white people are disproportionately primed to make this movement a national one.

A civic engagement gap has manifested in our schools: when compared with average socioeconomic status (SES) schools, low-income students are half as likely to study how laws are made, and they are 30 percent less likely to report having experiences with debates or panel discussions in social studies classes. Richer students are receiving more opportunities to become active than others.

But this isn't the whole story. The fact that these students were immediately elevated in the national media speaks to broader truths in the country. To say that low-income and young people of color do not receive equitable opportunities to learn the same civic knowledge and skills as their more affluent and white counterparts is not to say that they have not been organizing. In recent times, some of the most effective organizing has occurred in urban communities of color.

The responses to the spate of police shootings across the country have almost always been brought to the forefront by young people. Indisputably, young people who have been organizing in racial justice movements—as part of the #BlackLivesMatter movement or in protests against funding cuts in Chicago, Boston, and other urban districts nationwide—have not received the same amount of attention as the predominantly white Parkland students.

Harvard professor Meira Levinson, an expert on the civic empowerment gap, notes that we often elevate stories of white, more affluent students because most people in power can see themselves in these young people. Attempting to explain this racial phenomenon, she notes, "The people in power, including journalists and academics, tend to see young people like those in Parkland as being our kids and as representing nationwide concerns as opposed to kids protesting in Chicago, Philadelphia, New York."

The Stoneman Douglas young people recognized the importance of ensuring that their activism efforts were demographically intersectional, elevating other students who have not received the same amount of attention. In the weeks following the shooting in Parkland, many of the students visited youth activists in Chicago, who had been pushing for gun reform for years without receiving much media attention.

After meeting with the Chicago students, Emma Gonzalez noted the discrepancies in their activism efforts: "Those who face gun violence on a level that we have only just glimpsed from our gated communities have never had their voices heard in their entire lives the way that we have in these few weeks alone," she stated. "The platform us Parkland students have established is to be shared with every person, black or white, gay or straight, religious or not, who has experienced gun violence, and hand in hand, side by side, we will make this change together."

The reality that there are inequities of opportunity and representation in youth activism takes nothing away from the efficacy of the efforts of the Parkland kids. More than that, it demonstrates the extent to which we need to ensure that all young people can organize, use their voices, and take action on issues they care about, like the Stoneman Douglas students themselves have pledged.

And it becomes incumbent on society to ensure that we

elevate the political journeys of all young people—not just those that look like us, have access to copious amounts of money, or agree with us. We have a particular need to elevate the voices of those young people who have been most systematically targeted and marginalized in our society for decades upon decades: young people of color who come from lower-income backgrounds.

Imagine if all young people could organize politically in the same way. Imagine if we uplifted the voices of all young people. This activism, and this storytelling, is what our country desperately needs. All we have to do is to look at how effective the Stoneman Douglas students have been so quickly. They have succeeded in ways that the gun control movement could not for years before.

But in order for us to do this, and to inspire the youth of today to embrace living a political life, we are going to have to enact key reforms to ensure youth participation and protect the future of our democracy.

TIME FOR A (YOUTH-FOCUSED) CHANGE

Especially in the midst of an unprecedented political decline in the values of our democracy, young people taking action is not necessarily sufficient on its own. In order for those political journeys to happen effectively, we need to enact certain reforms to our democracy.

There are many potential changes that would create a more equitable and effective democracy in which all voices are represented in our government: better voting laws to ensure all individuals can vote, less gerrymandering and splitting up congressional districts to ensure certain parties remain in power, less money in politics to rig the game. Much has been written about these reforms. In keeping with the theme of elevating youth voices in politics, I argue for three specific but fundamental transformations we can make to help lift up young people as real and legitimate political players. These structural changes would ensure that more young people are able to live a political life.

1. ENSURE SCHOOLS PROMOTE DEMOCRACY

Generation Citizen works to educate young people to become active citizens through promoting civics education in the classroom. So, obviously, I'm going to be in favor of more civics education for young people. We need to make sure that an equitable, effective, and holistic civics education is available to all students. It would help us ensure that more young people are able to participate in our political process, just like the students we saw come out of Parkland.

At the same time, of course, a single civics class is not enough. A more comprehensive solution to ensuring that all young people have the potential to become active political citizens requires a revamped vision of the entire purpose of schools.

Currently, schools have become overly focused on preparing students for college and careers, with an extreme and misguided emphasis on high-stakes standardized testing. This obsession with testing leaves students inadequately prepared to participate in democracy.

The historic and ultimate mission of public schools is to educate the next generation of citizens to participate in and lead our democracy. That is, after all, why our founders created free public schools: to ensure that citizens would be capable of self-governance, from generation to generation.

We have not actualized that rhetoric and vision in our schools. Instead, schools today generally focus on subjects that have little relationship to one another. Content is emphasized over skills. Individual success over the collective well-being.

This starts with how we teach classes. Science, which, by its nature, involves observation, investigation, evidence, and application, is often taught in isolation from other subjects and in seats, rather than through exploration, experimentation, and evidence. The study of history too often involves reading brief paragraphs in a textbook; students aren't taught the complex history of their democracy.

A focus on rote learning, a staple of the American educational system, will not lead to the kind of citizenry necessary to maintain a democracy. Nor will an overemphasis on standardized tests lead to practiced real-life engagement in conflict resolution, research, and other activities that require critical thinking.

It is ineffective to teach civics in a public educational system that forces young people to demonstrate their abilities through standardized tests. Such a rigid intellectual climate is at odds with the democratic process and contrary to how many of the originators of the public school system envisioned the institution's role. While the Founders wanted to ensure that our democracy could continue to function through an informed citizenry, these visions were more words on paper than actual practices.

We need to articulate a more inspiring, citizen-centric vision to our public schools. We can, and must, reimagine schools as laboratories of democracy, enlisting young people as collaborators with educators and local community members to construct the better democracy that our country both needs and deserves. Rather than exhorting young people to understand a staid conceptualization that reduces their own agency in the ever-changing American narrative, there is an opportunity for schools to engage our young people as legitimate political actors.

We can transform schools into crucibles of democracy by enabling them to center education in the communities in which they are located, construct classes that are relevant to students' lives, and create a holistic democratic school culture.

This new vision of our schools begins with a greater respect for the local community in which schools are situated. Students need to understand that the community is a place where citizens make their wants and needs known and work together to solve communal challenges. Community members need to see the success of young people as relevant to the success of the community. Elected officials can learn to recognize students as purveyors of important local civic knowledge, capable of informing the most complex policy debates. Young people then have a real place in the community's discourse and action.

As an example, GC students in New York City recently lobbied the city to build memorials dedicated to African American abolitionists. The students studied historical movements, noted the lack of representation in monuments throughout the city, and met with the mayor's office to plot next steps. An education that focused on Action Civics allowed them to experience citizenship in their community while also studying the history of the abolitionist movement.

As a result, the students were excited. Education and democracy were not abstract. They were real concepts they were helping to mold, shape, and change.

This focus on the community also allows classes to become relevant and intersectional. Math transforms into a meaningful subject as students analyze traffic patterns and determine the ramifications of the local tax bond structure. English class involves analyzing articles in the local paper and learning persuasive communication skills through debating the merits of local policy.

Beyond classes, the school itself can fully embrace the community by becoming a place where students cocreate a culture that invites and nurtures their participation and that reflects the principles of democracy. In this type of school, students find meaning in education and become the producers and creators a democracy requires.

Too often, in our current day and age, schools and democracy are seen as boring and conventional, only telling young people what to do rather than inviting them in and listening to their concerns. By transforming schools into laboratories of democracy, and seeing students as real political actors, we can make school relevant, and even fun. And we can ensure that our education system returns to a focus that has oft been articulated but never totally reached: a public institution that molds and cultivates the next generation of citizens.

We need to bring civics back. Not just as a class in schools, but as the entire organizing principle into how our education system is structured.

2. LOWER THE VOTING AGE TO SIXTEEN

More and better comprehensive civics education is necessary. So is giving young people real ways to participate in the political process, starting now.

As we've discussed, the United States lowered the voting age to eighteen from twenty-one in 1971 after a decades-long fight to extend suffrage. The final, enduring argument was that if our young people were old enough to go off to battle, they should be able to vote for the elected representatives who were making the decision to go to war. The fight was led by young people.

New times call for new arguments—and a lower voting age.

Right now, with a democracy that is indisputably not working for young people, we need to offer young people the opportunity to fix our politics by lowering the voting age.

This idea almost immediately draws eye rolls when I first bring it up.

"Sixteen-year-olds? Voting? Give me a break. They can barely tie their shoes. And they're eating Tide pods. Why would we let them vote?" I hear versions of this argument whenever I trot out this idea from, well, older voters.

"In any case, they'd be liberal anyway. This is just a reform to create more Democrats," is another rebuttal I often hear.

This gut-instinct responses are logical, to an extent. Sixteen can seem young.

But when you witness the activism of the young people in Parkland, and acknowledge the fact that every single time we see change in this country, young people are at the forefront, you begin to see that sixteen-year-olds can be knowledgeable and effective. Almost every young person profiled in this book began his or her political activism before he or she turned eighteen.

Additionally, on the aggregate, young people are registering as independents much more than they are becoming Democrats and Republicans. This is not about creating more liberal voters. It's about enabling and educating more informed voters, period.

We need to overcome our paternalistic instincts that tell us these young people are too immature to have informed political opinions. On the contrary, they might be the best hope for us to improve our democracy.

Chiefly and crucially, if we were to lower the voting age to sixteen, schools would be incentivized to teach more and better civics education. If students could vote for local officials while they were still in school, the relevancy of civics classes would immediately be apparent. Democracy, as taught, would no longer be abstract, but rather a concrete idea in which students could immediately put their knowledge into practice. We don't learn to drive without being able to practice. Similarly, teaching civics while sixteen- and seventeen-year olds could vote would allow them to participate in our democracy in real time.

This idea is not new, and, like so many effective democratic reforms, it is not just American. Other countries, from Finland and Scotland to Argentina and Ecuador, already allow sixteen-year-olds to vote, and they see higher rates of participation among their youngest populations than we do in the United States. Additionally, numerous cities across the country, including Takoma Park and Hyattsville, Maryland, currently permit sixteen-year-olds to vote in local elections. This is not a radical reform. Rather, it is a necessary one given the state of our current democracy.

Voting Is a Habit—Start It Young

One of the arguments made against lowering the voting age is that young people don't currently vote at high levels. Why should we lower the voting age if eighteen-years-olds aren't even voting?

In reality, eighteen is a pretty terrible age to start enabling young people to go to the polls. Most young people are either in college or in the workforce for the first time; they are not thinking about their first election. Additionally, if young people are in college, outside of their home community or state, the laws about voter registration can be arcane and challenging to follow. At times, states have implemented explicit regulations to discourage young people from voting: some states have passed laws requiring eighteen-year-olds to register and vote in their home districts, even when they are off at college.

The idea that eighteen is not the ideal age to start the voting process is not just anecdotal. The overall voting rate has decreased steadily since the age was lowered in 1971, suggesting that voters are missing their first election and then unfortunately are establishing missing elections as a habit.

Allowing sixteen-year-olds to vote would ensure that young people are able to vote while they are still in school and living in their communities. Young people are more likely to vote in a more stable environment, in a community they have always known as home. Schools and parents alike could work to ensure that young people are aware of upcoming elections, educated on the issues, and are actually showing up and participating.

This is not just a theoretical argument. Statistics from countries and communities that have lowered the voting age indicate that sixteen-year-olds are far more likely to vote than eighteen-year-olds. In Takoma Park, Maryland, in the 2013 election (the first in which sixteen-year-olds could vote), the turnout rate for registered sixteen- and seventeen-year-olds far exceeded any other demographic.

Evidence from Europe is also positive. Austria lowered its voting age to sixteen for all of the country's elections in 2008, and turnout among that age group has been higher than for older first-time voters. In the 2011 local elections in Norway, twenty-one municipalities used a voting age of sixteen as a trial and found that turnout was also much higher than turnout among older first-time voters.

Just like any habit, individuals are more likely to continue the practice if they start it young. When eighteen-year-olds do not vote in their first election, because they are preoccupied with college or the workforce, they are significantly less likely to vote in subsequent elections.

By the same token, if young people do vote in their first election, they are significantly more likely to vote in all subsequent elections. Research indicates that voting in one election can increase the probability that a voter will participate in the next election by 50 percent.

It is this argument that serves as a rebuttal to the notion that lowering the voting age is a partisan campaign. All Americans should want a democracy in which more people participate—it will lead to more representative policies. Desiring a more robust, representative democracy with more holistic participation, especially in local elections, is not a partisan sentiment—it is an American one.

We are currently witnessing historically low voting rates across the country, especially in local elections (with an average rate hovering around 25 percent turnout). Lowering the voting age to sixteen would be an innovative, proven way to begin to rebuild an engaged electorate.

Young People Have the Capacity to Make Informed Political Decisions

Core to any argument against lowering the voting age is the myth that sixteen-year-olds do not have the political acumen to make informed decisions.

"You trust them with our country's future? I barely trust them to take out the trash" some parents have told me.

"They'll just follow their parents' decisions anyway: they won't make their own informed choices" goes another oft-heard argument.

The statistics don't back this up. Using the development of the brain's frontal cortex as a barometer, sixteen-year-olds have the same ability to process information and make decisions as twenty-one-year-olds. Additionally, research demonstrates that sixteen-year-olds possess the same level of civic knowledge as older young adults, and they also demonstrate equal levels of self-reported political skill and political efficacy of older adults.

Yes, there will inevitably be some young voters who go to the ballot box uninformed or who simply vote the way that others tell them to. But how is that reality different from regular voters? Just as there may be uninformed young voters, there are uninformed older voters.

Sixteen-year-olds do have the ability to make smart decisions. We just need to let them show up.

Our Youth Deserve the Right to Vote

Today, a sixteen-year-old can get a job, work hours without significant restrictions, pay taxes, and get behind the wheel of a car without any adult supervision. They deserve the right to have a say in the political issues that affect them on an everyday basis. Allowing them to work and pay taxes without an actual vote is equivalent to taxation without representation.

Additionally, young people feel challenges in their community the most acutely. They are directly impacted by changes in education funding, school board decisions, jobs initiatives, police programs, and public works projects. And, like the students in Parkland realized, gun violence affects our nation's schools, and young people, in disproportional and tragic ways.

Our tendency to look to the political issues of the moment, rather than the foundational challenges that face our future democracy, is an abdication of our responsibility to take care of our young people. We, as adults, have clearly not solved or made substantial progress on so many issues that affect our youngest generations. We should enlist young people as equals to help us solve our problems.

We need innovative ideas to spur political participation. Young people have the ability and acumen to make informed political decisions. And they deserve the right to have a say in issues that affect them. Lowering the voting age is not a ridiculous idea. It's a commonsense reform whose time is rapidly coming.

If we are serious about speaking truth to power and acknowledging the reality that young people always lead us forward, we need to lower the voting age to sixteen.

3. PUT EQUITY AT THE FOREFRONT

We need to ensure that we are creating a democracy that increasingly places equity at the forefront. And specifically, racial equity. Young people can help achieve this goal of ensuring that every single young person, irrespective of their background, can have a real voice and say in our country's future.

In our current lexicon, diversity, equity, and inclusion work has become increasingly important, with reason. But oftentimes, we do not actually dig into the definition of those three terms.

Diversity is quite literally the presence of difference within a given setting. You can have a diversity of opinions, a diversity of clothing brands in a closet, or a diversity of experiences on a team.

Inclusion refers to the diversity actually feeling integrated, valued, and leveraged within a given setting. In a team context, this means that the diversity of experiences, culture, and opinions is actually valued, rather than solely being present.

Equity is the process that ensures that everyone has access to the same opportunities. This is not equality, in which everyone literally has the same material goods. Rather, equity recognizes that inherent advantages and barriers are already in place that either promote or impede success. In our democracy's case, being white has led to certain ingrained advantages, especially because of the manner in which our very country was created. Recognizing the unequal starting place that our democracy has created, equity works to correct the imbalance.

In a new twenty-first-century democracy, the goal of equity must be front and center in any effort. We must recognize that the playing field is fundamentally unbalanced. When I started Generation Citizen, I did everything I could to ensure the organization succeeded. I had my fair share of challenges. But I also started with an inherent advantage—I was a white male with an Ivy League degree. Many of our original supporters were Brown

University alumni, and I had instant credibility when I walked into certain rooms because of my appearance and my pedigrees.

That intrinsically is not equitable. Thus, a principle goal of any democratic practice needs to be ensuring that diverse matters are included and valued toward an end goal of equity. This reality stems from two related truths.

First, our democracy continues to value certain voices over others. This is the result of being a country founded by white men that has labored under a patriarchal social system.

And second, our democracy looks, and will continue to look, a lot different than it ever has. In 2014, children of color became the new majority in the United States' public schools. Demographers predict that whites will make up less than half of the country's population by 2044, if not before. We'd be wise to put racial equity front and center now—not as a by-product of democracy, but a component of the process absolutely necessary in the ideal's next iteration.

LISTEN TO OUR YOUNG PEOPLE

As we focus on ways that young people can take their own political journeys, we need to put reforms in place that encourage and sustain active and equitable youth voices. We've seen throughout this book that young people have always been at the forefront of change in this country. To reach a better political future, young people need to lead us. But there are structural changes we can enact to help young people lead.

Lowering the voting age, ensuring schools are harbingers of democracy, and putting equity at the forefront are three critical ways that we can ensure that every young person can lead his or her own powerful political journey.

Politics doesn't have to suck. Our democracy can still work.

But only if we put young people at the center. And we help them get there.

16

A MANIFESTO FOR A NEW DEMOCRACY

Living Our Full Political Lives

This book has attempted to make two fundamental arguments. First, even in the midst of unprecedented political unrest, democracy can still work. A political system in which people are front and center, making decisions about their governance, is an idealistic but realistic concept. Democracy will never be perfect, but we can always seek to make it more perfect. We *need* to seek to make it more perfect.

And second, in order for democracy to work, young people must be at the forefront of change. They must become political. The more hopeless and entrenched our politics become, the more important it is for young people to engage in the process. Issue after issue is improved when young people deploy the unique but critical mixture of idealism and indignation it takes to become powerful. This change never happens overnight—failures and roadblocks are commonplace. But when young people live political lives, every single day, positive change always occurs.

We have made the case that democracy is a vibrant, living concept. It is not stagnant or certain. Rather, democracy is an ideal, molded and improved upon by citizens, constantly and always. To that end, the democracy we encounter at the onset of the twenty-first century is very distinctive from the one our founders envisioned almost 250 years ago.

The motley crew of wig-bearing colonists had some good, enduring ideas. But they were operating in a framework in which the only citizens with power were white male landowners (indeed, the Founders themselves were all white male landowners). Not so in our country today. And it's worth taking that difference into account as we imagine the future of our country's democracy.

Many of the Founders' original ideas remain relevant in our current context. The idea that every American has certain unalienable rights, and should have the opportunity for life, liberty, and the pursuit of happiness, is profound. So are the structures that emphasize the well-being of society over the power of an individual. This crucial democratic element stemmed from their original push against the monarchal dictatorial rule that had defined their previous lives in Great Britain, toward a more collective framework of governance, in which citizens reigned supreme.

But as much as our country's Founders trusted we, the people, and had foresight in molding a framework that has outlasted so many changes in society, they could not have been prescient about the unique challenges that confront our democracy today. They could not have predicted the advent of social media, which does democratize citizens' voices, but which also can cause individuals to segment their perspectives into silos. They could not have predicted the unprecedented diversity that would come to define this country's very fabric, with individuals hailing from every corner of the globe. They could not have predicted the growing and at times unabated economic and political inequality that threatens the ability to coexist in our society.

These unforeseen changes mean that we need a new framework for democracy. A new narrative. Because, for too many people, all these changes mean that the political process at usual is not working.

Walk into a classroom of high school students in the Bronx, or Oakland, or Oklahoma City. Tell them that their lives will be okay if only they participate in a political process that has continually and systematically oppressed them since the day they were born.

They will call out BS. As they should.

The reason that their peers have been shot is not because they are not participating in the political process. The reason their parents cannot obtain meaningful employment is not because they are not participating in the political process. The reason that their relatives are at risk of deportation or have already been deported is not because they are not participating in the political process.

Indeed, the United States of America, as a country built upon ideas rather than identities, has always oppressed some part of our population. Our nineteenth-century economy was predicated on enslaving an entire race of people. Women only won the right to vote at the beginning of the twentieth century.

Gay marriage only became legal in 2013. Systematic racial and gender oppression has defined our democracy since our very inception. Citizens have forced our country's arc to bend toward justice. But this bend doesn't happen easily. And it's difficult to solve these legacy challenges solely through political participation.

We do need to live our political journeys. Pushing the system to a more just equilibrium through gaining power is a critical part of building a better democracy. But we also need to think about a new manifesto for our democracy—a manifesto that describes the type of democracy we want to construct. We need one, through young people taking the lead, that is responsive to the needs of all people, rather than just a select few.

My ideas stem from the young people I have met throughout a decade of this work. These young people have helped to inform my belief in the promise of democracy. So as we live our political lives, here are some principles that we should build toward. Think of it as our manifesto for a new, twenty-first-century democracy. And think of this manifesto, as our democracy itself, as evolving. These ideas are only mine and will surely be strengthened when other people, especially young people, add to them.

1. THE MORE PERFECT UNION WILL NEVER BECOME PERFECT

The common strand that connects all of the stories presented by young people throughout this book is a constant push for more equality for every individual in our democracy. A more just immigration system. A more responsive criminal justice system. A more equitable labor force devoid of gender discrimination. In each of these stories, young people have played an instrumental role in pushing toward progress. And in each of these stories, there is more work to do.

Accepting and embracing the reality that the work will never end is both heartening and frustrating. But it is necessary.

Let's examine the maxim on which our very democracy is predicated: "We hold these truths to be self-evident, that all Men are created equal, that they are endowed by their Creator with certain unalienable Rights, that among these are Life, Liberty, and the Pursuit of Happiness."

The fact that the Founders said that "all Men" deserve these rights is proof itself of our never-ending, insurmountable push toward progress in its own right: the most foundational, inspirational premise of our democracy was completely biased from the start.

The road to ensuring that all people are created equal still holds promise. All of the youth-led activism we observed in this book works toward this premise: that we should all have the same opportunity to succeed. That premise is unbelievably powerful—that no matter where we are from, what we believe in, what we look like, or what we do, we are equal.

Right now, that idea sounds unbelievably utopian. In our rich-white-male-dominated society, the idea that all of us are equal might seem like an absurd premise. But it is a premise we should keep trying to reach.

And we will never, ever reach it.

That balance, of pushing for change while recognizing we'll never get where we want to go, is perhaps the most important, enduring idea of our democracy. It is an idea that holds true in every aspect of our lives.

The concept holds true in classrooms across this country.

Teachers prepare for their classes meticulously, writing out lessons plans, anticipating challenging students, crafting assessments. And inevitably, in every single class, something unexpected occurs. The class is not perfect. But the next day, teachers go to work again, trying to improve, getting closer to perfect.

We need to work toward perfection in our democracy, knowing it will never come. That might seem frustrating. But it can be motivational—we know we need to work every single day on our political journeys.

Langston Hughes's poem "Let America Be America Again" is perhaps the best way to illustrate the promise of a country we constantly yearn for but will never obtain:

O, let America be America again—
The land that never has been yet—
And yet must be—the land where every man is free.
The land that's mine—the poor man's, Indian's, Negro's, ME—
Who made America,
Whose sweat and blood, whose faith and pain,
Whose hand at the foundry, whose plow in the rain,
Must bring back our mighty dream again.

Sure, call me any ugly name you choose—
The steel of freedom does not stain.
From those who live like leeches on the people's lives,
We must take back our land again,
America!

O, yes,
I say it plain,

America never was America to me,
And yet I swear this oath—
America will be!

Our democracy has never been ideal. As Hughes says, the reality of the United States is of a country that has articulated the ideal of true equality, but one that has never met this lofty ideal. We can get closer to that mystic ideal. Only if we push.

2. GET POLITICAL EVERY SINGLE DAY

January 2 is always the busiest day of the year at the gym. Fresh off the holidays, and filled with New Year's resolutions, people everywhere decide they are going to make exercising a priority. The weight machines are crowded, there are lines for the treadmills, the locker rooms are packed. This is objectively a positive thing: exercising is good for you! We need more people engaged in this healthy behavior.

Some people do keep exercising. But a month later, inevitably, the gym is a lot more barren. The resolutions have not carried through.

Political engagement can sometimes feel like a lapsed resolution. After an election result we don't like, we act like it's January 2 at the gym, and we become more active. After Obama was elected in 2008, the right became animated. The Tea Party emerged, and Republicans took control of statehouse after statehouse across the country. They woke up after New Year's dedicated to the gym. Democrats, on the other hand, were relaxing, confident that our main man was in the White House. Democrats were already in shape. Democrats participated in historically low levels in the 2010 and 2014 midterm elections, and Republicans took control.

Similarly, after Trump was elected in 2016, the left has dedicated itself to becoming engaged like never before. We're back at the gym after a few years off. And to continue the metaphor, the Democrats are muscling up.

This contributes to the never-ending zigzag of history. One year, Republicans are incredibly active. The next year, Democrats have taken the mantle of activism. The engagement, however, on both sides does not sustain. We become active when we need to, and then we let former habits reemerge.

But if we want to have a healthy democracy, we need to go to the gym every day, not just after a period of ignoring our collective fitness.

All of the research demonstrates that the best way to live out resolutions is not to change behavior dramatically overnight. You can't go from not running to being a marathon runner—you need to gradually get into the practice.

Think about political engagement similarly. I'm not asking you to run for office tomorrow. I am asking you to make it a habit, just like exercising. Take steps to participate every single day.

You could start small: read the local paper every morning to keep apprised of local issues. Attend local town halls to learn about the issues affecting your community, and meet the neighbors taking action on the issues you care about.

And then, practice politics every day. This could be calling a local elected official to push for an issue. It could be chatting with a neighbor, or peer, or parent about an issue you care about and persuading him or her to adopt your position. It could be talking to someone you disagree with. It could be developing your expertise by reading newspapers and policy briefs.

Importantly, this engagement should not just occur around elections. And you cannot relax once your preferred candidates are in office. You need to get your daily exercise, regardless of the current state of your well-being.

We need to treat political engagement not just as something we practice only at election time, or every few years when our party's back is on the line. We should think about it every day of the year.

3. NONPARTISANSHIP IS OVERRATED

Democracy is about compromise and working past differences. But that does not mean that every opinion should be valued equally. Facts and basic decency still matter. Right now, there is a temptation to cry nonpartisanship as a plea for a bygone era that we pretend existed where we were all friends and collaborated all the time to move our democracy forward. But just like the Langston Hughes poem illustrates, that idealized version of the United States has never quite existed.

The challenge arises when we pretend that every perspective matters the same amount. If one citizen supported slavery, and one did not, does that mean that they should invoke nonpartisanship and aim for compromise? Perhaps only half of the country should be enslaved?

This argument is playing out with voting rights in this country right now. The objective of a democracy is that every citizen should have the opportunity to have their voices heard. Yet one party (Republicans) consistently attempts to restrict and constrain voting rights, while the other party (Democrats) consistently attempts to secure voting rights for all citizens. I don't care which party is trying to push reform—the fact of the matter is that expanding suffrage and ensuring that all citizens can participate is not a partisan issue. We cannot hide under the guise of nonpartisanship if one party is pushing for the restriction of participation in our very democracy.

Similarly, climate change is real. We don't need to have a debate over whether human behavior contributes to warming the environment: it does. The idea of an argument about whether climate change exists or not is a waste of time. Ninety-seven percent of scientists agree that it's real. Pretending to have a nonpartisan conversation based on that ratio is a lie.

It is worth having a political discussion on the types of reforms we put into place, and how much they will help ameliorate environmental conditions as opposed to adversely affecting current employment prospects. That is a nonpartisan debate.

This distinction is especially relevant for young people, who care less about party affiliation and the arbitrary policy perspectives that accompany formal membership and focus more on actual issues. Thus, as we engage in our political journeys, let's remain true to our values. Let's not pretend that nonpartisanship is a catchall solution to the problems of the day. Rather, let's adhere to our values and accept basic facts.

4. DEMOCRACY IS ABOUT PROCESS

We often cite specific outcomes when we talk about the problems in democracy. There is too much inequality. Not enough people have health care. Education is too unequal. The unemployment rate is too high. Why aren't our politicians doing anything about it?

But democracy itself is not about guaranteeing outcomes. A dictator could theoretically create more equitable conditions, provide better health care and education, and guarantee jobs. In some countries, this concept of a benevolent dictator does exist, and does actually obtain positive societal outcomes. (Rwanda under President Paul Kagame is an example.) But citizens would not be front and center. Democracy, on the other hand, is about guaranteeing that people can participate in the first place.

Fundamentally, democracy is a process—a citizen-centric process. The goal of a democracy is not to guarantee outcomes, but rather to ensure that people are front and center driving the process. In a democracy, the people are sovereign—the highest form of political authority. Power flows from the people to the leaders of government, who hold power only temporarily. It is not sufficient if a government guarantees basic rights for its people if citizens are not actively involved in the governance effort itself. Simultaneously, a government is not sufficiently listening to its citizens if it is not providing adequate basic social services and curbing economic inequality.

Thus, to improve democracy, we must focus on improving the process, with an end goal of robust citizen participation. A more robust and active citizenry will lead to more equitable and sustainable policies. A focus on process leads to better outcomes.

As an example of a focus on process over outcomes, we can look to the American health-care system. A debate has emerged as to whether a single-payer system would best provide health care to all. The argument, however, focuses on passing legislation and the actions of leaders. A focus instead on ensuring that all citizens are informed on the issue, and participate vigorously in the debate, would do more to advance the issue than a focus

on the opinions of elected officials and the movement of hypo-
thetical legislation.

A democracy in which citizens are not passive actors but
instead the most prominent actors will lead to the best and most
representative outcomes.

5. YOUNG PEOPLE MUST BE AT THE CENTER

This is the premise of this book. So it's not surprising that it
would be the finishing touch on our manifesto for democracy.
But it's worth repeating.

Whenever we see real change in this country, young people
are at the forefront. Every. Single. Time.

This book has tried to show, through history and the present
day, the extent to which that theory holds. It is not random that
progress occurs when young people become powerful and lead.
Rather, it is a truth, stemming from an idealism that pervades
the youth spirit that allows us to push for change when everyone
else thinks it is impossible.

Our country's very founding had young people at the center,
pushing back against the monarchical rule that had defined England and toward a more democratic future, with young people
at the helm.

Young people propelled the first-ever women's labor movement in Lowell in the mid-nineteenth century, pushing back
against a patriarchal society that had viewed and treated women
as solely pawns in factories.

Young people were instrumental in the civil rights movement: the first to sit in the back of the bus and the first to refuse
to get up from lunch counters in Greensboro, North Carolina.

Young people changed the very direction of the conservative

movement in this country, ensuring Ronald Reagan became president.

Young people have changed the terms of the immigration debate in this country, pushing for DREAMers to be seen as true Americans.

If we want to improve a democracy we see as faltering in today's tumultuous times, young people must be at the forefront.

The work won't be easy. We'll fail more times than we'll succeed. People will doubt our ability to succeed.

The journey, though, starts today. And it includes all of us.

Young people will be at the forefront of change. Take history's word for it. Our democracy's future depends on all of us starting our political journeys.

Let's get to it.

ACKNOWLEDGMENTS

Just as an effective democracy is dependent on the cumulative efforts of so many individuals, so is a book—or so I've continually learned throughout this entire process. I'm incredibly grateful to so many who helped me in my first foray into writing and the many hiccups as I tried to write that more perfect book, knowing that a perfect book will always be an elusive dream. I'm similarly thankful to all who have been part of the formation and growth of Generation Citizen. Both this book and the organization started purely as ideas and dreams, and they could not have become reality if so many did not believe in their importance and my idea to execute on them, perhaps more so than I believed in myself. A common theme throughout the Generation Citizen journey.

There are countless people to thank, and I'll be able to name only a few of them here. But know that every single person with whom I've come into contact during my life of democratic discovery has contributed to a better book and to a better organization. And in turn, I hope, to a better country.

The first note of thanks goes to all of the young people—those who I interviewed for this book, and those who Generation Citizen is lucky enough to work with on an everyday basis. I am not sure I am still privileged enough to consider myself young (I often say that I am not as young as I used to be). That said, there is nothing more inspiring than when I have the opportunity to engage with the generation that is actively building a better democracy. Talking with young people is a hell of a lot more inspiring than reading the daily political news and observing the horse race in action.

The opportunity to step into classrooms, talk to our students, hear their skepticism, their cynicism, their hopes, and their passion, and see this manifested into reality and true political change gives me energy and hope every single day. The GC students profiled in this book—Laila, A'Niya, Julian, Lexie, Carla—are wonderful exemplars of this dynamic. While the present of our democracy often seems dire, the opportunity to engage, and learn from, these young activists shows me that the future is a lot brighter than the present. A'Niya and Julian also helped to provide comments and thoughts on early drafts.

I'm also so grateful for all the youth activists and leaders I interviewed who are profiled in this book, and those who provided background. I am honored to help tell your stories. A special thank you to Themba Mzingwane: you have become a true friend, and your story inspires me every single day. I know you will be part of creating the new Zimbabwe you and your people do deserve.

While GC as an organization continues to grow, improve,

and hopefully flourish, taking our aims, goals, lessons, and achievements into a book was a journey in itself that I was not necessarily prepared for. I owe a huge amount of gratitude to Lauren LeBlanc, who met with me when this was all an idea, pushed my thinking and my writing, and edited draft upon draft upon draft. This book would not have occurred without Lauren's belief in the message and her ability to push me when I was tired of being pushed.

Dan Smetanka and the entire team at Counterpoint Press took a chance on me as a first-time author. Dan has spent countless hours talking me through the process of publishing, tightening this work, and calming my anxieties. Thank you for believing in this book. I am similarly appreciative of the rest of the team at Counterpoint for the incalculable edits, suggestions, and beautiful design work.

I wrote in this book about individuals receiving too much attention for change-making efforts and feel that the dynamic often occurs at Generation Citizen. I often receive too much of the credit for all the good work we've done. I wish I could thank every single person that has helped build the organization— know that I'm grateful. But to highlight a few: a huge thank-you to Anna Ninan, my cofounder. Without her belief in Generation Citizen, and her counsel at the beginning and now, the idea would have remained that. To Elizabeth Milligan, who helped to come up with this idea and got my hooked civcs education so long ago. To Molly Isenbarger—my first true partner at GC, whose wisdom and patience helped to propel us from a start-up to a real organization. To Sarah Andes, whom I consider a true cofounder at this point: GC would not be GC without your belief in what we do, and the values you bring to the table every day. To Josh Solomon, who is a true servant leader in the best sense of the phrase, and has been an indispensable part of our recent growth. To Caitlin Paul, who has been such a wonderful thought partner and is such a truly good person. To Molly Cohen, who pushes me in every single conversation I have with her and helped provide edits to early drafts of this book. And to all of the other organizational leaders: Andrew Wilkes, DeNora Getachew, Arielle Jennings, Tom Kerr-Vanderslice, Siobhan Brewer, Amy Curran, and Meredith Norris—you all make this organization work. And to every single person who has worked at GC—the belief that you all have in young people will make our democracy better.

We have been blessed with so many amazing supporters and a board of directors who believe in our mission and the power of young people. To all: thank you for believing in a better democracy. A special thank you to Mary Vascellaro, Lisa Issroff, and Kunal Modi, our successive board chairs, who have put up with me, pushed me, and made GC better. A special thanks also to David Flink, a board member and best friend who pushed me to think about this book when it was just an idea.

To Taylor: thank you for believing in me more than I believed in myself. For pushing me, every single day, to think about how to build that better democracy. You've made me a better person.

To Mom and Dad: when we moved abroad, I'm not sure how many times I told you that you had ruined my life. You know by now that is BS. I could not have asked for better and more supportive parents. You've taught me everything I know. You believed in me, and my voice, when I was young, and for that, this book is for you.

NOTES

1: A NEW POLITICS

17 **If you're like 90 percent of kids in this country, you're at a public school supported by taxpayer dollars:** Jack Jennings, "Proportion of U.S. Students in Private Schools Is 10 Percent and Declining," *HuffPost*, December 7, 2017, www.huffingtonpost.com/jack-jennings/proportion -of-us-students_b_2950948.html.

18 **Sometimes people even die from the flu because they cannot afford a $116 co-pay out of pocket:** Todd Unger, "Texas Teacher Dies after Opting Out of Tamiflu Because of Costly $116 Copay," *USA Today*, February 13, 2018.

2: DEMOCRACY IS US

30 *New York Times* columnist Thomas Friedman attempted to define my generation in an October 2007 column entitled "Generation Q": Thomas L. Friedman, "Generation Q," *New York Times*, October 10, 2007.

31 **Indeed, by a two-to-one margin, young people consider volunteering as a more effective way of finding change than participating in politics:** "Survey of Young Americans' Attitudes toward Politics and Public Service," Harvard Institute of Politics, April 29, 2015.

31 In the 2014 elections, 20 percent of eighteen- to thirty-year-olds voted—the lowest rate since the voting age was lowered to eighteen in 1971. Eighteen- to twenty-four-year-olds voted even less—at a 12 percent rate: "2014 Youth Turnout and Youth Registration Rates Lowest Ever Recorded; Changes Essential in 2016," CIRCLE, July 1, 2015, civicyouth.org/2014-youth-turnout-and-youth-registration-rates -lowest-ever-recorded-changes-essential-in-2016.

32 The reality is that a greater percentage of young people voted in the 1992 presidential election than in Obama's historic 2008 victory: Thom File, "Young-Adult Voting: An Analysis of Presidential Elections, 1964–2012," *Current Population Survey Reports*, P20-572. U.S. Census Bureau, Washington, D.C., 2013.

33 a 2014 study by the Brookings Institution found that 64 percent of millennials assert that it is a priority for them to make the world a better place: Morley Winograd and Michael Hais, "How Millennials Could Upend Wall Street and Corporate America," Brookings Institution, May 28, 2014, www.brookings.edu/research/how -millennials-could-upend-wall-street-and-corporate-america.

34 Despite living in a democracy, our government actively makes it more challenging for people to vote: German Lopez, "7 Specific Ways States Made It Harder for Americans to Vote in 2016," *Vox*, November 07, 2016, www.vox.com/policy-and-politics/2016/11/7/13545718 /voter-suppression-early-voting-2016.

35 In 2011, 25 percent of American millennials born in the 1980s said they did not believe democracy can work: Gwynn Guilford, "Harvard Research Suggests That an Entire Global Generation Has Lost Faith in Democracy," *Quartz*, November 30, 2016, qz.com/848031/harvard -research-suggests-that-an-entire-global-generation-has-lost-faith-in -democracy.

36 In 2010, two years after the Great Recession, the percentage of optimistic Americans fell dramatically, with only 35 percent believing that the government could help the economy show signs of promise: Jodie T. Allen, "How a Different America Responded to the Great Depression," Pew Research Center, December 14, 2010, www.pewresearch.org/2010/12/14 /how-a-different-america-responded-to-the-great-depression.

36 Today, only 19 percent of Americans say they can trust the government in Washington to do what is right and beneficial for all citizens: Uri Friedman, "Trust Is Collapsing in America," *The Atlantic*, January 21,

2018, www.theatlantic.com/international/archive/2018/01/trust-trump -america-world/550964.

37 In current times, in all elections, more than half of the young voting population is not showing up: File, "Young-Adult Voting."

37 Compared to developed democracies, the United States now ranks twenty-eighth out of thirty-five democracies in voter turnout: Drew DeSilver, "U.S. Trails Most Developed Countries in Voter Turnout," Pew Research Center, May 21, 2018, www.pewresearch.org/fact-tank /2018/05/21/u-s-voter-turnout-trails-most-developed-countries.

37 The average median age of a voter across all the cities in the study was fifty-seven years old: Phil Keisling, "Our Ever-Older Electorate and What It Means for Democracy," *Governing*, February 8, 2017, www .governing.com/columns/smart-mgmt/col-aging-electorate-voting -participation-democracy.html.

38 In a similar vein, a recent study indicated that 77 percent of citizens consider their political rivals to be less evolved humans than members of their own party: "The Primeval Tribalism of American Politics," *The Economist*, May 24, 2018, www.economist.com/united-states /2018/05/24/the-primeval-tribalism-of-american-politics.

38 In 1960, 5 percent of Republicans would be displeased if their child married a Democrat, and 4 percent of Democrats would be unhappy if their child married a Republican: Kevin Enochs, "In US, 'Interpolitical' Marriage Increasingly Frowned Upon," *VOA*, February 3, 2017, www .voanews.com/a/mixed-political-marriages-an-issue-on-rise/3705468 .html.

3: GENERATION CITIZEN

45 I was shocked that the international community allowed eight hundred thousand innocent civilians to die in less than ninety days: Rory Carroll, "US Chose to Ignore Rwandan Genocide," *The Guardian*, March 31, 2004, www.theguardian.com/world/2004/mar/31/usa.rwanda.

45 Similarly, during the first year of his presidency, President Bush wrote "Not on my watch" in the margins of a report describing the United States' lack of response to Rwanda: Associated Press, "Bush Honors Victims of Rwanda's Genocide," NBCNews.com, February 19, 2008, www.nbcnews.com/id/23230719/ns/world_news-africa/t/bush-honors -victims-rwandas-genocide.

46 We continued chanting until we were arrested for civil disobedience and

taken to the Anacostia prison. We received national press attention—this was the cause of the day: Megan Zingarelli, "18 Students Arrested in Darfur Protest at White House," CNN, April 13, 2008, www.cnn.com/2008/POLITICS/04/13/darfur.protest/index.html.

47 Due primarily to the efforts of young people across the country, the divestment movement rapidly gained traction, becoming the largest and fastest-moving divestiture campaign since the move to divest from South African companies during apartheid in the 1980s: Holly Hubbard Preston, "Sudan Divestment Campaigns Gain Momentum," *New York Times*, May 23, 2008, www.nytimes.com/2008/05/23/your-money/23iht-mdivest.1.13157602.html.

51 But this time, I was at a ceremony with the governor of Rhode Island, who was signing into law an unanimously passed piece of legislation that required the state to divest its holdings from companies doing business in Sudan—one of the first states in the country to do so: "Rhode Island Governor Signs Sudan Divestment Bill," *Sudan Tribune*, July 27, 2007, www.sudantribune.com/spip.php?article23025.

5: THE (REAL) POLITICAL JOURNEY

81 "We zig and zag, and sometimes we move in ways that some people think is forward and others think is moving back, and that's okay": Barack Obama, "Statement by the President," The White House Office of the Press Secretary, November 9, 2016, obamawhitehouse.archives.gov/the-press-office/2016/11/09/statement-president.

83 Approximately 12 percent of the American population is African American, but they make up 38 percent of prison inmates, largely because of the unjust way we treat mandatory minimum sentencing for minor crimes: Ellen A. Donnelly, "Racial Disparity Reform: Racial Inequality and Policy Responses in US National Politics," *Journal of Crime and Justice* 40, no. 4 (December 2016): 462–477, doi.org/10.1080/07356 48x.2016.1176950.

83 The unemployment rate for African Americans is more than double what it is for the rest of the country, and wage levels are much lower: P. R. Lockhart, "The Black Unemployment Rate Just Hit a Record Low, but There's a Catch," *Vox*, June 1, 2018, www.vox.com/policy-and-politics/2018/6/1/17417762/black-unemployment-rate-record-low-may-jobs-report.

91 "For a moment, I'd believed that the trip would change not only my life, but my family's life as well": Anthony Mendez, "The White House Made Me a Poster Child for Beating the Odds. Then I Dropped out of College," Vox, May 31, 2016, www.vox.com/2016/5/31/11785864 /reach-higher-initiative.

6: A POLITICAL AWAKENING IN KENYA

97 On television, for the first time in Kenya's history, prisoners cast their votes from jail: "Prisoners Vote for First Time in Kenya Elections," *The East African*, August 8, 2017, www.theeastafrican.co.ke/news/inmates -vote-prisons-Kenya-elections/2558-4049790-13j4v1z/index.html.

98 "I know now that something inside me was stirring at that time, something important. And that was the belief that I could be part of something bigger than myself; that my own salvation was bound up with those of others": Jacki Lyden and Ari Shapiro, "Obama Lays Out Africa Plan," NPR, June 30, 2013, www.npr.org/templates/story/story .php?storyId=197369939.

100 Moi had "won" a total of five elections from his perch as leader of the Kenyan African National Unity (KANU) party. Objectively, none of the elections were free and fair, or had any semblance of real opposition: "A Look at Kenya's Elections History since Independence in 1964," Africanews, August 6, 2017, www.africanews.com/2017/10/25/a-look-at -kenya-s-elections-history-since-independence-in-1964.

101 Many doubted that a free and fair election could occur: "Kenya's Election Violence Condemned," BBC News, December 23, 2002, news.bbc .co.uk/2/hi/africa/2602819.stm.

101 Leading up to the election, informal polls, conducted by international groups like the European Union and National Democratic Institute, indicated Kibaki held a wide lead: "Election Watch: Kenya," Report no. 6, National Democratic Institute, 2002. www.ndi.org/sites/default /files/1518_ke_electionwatch_112002_0.pdf

113 "Corruption will now cease to be a way of life in Kenya," Kibaki declared in his inaugural remarks: "New Kenya Leader Promises Reform," BBC News, December 30, 2002, news.bbc.co.uk/2/hi/africa/2614963 .stm.

114 In the end, over one thousand people died in Kenya in postelection violence: Jeffrey Gettleman, "Disputed Vote Plunges Kenya Into

Bloodshed," *New York Times*, December 31, 2007, www.nytimes.com /2007/12/31/world/africa/31kenya.html.

115 **Many blamed international observers for too quickly declaring that the results were fair and free:** Lily Kuo and Abdi Latif Dahir, "Foreign Election Observers Endorsed a Deeply Flawed Election in Kenya. Now They Face Questions," *Quartz*, September 06, 2017, qz.com/1068521 /kenya-elections-deeply-flawed-questions-foreign-observers.

7: "OUR WORST FEAR BECAME OUR REALITY"

118 **"My parents tried everything to give us a better life," Cristina reflects now. "It was really difficult. Their sacrifice inspires me to this day":** Cristina Jiménez, telephone interview by author, April 9, 2018.

121 **"I was very disappointed," she told me. "Educators are there to help you. This one did not":** Jiménez, interview by author.

122 **Led by youth activism, the bill, SB 7784, passed in the state of New York in 2002:** H. Kenny Nienhusser, "Undocumented Immigrants and Higher Education Policy: The Policymaking Environment of New York State," *Review of Higher Education* 38, no. 2 (Winter 2015): 271–303, doi.org/10.1353/rhe.2015.0006.

127 **If you decide that climate change is the issue that you want to focus on, you will find that the changing climate disproportionately affects poverty-stricken populations:** J. L. Gamble, J. Balbus, M. Berger, K. Bouye, V. Campbell, K. Chief, K. Conlon, A. Crimmins, B. Flanagan, C. Gonzalez-Maddux, E. Hallisey, S. Hutchins, L. Jantarasami, S. Khoury, M. Kiefer, J. Kolling, K. Lynn, A. Manangan, M. McDonald, R. Morello-Frosch, M. H. Redsteer, P. Sheffield, K. Thigpen Tart, J. Watson, K. P. Whyte, and A. F. Wolkin, "Populations of Concern. The Impacts of Climate Change on Human Health in the United States: A Scientific Assessment," *Climate Health Assessment*, U.S. Global Change Research Program, Washington, D.C., 247–286, dx.doi.org/10.7930 /J0Q81B0T.

128 **It is impossible to level the educational playing field without taking into account issues like poverty, racism, housing situations, or access to healthy food. All of these public problems are related to young people receiving high-quality educations, in addition to the types of schools they attend:** Julia Fisher, "Schools That Accept 'No Excuses' from Students Are Not Helping Them," *Washington Post*, August 11, 2016, www .washingtonpost.com/posteverything/wp/2016/08/11/schools-that

-accept-no-excuses-from-students-are-not-helping-them/?utm
_term=.48bb017bbcfa.

131 DACA ensures that young people like Cristina will be able to stay without threat of deportation, work legally, and attend colleges across the country at in-state tuition prices: Julia Preston and John H. Cushman Jr., "Obama to Permit Young Migrants to Remain in U.S.," *New York Times*, June 15, 2012, www.nytimes.com/2012/06/16/us/us-to-stop-deporting-some-illegal-immigrants.html.

8: "OUR CONDITIONS WERE NOT RANDOM"

137 "I actually befriended a few students from these neighborhoods," Darius told me. "It was then that I realized just how sheltered they were from disadvantaged neighborhoods in Baltimore. Many of them usually didn't travel deep into the city": Darius Craig, telephone interview by author, February 7, 2018.

138 He realized that, according to a 2013 American Civil Liberties Union report, Baltimore had Maryland's highest rate of arrests for marijuana possession, and Maryland had one of the highest rates in the country for such petty drug offenses: "Report: The War on Marijuana in Black and White," American Civil Liberties Union, accessed June 15, 2018, www.aclu.org/report/report-war-marijuana-black-and-white.

139 As a result, the schools were becoming more segregated than they had been in decades. More affluent parents would move their children away when they could, exacerbating the problem by further segregating the schools and decreasing the property-tax income the city used to help fund Darius's school: "School Segregation: The Injustice We Can't Afford to Ignore," *Baltimore Sun*, March 28, 2017, www.baltimoresun .com/news/opinion/editorial/bs-ed-segregation-20170328-story.html.

139 Additionally, he found that 59 percent of black men between the ages of twenty-five and fifty-four were employed, compared with 79 percent of white men between the same ages. Only 10 percent of black men in Baltimore have a college degree, compared to more than 50 percent of white men. The median income for black households in Baltimore is less than $33,000. For white families, it's over $65,000: Ben Casselman, "How Baltimore's Young Black Men Are Boxed In," *FiveThirtyEight*, April 28, 2015, fivethirtyeight.com/features/how -baltimores-young-black-men-are-boxed-in.

141 In this case, the police turned and sped up the van in an attempt to harm

Gray on the ride to the station. The city coroner officially concluded that the ride caused his death: David A. Graham, "The Mysterious Death of Freddie Gray," *The Atlantic*, April 22, 2015, www.theatlantic.com /politics/archive/2015/04/the-mysterious-death-of-freddie-gray/391119.

143 The situation became so chaotic that Maryland governor Larry Hogan issued a state of emergency and called in the National Guard, and Baltimore mayor Stephanie Rawlings-Blake established a curfew: Justin Fenton, Yvonne Wenger, and Colin Campbell, "After Protests, Baltimore Curfew Meets Resistance," *Baltimore Sun*, April 29, 2015, www .baltimoresun.com/news/maryland/baltimore-city/bs-md-ci-protest -curfew-20150427-story.html.

144 "We, the youth of Baltimore, hold the responsibility of taking the lead of Baltimore's future. The only way to fix a broken system is by working the system yourself": Emma Brown, "This Baltimore Teen Will Give You Hope for the Future," *Washington Post*, May 2, 2015, www .washingtonpost.com/news/local/wp/2015/05/02/this-baltimore-teen -will-give-you-hope-for-the-future.

145 Indeed, research demonstrates that while Baltimore schools account for 10 percent of Maryland's students, the district accounts for 90 percent of Maryland's school-based criminal referrals: Emma Brown, "Some Baltimore Youth Have Fears of Police Reinforced in Their Schools," *Washington Post*, May 2, 2015, www.washingtonpost.com /local/education/some-baltimore-youth-have-fears-of-police-reinforced -in-their-schools/2015/05/02/8bc837e8-f019-11e4-a55f-38924fca94f9 _story.html.

149 Diving into criminal justice reform, the statistics become overwhelming. In 2015, while racial minorities comprised 37 percent of the U.S. population, they accounted for 63 percent of victims killed by police: German Lopez, "There Are Huge Racial Disparities in How US Police Use Force," *Vox*, December 17, 2015, www.vox.com/cards /police-brutality-shootings-us/us-police-racism.

150 The ten distinct policy solutions all stem from an analysis of some of the different causes of police violence. They all go beyond the broad poles of the Advocacy Hourglass and into the narrow middle: "Solutions," Campaign Zero, accessed February 22, 2018, www.joincampaignzero .org/solutions.

154 Indeed, the *New York Times* story the day after the rally noted that the

thousands on the mall "urged the American people and the Bush administration to do more to help end the ethnic and political conflict in the Darfur region of Sudan": Holli Chmela, "Thousands Rally in Support of American Aid to Darfur," *New York Times*, May 1, 2006, www .nytimes.com/2006/05/01/us/01rally.html.

156 One Darfurian refugee knowingly articulated in the wake of the agreement's signing, "This will lead nowhere": Rebecca Hamilton, *Fighting for Darfur: Public Action and the Struggle to Stop Genocide* (New York: Palgrave Macmillan, 2011). 98.

157 "For those who believed that building a mass constituency of regular citizens was the way to build political will, there was no good alternative to simplification at the beginning. But 18 months into their organizing, it was reasonable to expect the movement's leaders to have started educating their constituents on the way that the conflict was changing over time": Hamilton, *Fighting for Darfur*. 130.

9: "THEY WERE MOVED BY MY STORY"

163 like all six-year-olds across the country, Ruby was walking to school. But this morning was a little different. On this morning, Ruby was challenging segregationist school policies, and she was on the way to permanently changing public education in this country: Ruby Bridges and Margo Lundell, *Through My Eyes* (New York: Scholastic Press, 2009), 30.

164 Ruby walked forward, becoming stronger and more resolute with each step, only growing nervous when she saw a woman holding a black baby doll in a coffin. The doll gave her nightmares for the rest of her childhood: Associated Press, "Civil Rights Icon Ruby Bridges Thanks US Marshal Who Protected Her so She Could Attend All-White School in 1960," *Daily Mail Online*, September 6, 2013, www.dailymail.co.uk /news/article-2413509/Civil-rights-icon-Ruby-Bridges-thanks-US -Marshal-protected-attend-white-school-1960.html.

165 The Eisenhower and Kennedy presidential administrations were forced to continually, and often times ineffectively, grapple with their role of enforcing the Supreme Court decision at the local level and effectively ensuring Southern states were compliant: "'With an Even Hand'; The Aftermath," Library of Congress, accessed March 23, 2018, www.loc .gov/exhibits/brown/brown-aftermath.html.

166 Hundreds of students took the test. Ruby, along with five other students, passed. Technically speaking, Ruby was now free to attend the school of her choosing: "Ruby Bridges Biography," Biography.com, accessed January 18, 2018, www.biography.com/people/ruby-bridges-475426.

166 He went as far as to threaten to close down all public schools in the state if the federal law was implemented: Bridges and Lundell, *Through My Eyes*. 38.

167 "We have Mardi Gras and the street is blocked off and people are standing there and there's police officers everywhere and they're throwing things, it's a huge celebration. So in my six-year-old mind, we stumbled into a Mardi Gras parade": Mia Summerson, "Ruby Bridges Brings Message to NU," *Niagara Gazette*, January 31, 2018, www.niagara -gazette.com/news/local_news/ruby-bridges-brings-message-to-nu /article_6d6cc127-8d1c-5b44-811f-55f711a41b12.html.

167 "The only thing they said to me is, 'You're gonna go to the new school today and you better behave.' That is what I was concentrating on": Summerson, "Ruby Bridges."

168 All because a six-year-old girl had torn down the artificially imposed walls that had come to define education in the United States: Bridges and Lundell, *Through My Eyes*.83.

170 Using the art of storytelling, Ganz and Chavez helped to tell the real story of the migrant workers, ensuring that the American people saw them as laudable individuals who merited equal treatment under the law: Sasha Abramsky, "A Conversation with Marshall Ganz," *The Nation*, February 3, 2011, www.thenation.com/article/conversation -marshall-ganz.

170 "Stories not only teach us how to act—they inspire us to act. Stories communicate our values through the language of the heart, our emotions. And it is what we feel—our hopes, our cares, our obligations— not simply what we know that can inspire us with the courage to act": Marshall Ganz, "Telling Your Public Story: Self, Us, Now," worksheet, Kennedy School of Government, 2007.

171 The second is "peripherally," in which we do not pay substantive attention to the message and focus more on the speaker or our mood: R. E. Petty and J. T. Cacioppo, *Attitudes and Persuasion: Classic and Contemporary Approaches* (Dubuque, Iowa: Wm. C. Brown, 1981), 10.

171 This type of visceral immersion can lend itself to persuasion and the

changing of opinions, even when people are not personally invested in the subject. The brain itself processes stories empathetically, relating to the narrator and diving to a level deeper than solely connecting to the facts at hand: Kelly Ann Kane, "Don't Judge a Book by Its Author: Central and Peripheral Processing in Narrative Persuasion," (master's thesis, Iowa State University, 2017), 4, lib.dr.iastate.edu/etd/15335.

172 Research has also demonstrated that stories actually have no effect if the message is too explicit: John Baldoni, "Using Stories to Persuade," *Harvard Business Review*, March 24, 2011, hbr.org/2011/03/using-stories-as-a-tool-of-per.

173 "The single story creates stereotypes, and the problem with stereotypes is not that they are untrue, but that they are incomplete. They make one story become the only story": Chimamanda Adichie, "The Danger of a Single Story," TED Talks, July 2009, www.ted.com/talks/chimamanda_adichie_the_danger_of_a_single_story.

177 In other words, schools are becoming segregated by race anew. And the issue is not particular to the South—school resegregation is happening across the country: Beverly Daniel Tatum, "America Is More Diverse than Ever Before, but Its Schools Are Growing More Segregated," *Los Angeles Times*, September 12, 2017, www.latimes.com/opinion/op-ed/la-oe-tatum-school-segregation-20170912-story.html.

178 "In one of the most diverse cities in the world, the children who attend these schools learn in classrooms where all of their classmates—and I mean, in most cases, every single one—are black and Latino, and nearly every student is poor": Nikole Hannah-Jones, "Choosing a School for My Daughter in a Segregated City," *New York Times Magazine*, June 9, 2016, www.nytimes.com/2016/06/12/magazine/choosing-a-school-for-my-daughter-in-a-segregated-city.html.

178 According to a report released by the Civil Rights Project at UCLA, 85 percent of black students and 75 percent of Latino students attend "intensely" segregated schools in New York City, which are less than 10 percent white: John Kucsera Gary Orfield, "New York State's Extreme School Segregation Inequality, Inaction and a Damaged Future," The Civil Rights Project, UCLA, March 26, 2014, www.civilrightsproject.ucla.edu/research/k-12-education/integration-and-diversity/ny-norflet-report-placeholder.

181 "I did not understand why," she told me. "Why would they take my

home from me and my family? I was really confused. I was upset at the system": Alexandra Tesch, interview by author, February 12, 2018.

184 As a result, in 2017, more than fifteen hundred young people in the Bay Area were homeless, one of the worst per capita rates in the entire country: Carolyn Jones and Daniel J. Willis. "Amid Affluence, Youth Homelessness Surges in the Bay Area," EdSource, October 2, 2017, edsource .org/2017/homeless-bay-area/588094.

185 "I am not going to stand up to show pride in a flag for a country that oppresses black people and people of color. To me, this is bigger than football and it would be selfish on my part to look the other way. There are bodies in the street and people getting paid leave and getting away with murder": Charles Curtis, "Colin Kaepernick: I Won't Stand 'to Show Pride in a Flag for a Country That Oppresses Black People,'" *USA Today*, August 27, 2016, ftw.usatoday.com/2016/08/colin -kaepernick-49ers-national-anthem-sit-explains.

10: "LET OPPRESSION SHRUG HER SHOULDERS"

191 The town was named after American businessman Francis Cabot Lowell, who, after learning about textiles and the emerging mill-factory industry through his travels across Europe, became one of the leaders of bringing the manufacturing industry into the American economy: "Francis Cabot Lowell (1775–1894) papers," Massachusetts Historical Society, accessed July 14, 2018, www.masshist.org/collection-guides /view/fa0251.

191 Just in Lowell, between 1840 and 1860, the number of spindles in use increased from 2.25 million to more than 5.25 million. During the same time period, the bales of cotton produced annually increased from three hundred thousand to more than a million. This production directly translated into increased revenues for factory owners—profits increased at an average of 14 percent per year for textile-related investors between 1840 and 1850: Allan Pred, "Manufacturing in the American Mercantile City: 1800–1840," *Annals of the Association of American Geographers* 56, no. 2 (1966): 307–38, doi.org/10.1111/j.1467-8306.1966 .tb00560.x.

192 It is estimated that by 1840, more than eight thousand women were employed at Lowell factories, comprising more than 75 percent of all the workers. The women, primarily daughters of farmers from the region,

were also young: mostly between the ages of fifteen and twenty-five. A small number of workers even migrated from Canada, eager to take part in the emerging industry: Mark Newman and James L. Roark, *The American Promise: A History of the United States* (Boston: Bedford, 1998), 8.

193 "At the time the Lowell cotton mills were started, the caste of the factory girl was the lowest among the employments of women . . . She was represented as subjected to influences that must destroy her purity and self-respect. In the eyes of her overseer she was but a brute, a slave, to be beaten, pinched, and pushed about": Harriet Jane Hanson Robinson and Carroll D. Wright, *Early Factory Labor in New England* (Boston: Wright & Potter, 1889), 3.

194 As one girl, Amelia, noted of the conditions, it was worse than "the poor peasant of Ireland or the Russian serf who labors from sun to sun": Constance L. Shehan, *Gender Roles in American Life: A Documentary History of Political, Social, and Economic Changes* (Santa Barbara, CA: ABC-CLIO, 2018).

194 "Then too, when she is at last released from her wearisome day's toil, still may she not depart in peace. No! her footsteps must be dogged to see that they do not stray beyond the corporation limits, and she must, whether she will or no, be subjected to the manifold inconveniences of a large crowded boarding-house, where too, the price paid for her accommodation is so utterly insignificant, that it will not ensure to her the common comforts of life; she is obliged to sleep in a small comfortless, half ventilated apartment containing some half a dozen occupants each": "The Voice of Industry," Factory Tracts, Female Labor Reform Association, 1845, lostmuseum.cuny.edu/archive/factory-tracts-factory-life-as-it-is-by-an.

195 In 1834, using the same exploitative logic that they deployed when starting the factories, the owners unilaterally decided to cut the wages for the women by 15 percent: Ian Schlom, "The Struggle of the 'Mill Girls': Class Consciousness in Early 19th Century New England," Libcom.org, April 2, 2014, libcom.org/history/struggle-mill-girls-class-consciousness-early-19th-century-new-england.

195 They decided to "turn out"—or essentially go on strike—to protest the wage cuts and refuse to work until their salaries were reinstated: Robinson and Wright, *Early Factory Labor*, 10.

196 "A procession was formed, and they marched about the town, to the amusement of a mob of idlers and boys. We are told that one of the leaders

mounted a stump and made a flaming speech on the rights of women and the iniquities of the 'monied aristocracy,' which produced a powerful effect on her auditors, and they determined to 'have their way if they died for it'": "Turn-Out at Lowell," *Boston Evening Transcript*, February 17, 1834, sites.fasharvard.edu/~hsb41/course_resources/documents.html.

197 Let oppression shrug her shoulders . . . O'er our noble nation flies: Philip S. Foner, *American Labor Songs of the Nineteenth Century* (London: University of Illinois Press, 1975), 10.

198 "an Amazonian display" and noted that "a spirit of evil omen has prevailed," chauvinistic language that may not be unfamiliar to women's rights activists today: James MacGregor Burns, *The Vineyard of Liberty* (New York: Knopf, 1981), 22.

199 "As I looked back at the long line that followed me, I was more proud than I have ever been since at any success I may have achieved, and more proud than I shall ever be again until my own beloved State gives to its women citizens the right of suffrage": Robinson and Wright, *Early Factory Labor*, 8.

200 As one of the Mill Girls noted, "[the men] have at last learnt the lesson which a bitter experience teaches, not to those who style themselves their 'natural protectors' are they to look for the needful help, but to the strong and resolute of their own sex": "Lowell Mill Women Create the First Union of Working Women," AFL-CIO, accessed July 14, 2018, aflcio.org/about/history/labor-history-events/lowell-mill-women -form-union.

203 A 2015 Council of the Great City Schools study found that a student takes approximately 112 mandated standardized tests between pre-kindergarten classes and twelfth grade: Ray Hart, "Student Testing in America's Great City Schools: An Inventory and Preliminary Analysis," Council of Great City Schools, October 2015.

203 Qi Wang, a professor of psychology at Cornell, asserts that the uniquely American focus on the individual narrative occurs because of our country's distinctive emphasis on the combination of rugged individualism and storytelling. American society has, both implicitly and explicitly, according to Wang, created the model of the heroic individual, who happens to pull him or herself up by his or her own bootstraps: Qi Wang, *The Autobiographical Self in Time and Culture* (New York: Oxford University Press, 2013), 87.

205 "So, as we're told that we should all be leaders, that would be really in-effective. If you really care about starting a movement, have the courage to follow and show others how to follow": Derek Sivers, "How to Start a Movement," TED Talks, February 2010, www.ted.com/talks /derek_sivers_how_to_start_a_movement.

207 Latinos, like Julian and his family, comprise 17 percent of the population: Lori Weeden, "Eastern Massachusetts Geology, The Colonial Expansion And Industrial Revolution In And Around Lowell, Massachusetts," (presentation, The Geological Society of America, Northeastern Section, 53rd Annual Meeting, 2018), doi.org/10.1130 /abs/2018ne-310690.

207 "I was not interested in politics," he said. "As a nonvoter, and a Colombian, I did not think that my voice could matter": Julian Viviescas, telephone interview by author, April 9, 2018.

208 "This past October a third-grader here in Lowell brought a gun to school. He thought it was a toy gun. It was in fact a loaded .25 caliber pistol. After school the boy brought the gun out on the school bus, passing it around to show to his classmates. What would have happened if a child pulled the trigger?": Julian Viviescas, "Got a Gun in Your Home? Read This," *Lowell Sun Online*, May 2, 2017, www.lowellsun.com /opinion/ci_30960511/got-gun-your-home-read-this.

11: "MORE PROVOCATIVE, MORE IRREVERENT, AND MORE CONFRONTATIONAL"

214 "It doesn't really have anything to do with how we change the world": Jillian Jorgensen, "De Blasio Lectures on Climate Change, Says Regular 12-Mile SUV Trek to Gym 'Doesn't Really' Matter to Climate," *New York Daily News*, June 2, 2017, www.nydailynews.com/new-york /environmental-crusader-de-blasio-daily-suv-trips-not-issue-article -1.3215848.

215 Defining power as a concept that anyone can practice, Liu presents three principles of using power that are relevant to our political journeys: Eric Liu, *You're More Powerful than You Think: A Citizen Guide to Making Change Happen* (New York: Public Affairs, 2018), 46.

217 "There is no inherent cap on the amount of power citizens can generate": Liu, *You're More Powerful*, 42.

220 Randolph based his support on a belief in the power and abilities of

the country's youth, declaring upon introducing legislation that young people "possess a great social conscience, are perplexed by the injustices in the world, and are anxious to rectify those ills": George C. Edwards, Martin P. Wattenberg, and William G. Howell, *Government in America: People, Politics, and Policy* (New York: Pearson Education, 2018), 21.

221 The *Washington Post* wrote that the youth activists were politically inexperienced and looked decidedly "un-hip" in their earnest "gray-flannel suits." *The Christian Science Monitor* reported that political operatives cast them as "another children's crusade enlisting volunteers": Rebeca Logan, "Project 18: How a Group of How a Group of 'Un-Hip' Student Activists Changed the Constitution," NEA, accessed August 23, 2018, www.nea.org/home/48410.htm.

222 Other young people wrote opinion articles in local and national newspapers in which they pointed out the moral urgency of lowering the voting age. Before long, the issue began to transform from an absurdity into a potential reality: Sylvia Engdahl, *Amendment XXVI: Lowering the Voting Age* (Detroit: Greenhaven Press, 2010), 5.

222 In June 1939, before the movement had really taken off, only 17 percent of the American public was in favor of lowering the voting age. By 1967, this had changed dramatically: 64 percent of Americans were in favor of the change: Thomas Neale, "The Eighteen Year Old Vote: The Twenty-Sixth Amendment and Subsequent Voting Rates of Newly Enfranchised Age Groups" (report 83-103), Congressional Research Service, The Library of Congress, May 20, 1983.

222 "For years our citizens between the ages of eighteen and twenty-one have, in time of peril, been summoned to fight for America. They should participate in the political process that produces this fateful summons. I urge Congress to propose to the States a constitutional amendment permitting citizens to vote when they reach the age of eighteen": Barbara Quinn and Claudia Isler, *Understanding Your Right to Vote* (New York: Rosen, 2012), 8.

224 "As I meet with this group today, I sense that we can have confidence that America's new voters, America's young generation, will provide what America needs as we approach our two hundredth birthday, not just strength and not just wealth but the 'Spirit of '76,' a spirit of moral courage, a spirit of high idealism in which we believe in the American dream, but in which we realize that the American dream can never be

fulfilled until every American has an equal chance to fulfill it in his own life": Richard Nixon, "Remarks at a Ceremony Marking the Certification of the 26th Amendment to the Constitution," The American Presidency Project, July 5, 1971, www.presidency.ucsb.edu/ws/index .php?pid=3068.

226 They also advocated for staunchly defeating communism rather than coexisting with the governmental philosophy. Consequently, YAF supported robust military action in Vietnam as a critical component to stopping the spread of communism. These young people were pro-war, and they wanted to make their voices, which they felt were in the minority, heard: John A. Andrew, *The Other Side of the Sixties: Young Americans for Freedom and the Rise of Conservative Politics* (New Brunswick, NJ: Rutgers University Press, 1997), 14.

226 "What is so striking in the students who met at Sharon is their appetite for power . . . It is quixotic to say that they or their elders have seized the reins of history. But the difference in psychological attitude is tremendous. They talk about affecting history; we have talked about educating people to want to affect history": National Review Staff, "The Young Americans for Freedom," *National Review*, October 30, 2017, www.nationalreview.com/2017/10 /young-americans-freedom-sharon-statement-1960.

228 "We have not been heard because we were studying. Now we must be heard!": Robert Walters, "Young Americans for Freedom," First Principles, March 22, 2012, www.firstprinciplesjournal.com/articles .aspx?article=363&theme=home&page=2&loc=b&type=cbtb.

230 When Reagan was inaugurated, at least fifty graduates or members of YAF were appointed to the White House staff, with others sprinkled throughout outer layers of the administration: Dudley Clendinen, and Special to the New York Times, "After 20 Years, Young Conservatives Enjoy a Long-Awaited Rise to Power," *New York Times*, August 22, 1981, www.nytimes.com/1981/08/22/us/after-20-years-young-conservatives -enjoy-a-long-awaited-rise-to-power.html.

231 The 115th Congress, which began in 2017, is one of the oldest in American history. The average age of a representative is fifty-seven. The average age of a senator is sixty-one. Compare this to 1981: the respective average ages were forty-nine and fifty-three: Jennifer Manning, "Membership of the 115th Congress: A Profile" (report 7-5700) Congressional

Research Service, February 17, 2017, digital.library.unt.edu/ark:/67531 /metadc980463/m1/1.

231 According to American University professor Jennifer Lawless, as of 2012 there were over 519,000 elected officials in the United States, from the Senate and the House of Representatives to school boards and city councils: Jennifer L. Lawless and Richard Logan Fox, *Running from Office: Why Young Americans Are Turned Off to Politics* (Oxford: Oxford University Press, 2017), 62.

232 "It was an awesome experience," Saira said. "It made me want to run for office myself": Saira Blair, telephone interview by author, March 2, 2018.

235 The complex, isolated and a forty-minute walk from the nearest subway stop, was in terrible shape: Jennifer Gonnerman, "Fighting for the Poor Under Trump," *The New Yorker*, December 12, 2016, www.newyorker .com/magazine/2016/12/12/fighting-for-the-poor-under-trump.

235 "Your home is supposed to be a sanctuary," he said. "I didn't feel safe in mine": Ritchie Torres, interview by author, May 2, 2018.

12: "IT'S TOO HARD"

248 "Can you imagine all of that in my head? My head was just too full of black history, the oppression we went through," she reflected in a recent interview: Margot Alder, "Before Rosa Parks, There Was Claudette Colvin," WBUR, March 15, 2009, www.wbur.org/npr/101719889 /before-rosa-parks-there-was-claudette-colvin.

249 "He shut it hard behind me and turned the key. The lock fell into place with a heavy sound. It was the worst sound I ever heard. It sounded final. It said I was trapped": Phillip M. Hoose, *Claudette Colvin: Twice Toward Justice* (New York: Farrar, Straus and Giroux, 2014), 43.

249 "I'm so proud of you. Everyone prays for freedom. We've all been praying and praying. But you're different—you want your answer the next morning. And I think you just brought the revolution to Montgomery": Hoose, *Claudette Colvin*. 10.

250 "I didn't fit the image either of, you know, someone they would want to show off," she suggested: "Before Rosa Parks, A Teenager Defied Segregation on an Alabama Bus," *All Things Considered*, NPR, March 2, 2015, www.npr.org/sections/codeswitch/2015/02/27/389563788/before -rosa-parks-a-teenager-defied-segregation-on-an-alabama-bus.

251 "So now, I hope [my story] inspires the young groups, that they should use every resource available to them so they can reach their fullest potential and become very productive in this so-called—well, America isn't flawless, but I still love America—this democratic society that we live in": Jeff Coltin, "The Original Rosa Parks: A Q&A with Claudette Colvin," *City & State New York*, February 8, 2016, www.cityandstateny .com/articles/politics/new-york-city/the-original-rosa-parks-a-q-and-a -with-claudette-colvin.html.

253 They arrested thirteen people for violating New York's gender-appropriate clothing laws. At one point, an officer hit a woman on the head with a baton as he forced her into his car: David Carter, *Stonewall: The Riots That Sparked the Gay Revolution* (New York: Griffin, 2011), 28.

254 As historian Michael Bronski noted, in the wake of Stonewall, "gay liberation was a youth movement whose sense of history was defined to a large degree by rejection of the past": Michael Bronski, *Pulp Friction: Uncovering the Golden Age of Gay Male Pulps* (New York: St. Martin's Griffin, 2003), 38.

254 Indeed, the day after the election, while many in the liberal parts of the United States were celebrating Obama's win, groups of determined Californians took to the streets: Associated Press, "In California, Protests Over Gay Marriage Vote," *New York Times*, November 09, 2008, www.nytimes.com/2008/11/10/us/10protest.html.

256 Rustin was a gay man, and due to the stigma associated with homosexuality at the time, he is not widely known as a leader in the movement. Like Claudette Colvin, Rustin and his role in the movement has too often been marginalized: Steven Thrasher, "Bayard Rustin: The Man Homophobia Almost Erased From History," *BuzzFeed*, August 27, 2013, www.buzzfeed.com/steventhrasher/walter-naegle-partner-of-the-late -bayard-rustin-talks-about.

256 Leaders in the movement felt the rally had actually set them back: the students came across as muddled and unprofessional, with disparate messages: Calvin Craig Miller, *No Easy Answers: Bayard Rustin and the Civil Rights Movement* (Greensboro, NC: Morgan Reynolds, 2005), 38.

257 King called off the march and publicly distanced himself from Rustin. For three years, Rustin was largely ostracized from the movement: Henry Louis Gates Jr., "Who Designed the March on Washington?" *The African Americans* (blog), accessed August 23, 2018, www.pbs.org/wnet

/african-americans-many-rivers-to-cross/history/100-amazing-facts
/who-designed-the-march-on-washington.

13: THE PEACEFUL PLAY OF POWER

262 **Sixty percent of Clinton supporters had not talked to any Trump supporters**: Laura Vozzella and Emily Guskin, "In Virginia, a State of Political Separation: Most Clinton Voters Don't Know Any Trump Voters, and Vice Versa," *Washington Post*, September 14, 2016, www .washingtonpost.com/local/virginia-politics/in-virginia-a-state-of -political-separation-most-clinton-voters-dont-know-any-trump -voters-and-vice-versa/2016/09/14/f617a2b8-75e8-11e6-b786-19d0cb 1ed06c_story.html.

264 **The democratic watchdog organization Freedom House estimates that 26 percent of countries across the world today are "not free"**: Emily Tamkin, "New Freedom House Rankings Show Democracy Ebbing," *Foreign Policy*, April 4, 2017, foreignpolicy.com/2017/04/04 /new-freedom-house-rankings-show-democracy-ebbing.

265 **An example of such a country is Turkey, in which President Recep Tayyip Erdoğan has consolidated unilateral power and recently engaged in a flawed constitutional referendum that provided his office with expanded authority**: Nicholas Danforth, "Turkish Democracy Might Be Dead—And Things Could Soon Get a Lot Worse," *Washington Post*, August 16, 2017, www.washingtonpost.com/news/democracy-post /wp/2017/08/16/turkish-democracy-might-be-dead-and-things-could -soon-get-a-lot-worse.

265 **According to Freedom House's *Freedom in the World* report, which uses hundreds of experts to assess metrics on basic democratic functions like an independent press and freedom of speech, the world has witnessed twelve straight years during which the number of countries who suffered democratic setbacks outnumbered those who registered gains**: "Freedom in the World 2018," Freedom House, accessed May 08, 2018, freedomhouse.org/report/freedom-world/freedom-world-2018.

266 **"The alternate domination of one faction over another, sharpened by the spirit of revenge, natural to party dissension, which in different ages and countries has perpetrated the most horrid enormities"**: "Washington's Farewell Address 1796," Avalon Project, Documents in Law, History and Diplomacy, Yale Law School, accessed August 23, 2018, avalon.law.yale.edu/18th_century/washing.asp.

266 "A stable democracy requires the manifestation of conflict or cleavage so that there will be struggle over ruling positions, challenges to parties in power, and shifts of parties in office": Seymour Martin Lipset, *Political Man: The Social Bases of Politics* (Ancho Books, 1963).

269 "The simple fact of the matter is that the world has never built a multiethnic democracy in which no particular ethnic group is in the majority and where political equality, social equality, and economies that empower all have been achieved": Steven Levitsky and Daniel Ziblatt, *How Democracies Die* (New York: Crown, 2018), 210.

270 By 2016, that rating had dropped five points, mostly because the most common answer given in the survey was zero: Hannah Fingerhut, "Feelings about Partisans and the Parties," Pew Research Center, June 22, 2016, www.people-press.org/2016/06/22/1-feelings-about-partisans-and-the-parties.

270 A 2017 Stanford study demonstrated that partisan hatred and prejudice now exceeds racial hostility in this country, as measured by implicit-association group tests: Sean J. Westwood, Shanto Iyengar, Stefaan Walgrave, Rafael Leonisio, Luis Miller, and Oliver Strijbis, "The Tie That Divides: Cross-national Evidence of the Primacy of Partyism," *European Journal of Political Research* 57, no. 2 (2017): 333–54, doi.org/10.1111/1475-6765.12228.

270 political scientist Lilliana Mason argues that "the more sorted we become, the more emotionally we react to normal political events": Lilliana Mason, *Uncivil Agreement: How Politics Became Our Identity* (Chicago; London: University of Chicago Press, 2018), 8.

271 In the 1992 presidential election, 38 percent of voters lived in a "landslide county," defined as an area that voted for one of the presidential candidates by twenty percentage points or more: David Wasserman, "Purple America Has All But Disappeared," *FiveThirtyEight*, March 8, 2017, fivethirtyeight.com/features/purple-america-has-all-but-disappeared.

271 a 2014 Pew survey indicated that 50 percent of conservatives and 35 percent of liberals agree that "it's important to me to live in a place where most people share my political views": Nicholas Kristof, "You're Wrong! I'm Right!" *New York Times*, February 17, 2018, www.nytimes.com/2018/02/17/opinion/sunday/liberal-conservative-divide.html.

271 In a 2016 paper entitled "Echo Chambers on Facebook," social scientists used a variety of tests to confirm that online users promote their favorite narratives, form and belong to polarized groups, and reject

information that does not neatly fit into their preexisting beliefs: Walter Quattrociocchi, Antonio Scala, and Cass R. Sunstein, "Echo Chambers on Facebook," *SSRN Electronic Journal*, June 13, 2016, doi.org/10.2139 /ssrn.2795110.

272 According to Pew Research, 61 percent of millennials use Facebook as their primary source for news about politics and government, a number that is only increasing: Tom Kludt, "For Millennials, Facebook Is Political," CNNMoney, June 1, 2015, money.cnn.com/2015/06/01/media /pew-study-millennials-facebook/index.html.

275 "I was generally surrounded by people that all think similarly," Turnbull said of the reason for creating the forum. "This led me to wonder, what does someone actually do when they want to hear a different perspective or change their mind?": Virginia Heffernan, "Our Best Hope for Civil Discourse on the Internet Is on ... Reddit," *Wired*, February 15, 2018, www.wired.com/story/free-speech-issue-reddit-change-my-view.

277 "Everybody believes they are the good guy. The only way to disarm your enemy is to listen to them. If you hear them out, if you're brave enough to really listen to their story, you can see that more often than not, you might have made some of the same choices if you'd lived their life instead of yours": Cavan Sieczkowski, "Former CIA Officer: Listen To Your Enemy, Because 'Everybody Believes They Are The Good Guy,'" *HuffPost*, June 14, 2016, www.huffingtonpost.com/entry /amaryllis-fox-undercover-cia-video_us_57600d31e4b0e4fe5143afc6.

278 "The African American retiree in Brooklyn who fears gentrification is whitening her borough beyond recognition probably votes differently from the white foreman in Arizona who fears immigration is browning his state. Yet their worries echo": Anand Giridharadas, "Democracy Is Not a Supermarket," *Medium*, November 1, 2017, medium.com /@AnandWrites/why-real-change-escapes-many-change-makers-and -why-it-doesnt-have-to-8e48332042a8.

14: "BY ANY MEANS NECESSARY"

286 The Democratic Republic of the Congo suffered through decades of brutal authoritarian colonialism at the hands of Belgium, and its citizens have been trying to fight through the aftermath of their past since independence in 1960: Jason K. Stearns, *Dancing with Monsters: The Collapse of the Congo and the Great War of Africa* (New York: PublicAffairs, 2011), 62.

287 of the thirty-five countries in the Organisation for Economic Co-operation and Development, the United States ranks thirty-first in terms of voter participation: Michael D. Regan, "Why Is Voter Turnout so Low in the U.S.?" PBS, November 6, 2016, www.pbs.org/newshour /politics/voter-turnout-united-states.

289 Mugabe retained power through the chaos by continuously rigging elections. He attempted to demonstrate to the outside world that Zimbabwe was a democracy. In reality, he became one of the more autocratic rulers in the world: David Coltart, *A Decade of Suffering in Zimbabwe: Economic Collapse and Political Repression under Robert Mugabe* (Washington, D.C.: CATO Institute, 2008), 73.

291 "I realized that politics mattered and affected my life": Themba Mzingwane, interview by author, June 9, 2017.

291 At its peak, Zimbabwe's inflation reached 79.6 billion percent in November of 2008. It is one of the highest inflation rates in the history of the world: Matt Vasilogambros, "Zimbabwe's Own U.S. Dollar Bills," *The Atlantic*, May 06, 2016, www.theatlantic.com/international /archive/2016/05/zimbabwe-money/481518.

301 "You may be disillusioned with the Church but still believe in God," he explains. "The same is true for democracy—you can be disenchanted with the institutions but still believe in a government in which people are front and center at the push for change": Srđa Popović, interview by author, May 9, 2018.

302 "Young people just want to live and not make trouble, but they are unable to break into the political, social, economic systems of their countries," says Rami Khouri, of the American University of Beirut, a journalist with joint Palestinian-Jordanian and United States citizenship: "Look Forward in Anger," *The Economist* (US), August 6, 2016, www.economist.com/briefing/2016/08/06/look-forward-in-anger.

15: "OUR VOICES MUST BE TAKEN SERIOUSLY"

312 Census data shows that the median household income in the city is just over $128,000 and 84 percent is white, compared with less than $53,000 for the rest of Broward County, which is 63 percent white: Alia Wong, "The Parkland Students Aren't Going Away," *The Atlantic*, February 24, 2018, www.theatlantic.com/education/archive/2018/02 /the-parkland-students-arent-going-away/554159/.

313 "Citizens with low or moderate incomes speak with a whisper that is lost

on the ears of inattentive government, while the advantaged roar with the clarity and consistency that policymakers readily heed": "American Democracy in an Age of Rising Inequality." *Perspectives on Politics* 2, no. 04 (2004): 651-66. www.apsanet.org/portals/54/Files/Task%20 Force%20Reports/taskforcereport.pdf.

314 A civic engagement gap has manifested in our schools: when compared with average socioeconomic status (SES) schools, low-income students are half as likely to study how laws are made, and they are 30 percent less likely to report having experiences with debates or panel discussions in social studies classes: Meira Levinson, *No Citizen Left Behind* (Cambridge, MA: Harvard University Press, 2012), 84.

315 The people in power, including journalists and academics, tend to see young people like those in Parkland as being our kids and as representing nationwide concerns as opposed to kids protesting in Chicago, Philadelphia, New York": Wong, "The Parkland Students."

315 "The platform us Parkland Students have established is to be shared with every person, black or white, gay or straight, religious or not, who has experienced gun violence, and hand in hand, side by side, we will make this change together": P. R. Lockhart, "Students from Parkland and Chicago Unite to Expand the Gun Control Conversation," *Vox*, March 6, 2018, www.vox.com/identities/2018/3/6/17086426/parkland -chicago-students-gun-violence-race-activism.

323 Statistics from countries and communities that have lowered the voting age indicate that sixteen-year-olds are far more likely to vote than eighteen-year-olds. In Takoma Park, Maryland, in the 2013 election (the first in which sixteen-year-olds could vote), the turnout rate for registered sixteen- and seventeen-year-olds far exceeded any other demographic: Zachary Crockett, "The Case for Allowing 16-Year-Olds to Vote," *Vox*, November 7, 2016, www.vox.com/policy-and-politics/2016 /11/7/13347080/voting-age-election-16.

324 Evidence from Europe is also positive. Austria lowered its voting age to sixteen for all of the country's elections in 2008, and turnout among that age group has been higher than for older first-time voters. In the 2011 local elections in Norway, twenty-one municipalities used a voting age of sixteen as a trial and found that turnout was also much higher than turnout among older first-time voters: Generation Citizen, "Young Voices at the Ballot Box: Advancing Efforts to Lower the Voting

Age," Vote16USA, 2017. vote16usa.org/wp-content/uploads/2016/01 /Vote16USA-white-paper.pdf.

325 Using the development of the brain's frontal cortex as a barometer, sixteen-year-olds have the same ability to process information and make decisions as twenty-one-year-olds. Additionally, research demonstrates that sixteen-year-olds possess the same level of civic knowledge as older young adults, and they also demonstrate equal levels of self-reported political skill and political efficacy of older adults: Daniel Hart and Robert Atkins, "American Sixteen- and Seventeen-Year-Olds Are Ready to Vote." *The ANNALS of the American Academy of Political and Social Science* 633, no. 1 (December 2010): 201–22, doi.org/10.1177/0002716210382395.

SCOTT WARREN is the cofounder and chief executive officer of Generation Citizen. He has been named an Echoing Green Fellow, a Draper Richards Kaplan Fellow, and a *Forbes* 30 under 30 for Social Entrepreneurship. He has also been a social entrepreneur in residence at Brown University, and a social entrepreneur in residence at Tufts University. He is currently a democracy fellow at Brown University. Visit www.GenerationCitizen.org.